Family Values **FRANK MILLER**

DARK HORSE BOOKS®

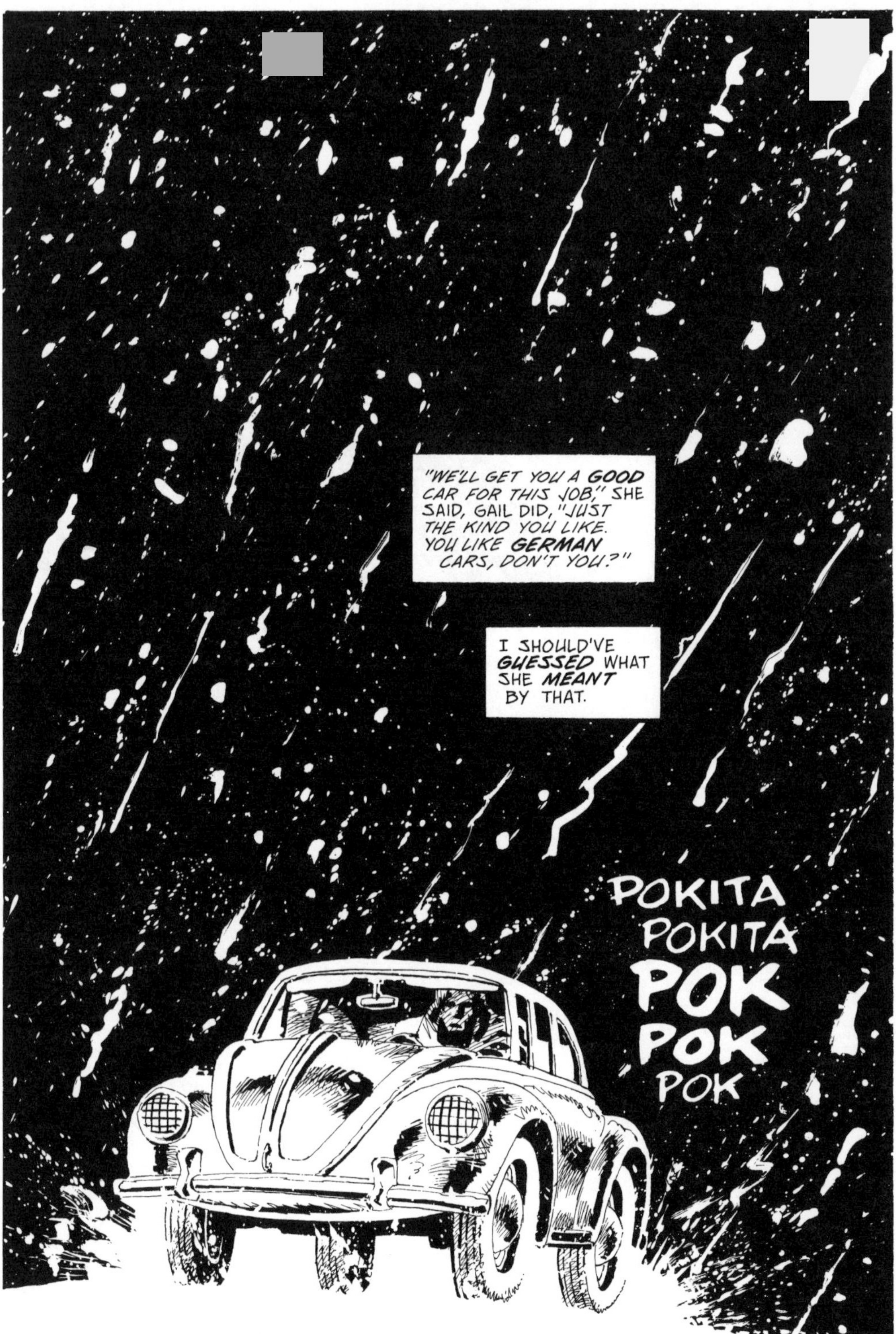
"WE'LL GET YOU A GOOD CAR FOR THIS JOB," SHE SAID, GAIL DID, "JUST THE KIND YOU LIKE. YOU LIKE GERMAN CARS, DON'T YOU?"
I SHOULD'VE GUESSED WHAT SHE MEANT BY THAT.
POKITA
POKITA
POK
POK
POK

Publisher MIKE RICHARDSON
Editor DIANA SCHUTZ
Logo design STEVE MILLER
Book design FRANK MILLER and JOSH ELLIOTT

Published by Dark Horse Books
A division of Dark Horse Comics, Inc.
10956 SE Main Street, Milwaukie, Oregon 97222
United States of America

darkhorse.com

Third Edition: November 2010
ISBN 978-1-59307-297-1

10 9 8 7 6 5

Printed at Lake Book Manufacturing, Inc., Melrose Park, IL, USA

FRANK MILLER'S SIN CITY® VOLUME 5: FAMILY VALUES

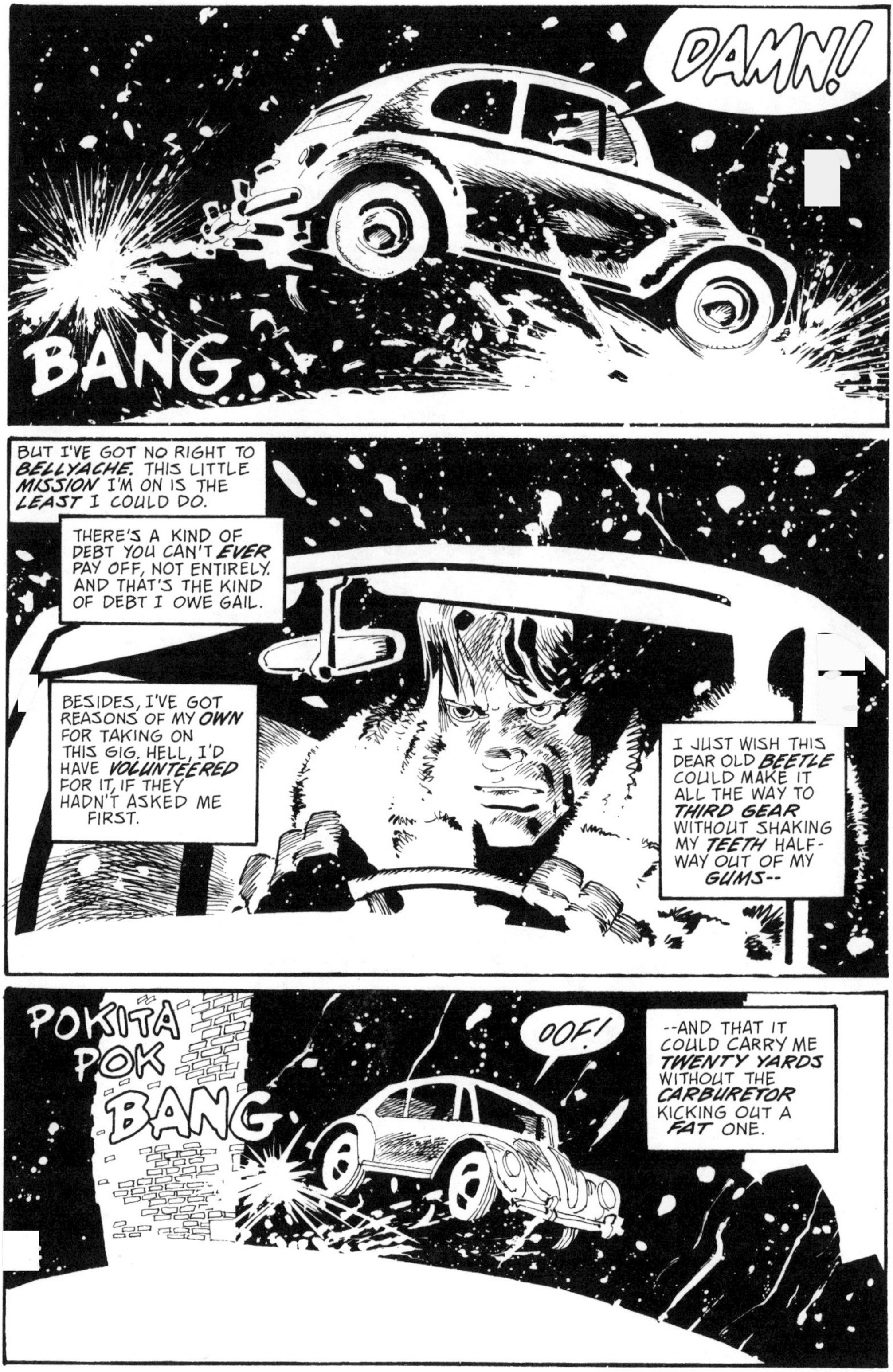

DAMN!
BANG
BUT I'VE GOT NO RIGHT TO BELLYACHE. THIS LITTLE MISSION I'M ON IS THE LEAST I COULD DO.
THERE'S A KIND OF DEBT YOU CAN'T EVER PAY OFF, NOT ENTIRELY. AND THAT'S THE KIND OF DEBT I OWE GAIL.
BESIDES, I'VE GOT REASONS OF MY OWN FOR TAKING ON THIS GIG. HELL, I'D HAVE VOLUNTEERED FOR IT, IF THEY HADN'T ASKED ME FIRST.
I JUST WISH THIS DEAR OLD BEETLE COULD MAKE IT ALL THE WAY TO THIRD GEAR WITHOUT SHAKING MY TEETH HALF-WAY OUT OF MY GUMS--
POKITA POK BANG
OOF!
--AND THAT IT COULD CARRY ME TWENTY YARDS WITHOUT THE CARBURETOR KICKING OUT A FAT ONE.

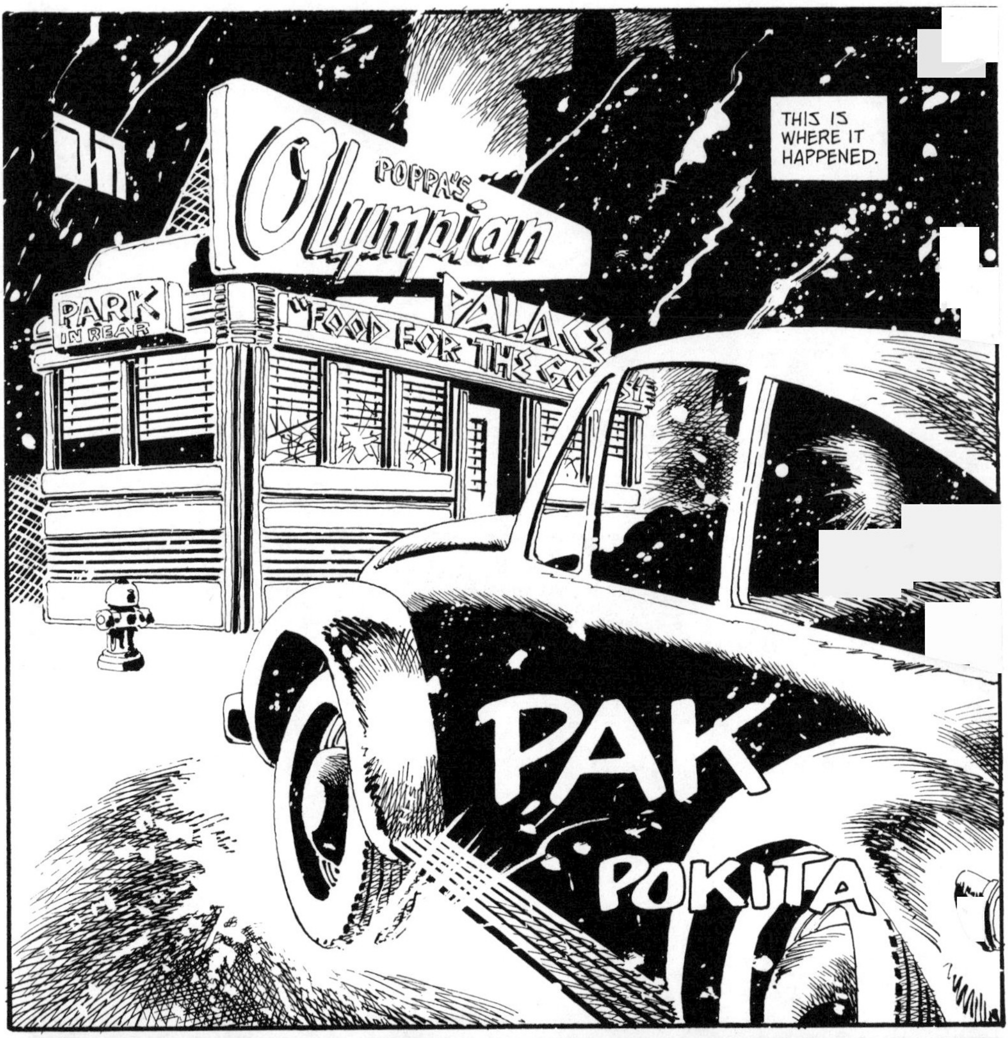
THIS IS WHERE IT HAPPENED.
POPPA'S Olympian PALACE
"FOOD FOR THE GODS"
PARK IN REAR
PAK
POKITA

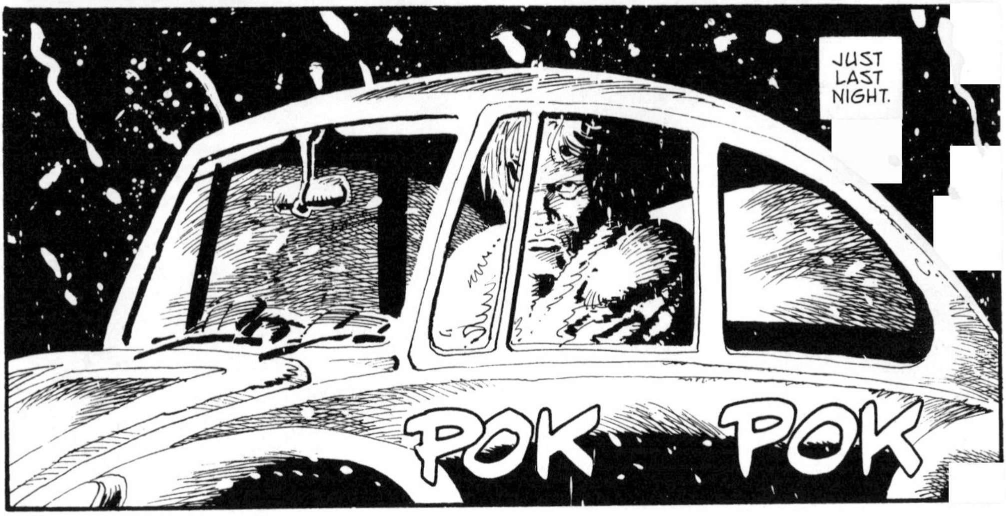
JUST LAST NIGHT.
POK POK

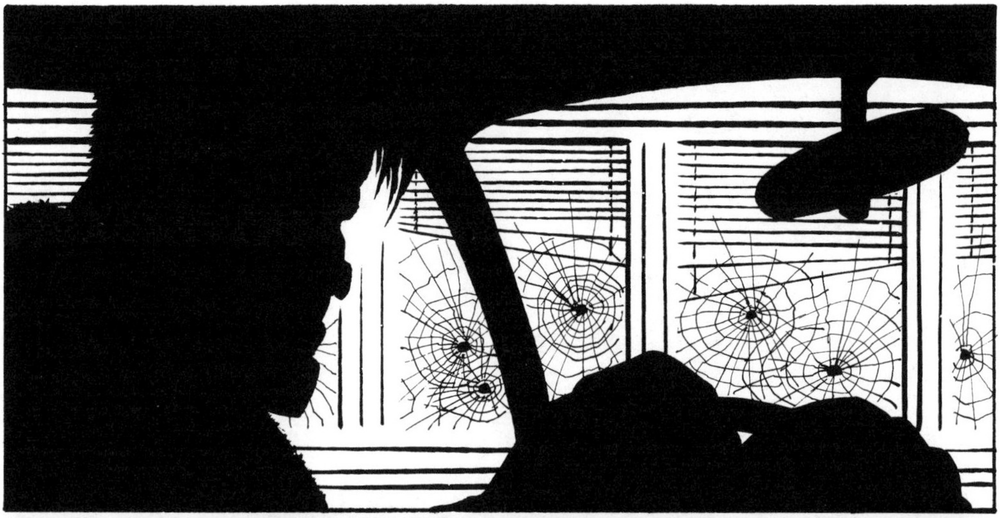

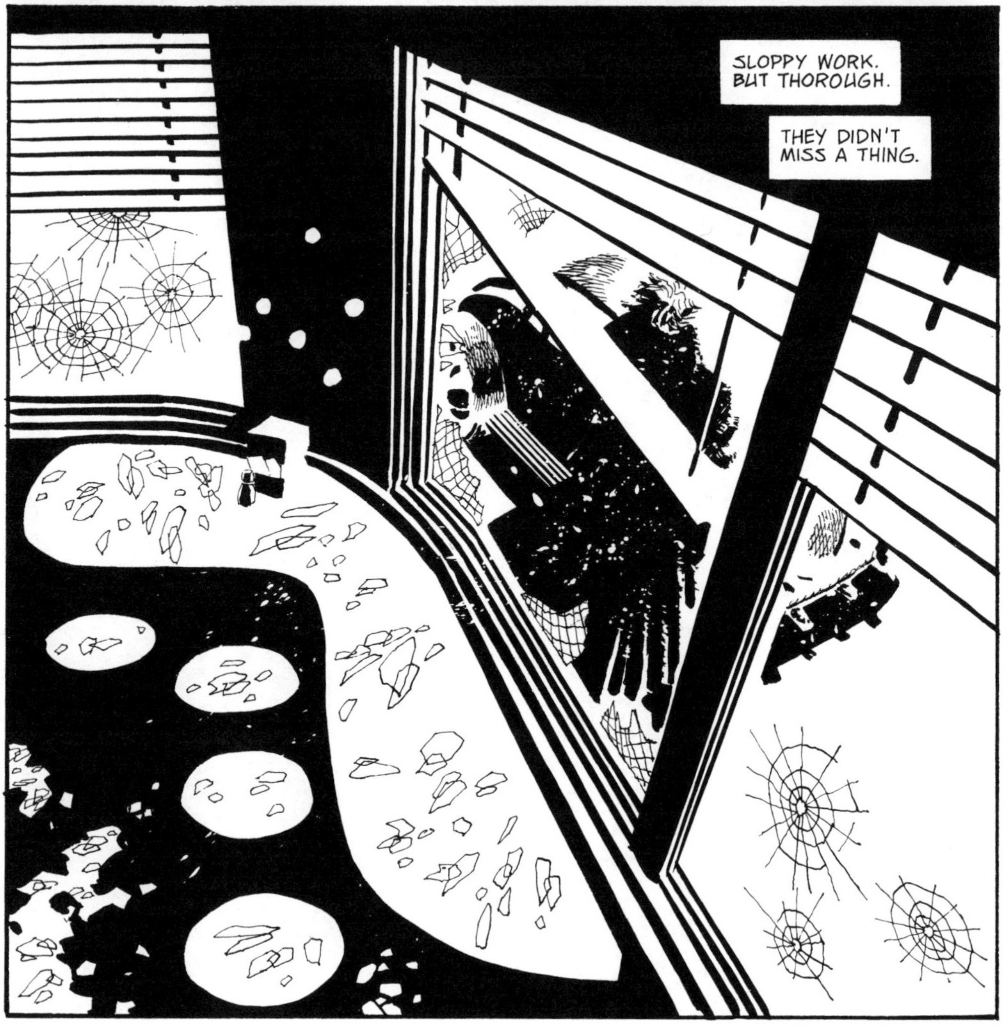
SLOPPY WORK. BUT THOROUGH.
THEY DIDN'T MISS A THING.

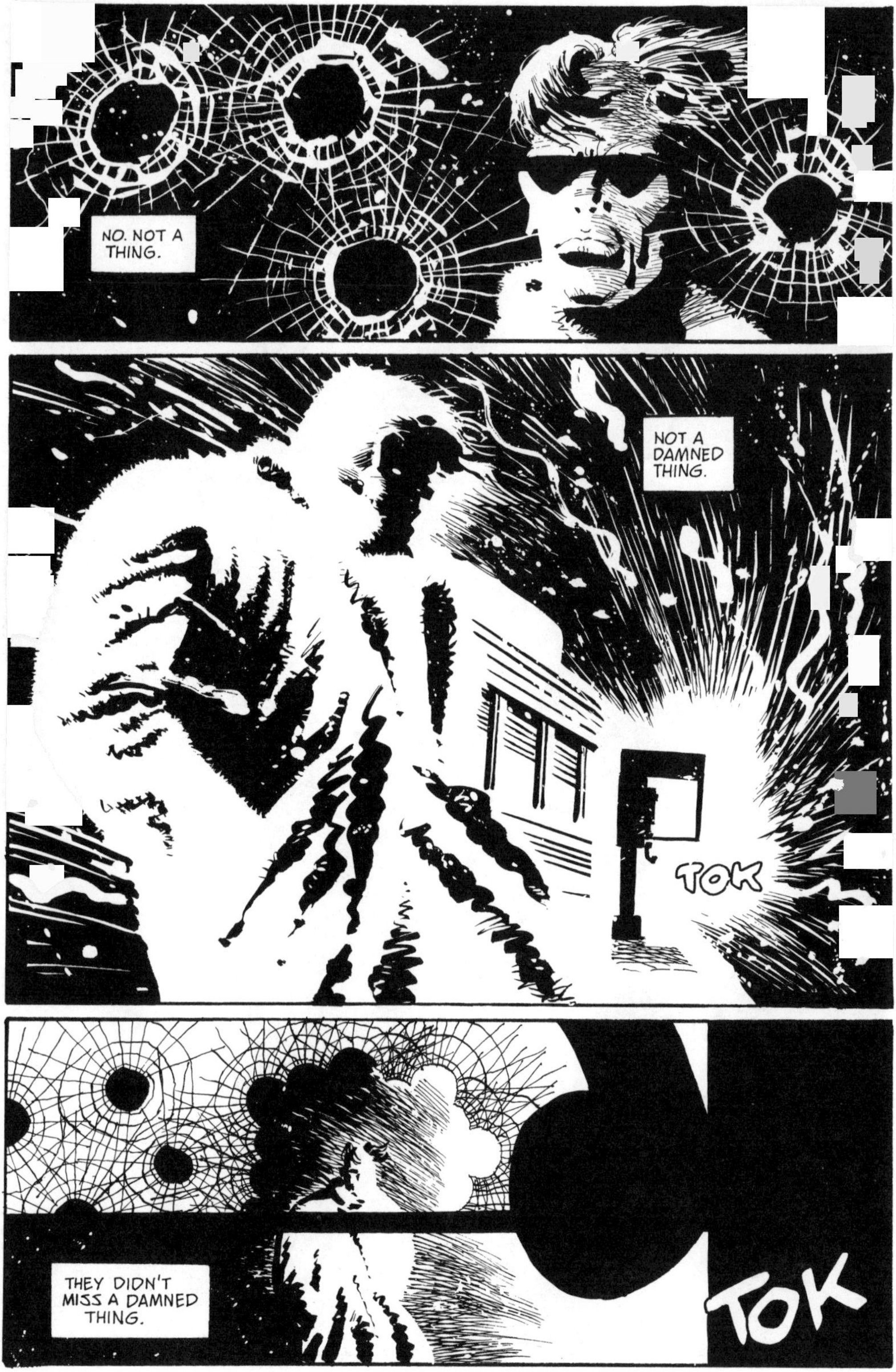

NO. NOT A THING.
NOT A DAMNED THING.
TOK
THEY DIDN'T MISS A DAMNED THING.
TOK

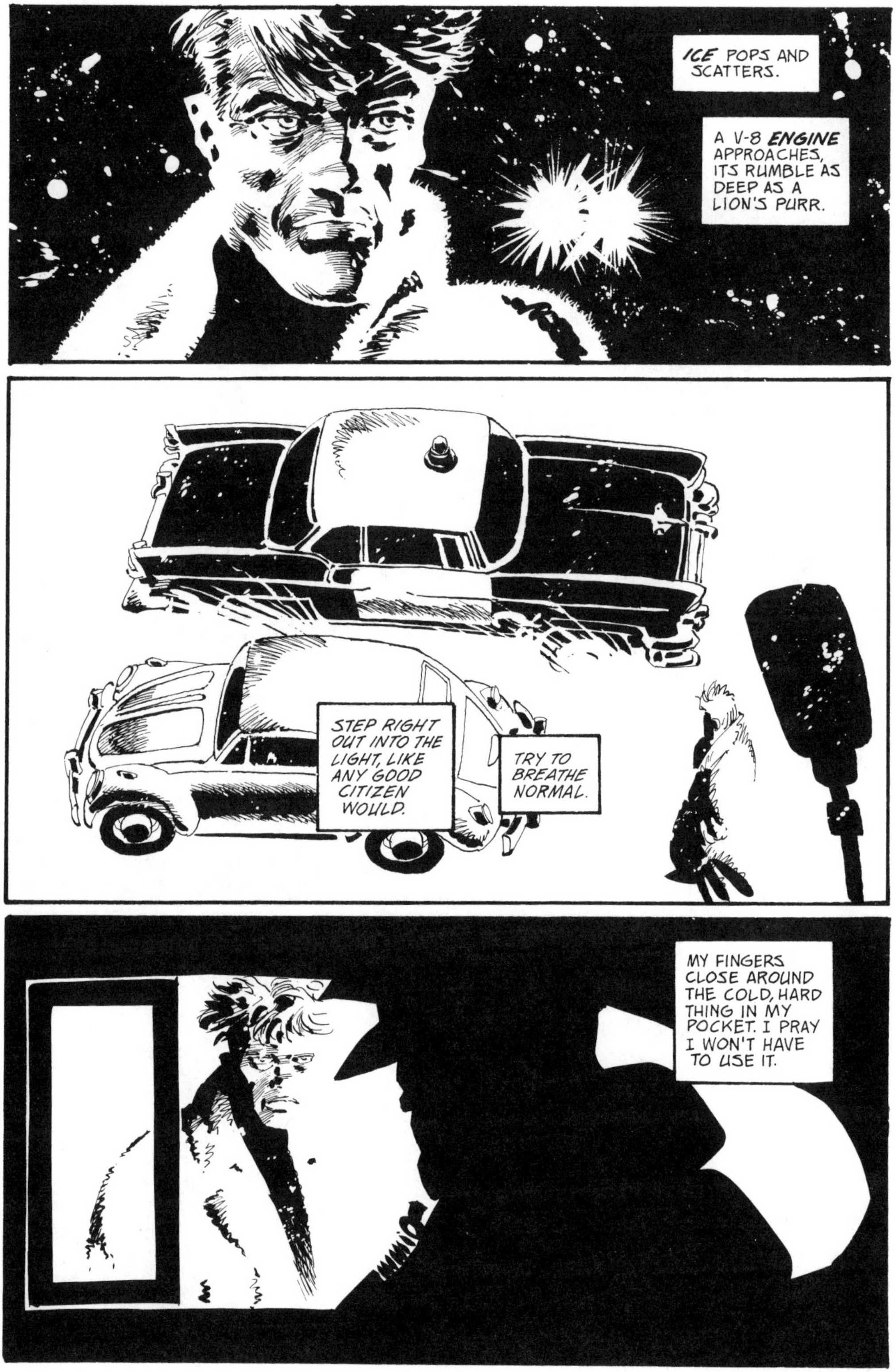
ICE POPS AND SCATTERS.
A V-8 ENGINE APPROACHES, ITS RUMBLE AS DEEP AS A LION'S PURR.
STEP RIGHT OUT INTO THE LIGHT, LIKE ANY GOOD CITIZEN WOULD.
TRY TO BREATHE NORMAL.
MY FINGERS CLOSE AROUND THE COLD, HARD THING IN MY POCKET. I PRAY I WON'T HAVE TO USE IT.

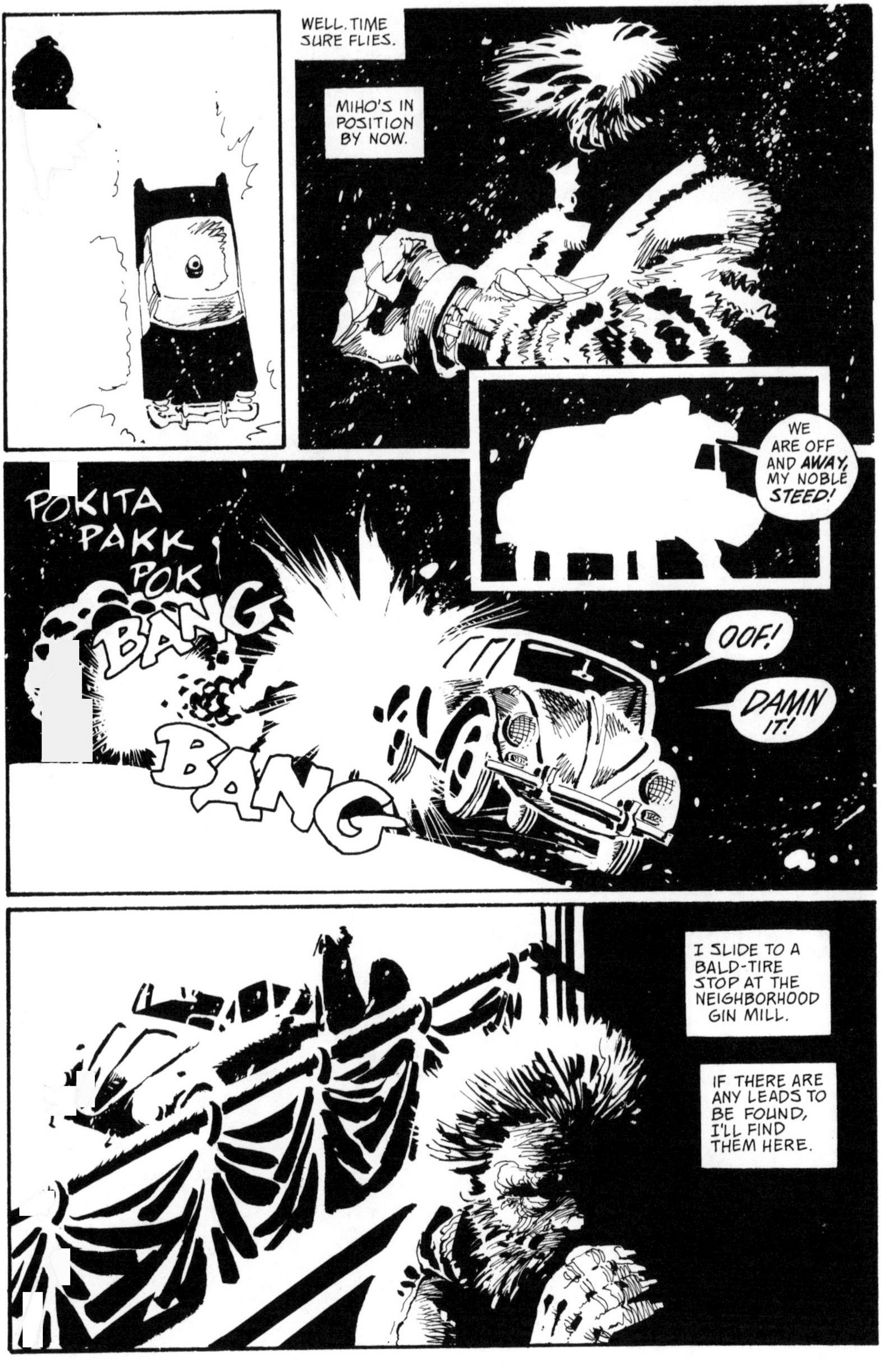
WELL. TIME SURE FLIES.
MIHO'S IN POSITION BY NOW.
WE ARE OFF AND AWAY, MY NOBLE STEED!
POKITA PAKK POK
BANG
BANG
OOF!
DAMN IT!
I SLIDE TO A BALD-TIRE STOP AT THE NEIGHBORHOOD GIN MILL.
IF THERE ARE ANY LEADS TO BE FOUND, I'LL FIND THEM HERE.

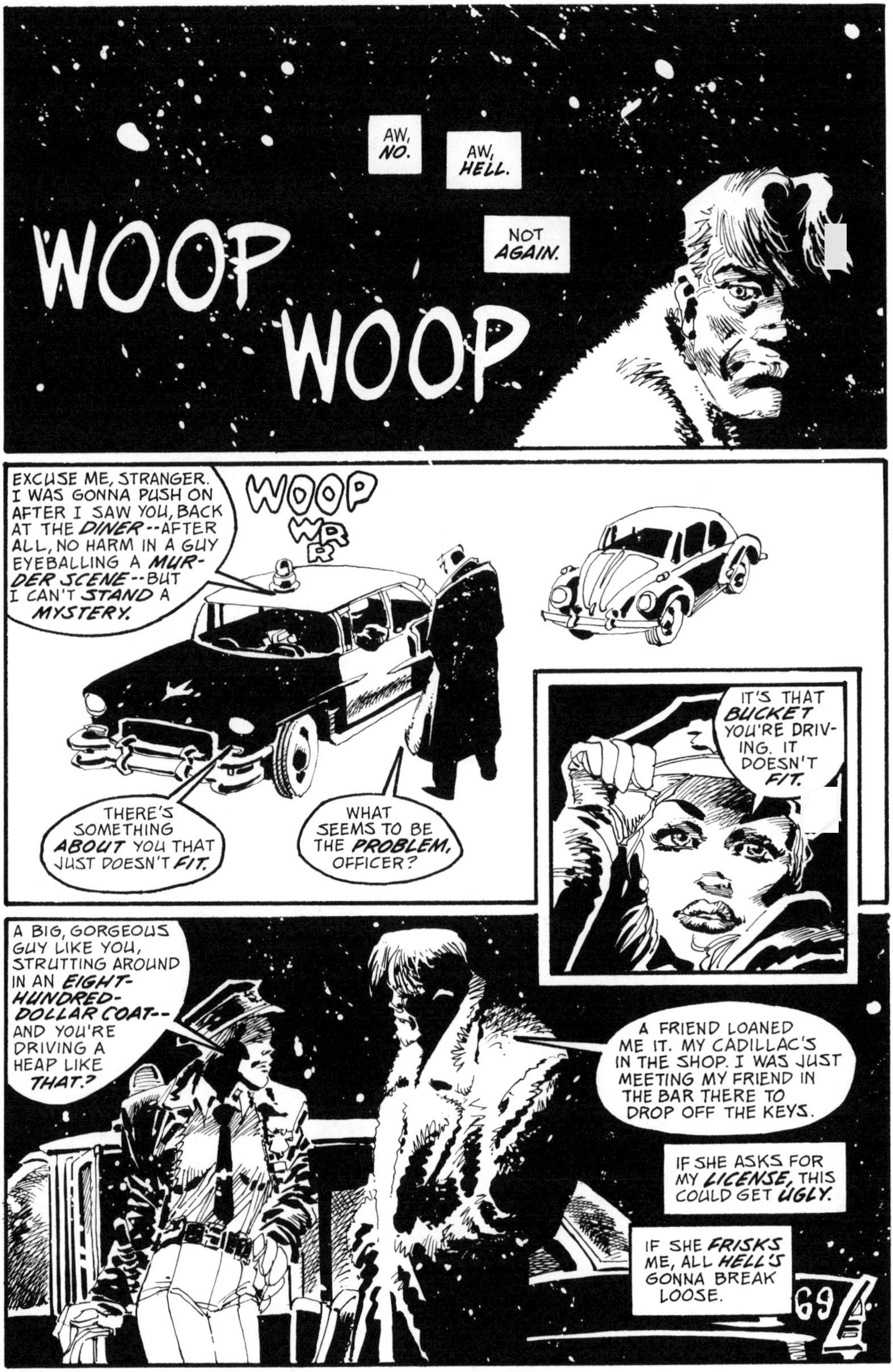
AW, NO.
AW, HELL.
NOT AGAIN.
WOOP WOOP
EXCUSE ME, STRANGER. I WAS GONNA PUSH ON AFTER I SAW YOU, BACK AT THE DINER--AFTER ALL, NO HARM IN A GUY EYEBALLING A MURDER SCENE--BUT I CAN'T STAND A MYSTERY.
WOOP
WRR
THERE'S SOMETHING ABOUT YOU THAT JUST DOESN'T FIT.
WHAT SEEMS TO BE THE PROBLEM, OFFICER?
IT'S THAT BUCKET YOU'RE DRIVING. IT DOESN'T FIT.
A BIG, GORGEOUS GUY LIKE YOU, STRUTTING AROUND IN AN EIGHT-HUNDRED-DOLLAR COAT--AND YOU'RE DRIVING A HEAP LIKE THAT?
A FRIEND LOANED ME IT. MY CADILLAC'S IN THE SHOP. I WAS JUST MEETING MY FRIEND IN THE BAR THERE TO DROP OFF THE KEYS.
IF SHE ASKS FOR MY LICENSE, THIS COULD GET UGLY.
IF SHE FRISKS ME, ALL HELL'S GONNA BREAK LOOSE.
69

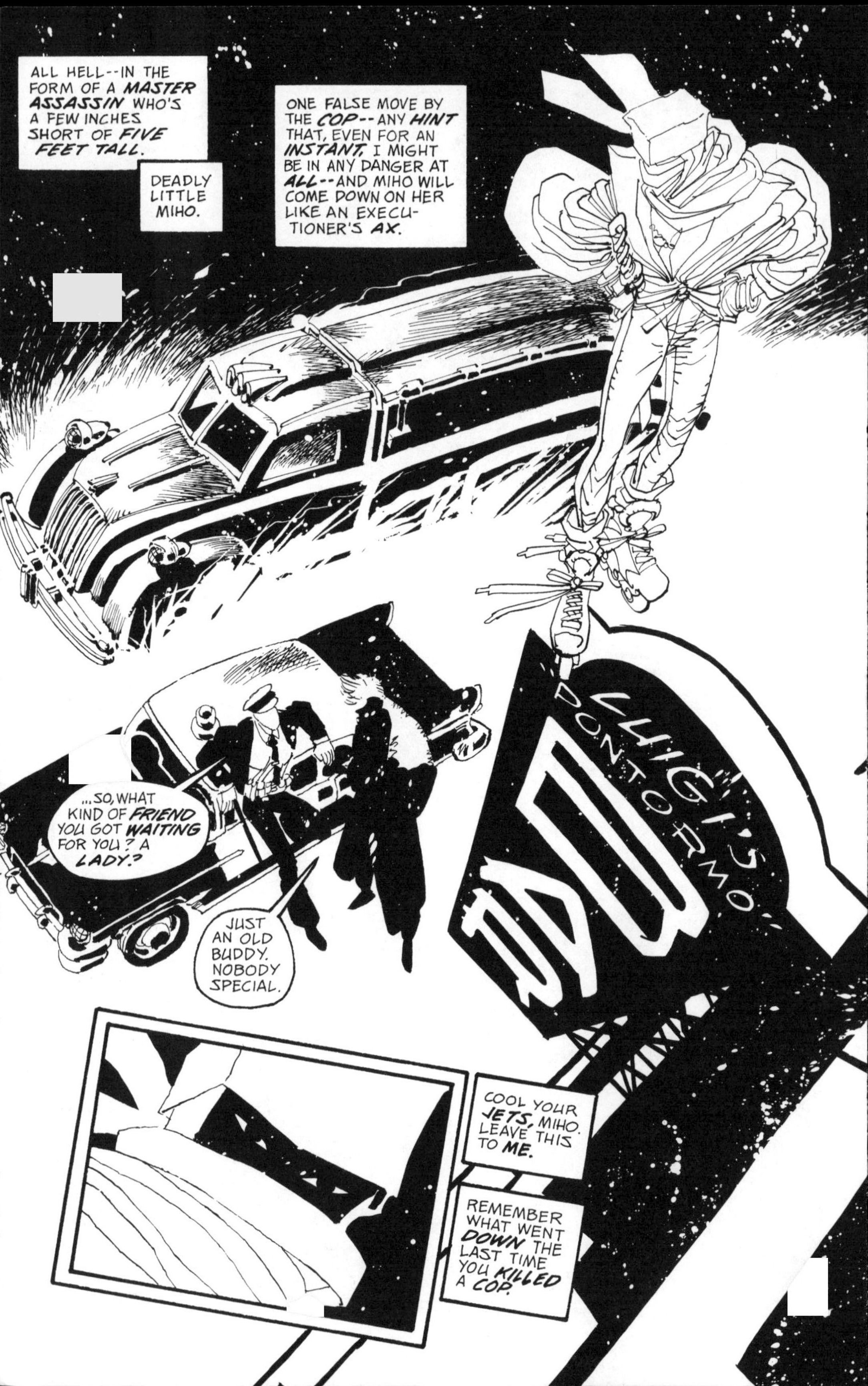
ALL HELL--IN THE FORM OF A MASTER ASSASSIN WHO'S A FEW INCHES SHORT OF FIVE FEET TALL.
DEADLY LITTLE MIHO.
ONE FALSE MOVE BY THE COP--ANY HINT THAT, EVEN FOR AN INSTANT, I MIGHT BE IN ANY DANGER AT ALL--AND MIHO WILL COME DOWN ON HER LIKE AN EXECUTIONER'S AX.
LUIGI'S
PONTORMO
...SO, WHAT KIND OF FRIEND YOU GOT WAITING FOR YOU? A LADY?
JUST AN OLD BUDDY. NOBODY SPECIAL.
COOL YOUR JETS, MIHO. LEAVE THIS TO ME.
REMEMBER WHAT WENT DOWN THE LAST TIME YOU KILLED A COP.

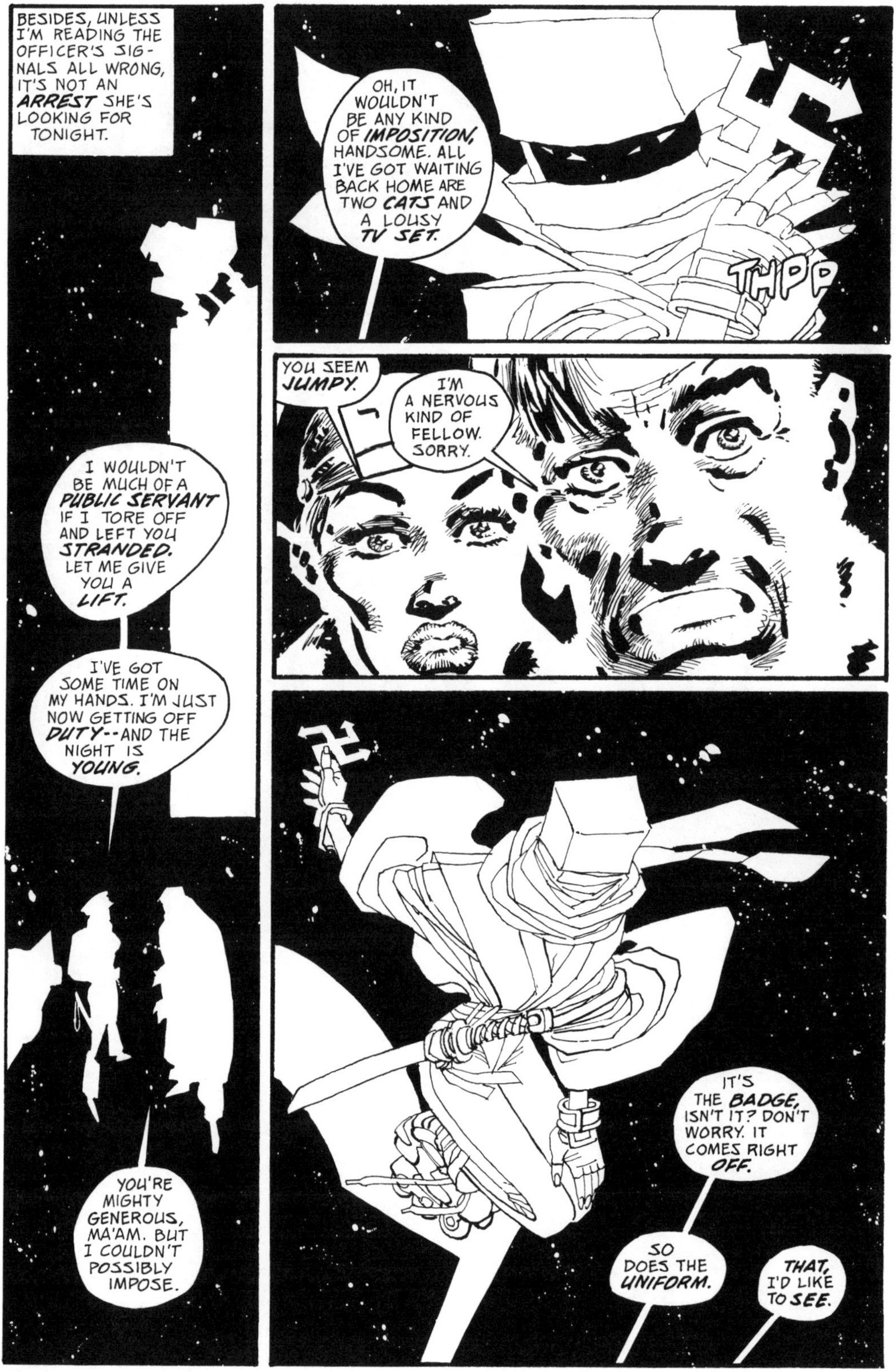

BESIDES, UNLESS I'M READING THE OFFICER'S SIG- NALS ALL WRONG, IT'S NOT AN ARREST SHE'S LOOKING FOR TONIGHT.
I WOULDN'T BE MUCH OF A PUBLIC SERVANT IF I TORE OFF AND LEFT YOU STRANDED. LET ME GIVE YOU A LIFT.
I'VE GOT SOME TIME ON MY HANDS. I'M JUST NOW GETTING OFF DUTY--AND THE NIGHT IS YOUNG.
YOU'RE MIGHTY GENEROUS, MA'AM. BUT I COULDN'T POSSIBLY IMPOSE.
OH, IT WOULDN'T BE ANY KIND OF IMPOSITION, HANDSOME. ALL I'VE GOT WAITING BACK HOME ARE TWO CATS AND A LOUSY TV SET.
THPP
YOU SEEM JUMPY.
I'M A NERVOUS KIND OF FELLOW. SORRY.
IT'S THE BADGE, ISN'T IT? DON'T WORRY. IT COMES RIGHT OFF.
SO DOES THE UNIFORM.
THAT, I'D LIKE TO SEE.

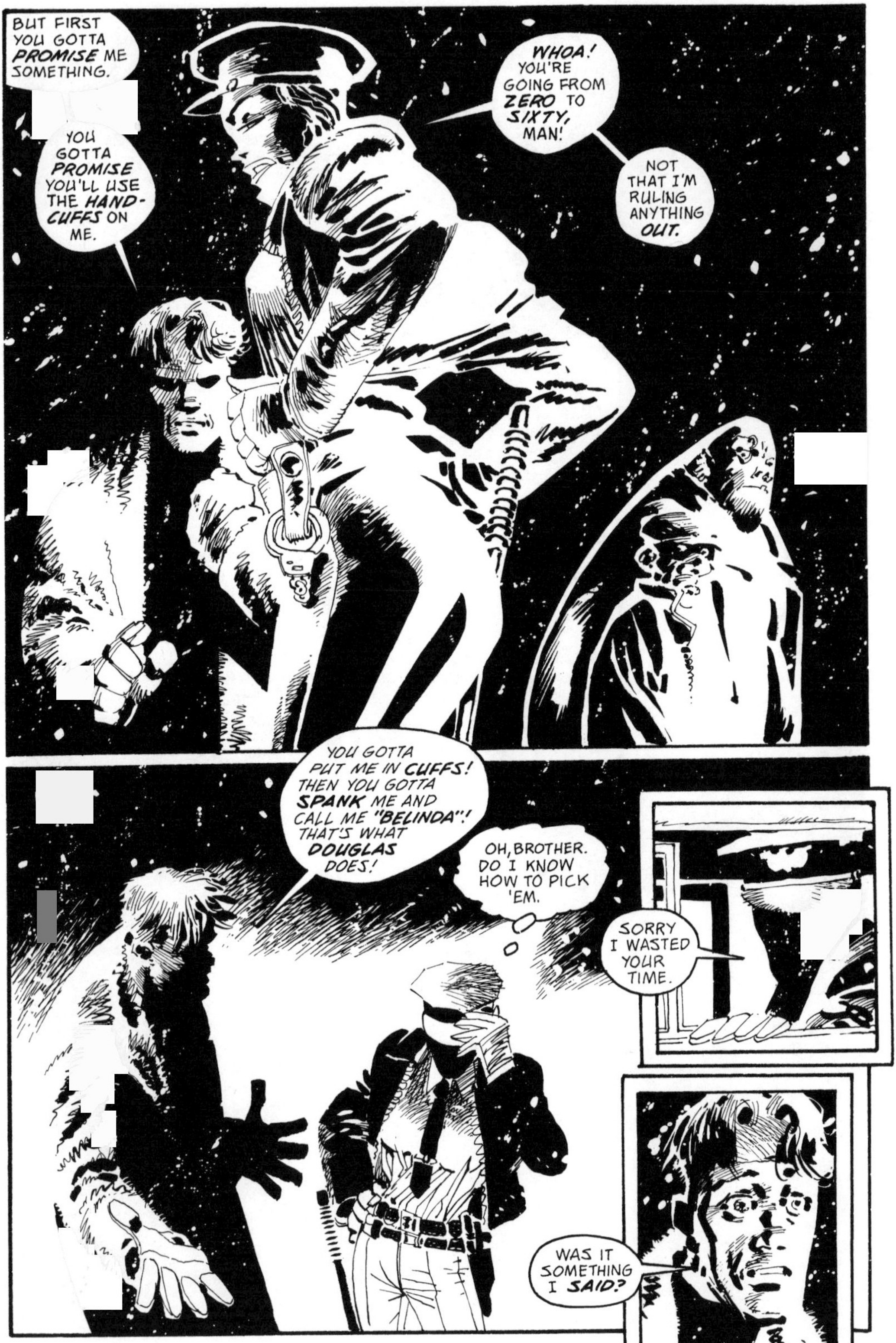

BUT FIRST YOU GOTTA PROMISE ME SOMETHING.
YOU GOTTA PROMISE YOU'LL USE THE HAND-CUFFS ON ME.
WHOA! YOU'RE GOING FROM ZERO TO SIXTY, MAN!
NOT THAT I'M RULING ANYTHING OUT.
YOU GOTTA PUT ME IN CUFFS! THEN YOU GOTTA SPANK ME AND CALL ME "BELINDA"! THAT'S WHAT DOUGLAS DOES!
OH, BROTHER. DO I KNOW HOW TO PICK 'EM.
SORRY I WASTED YOUR TIME.
WAS IT SOMETHING I SAID?

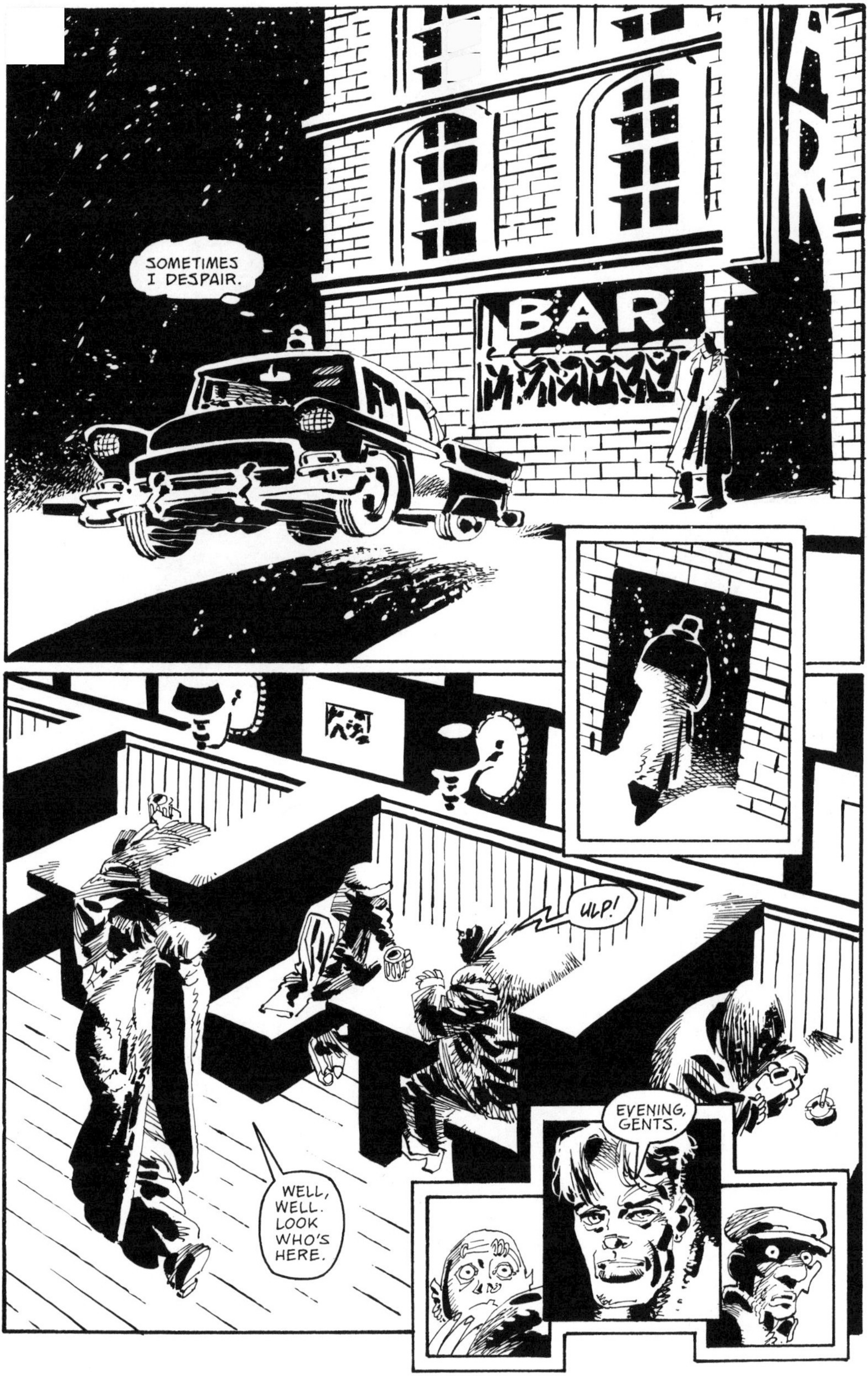
SOMETIMES I DESPAIR.
BAR
ULP!
WELL, WELL. LOOK WHO'S HERE.
EVENING, GENTS.

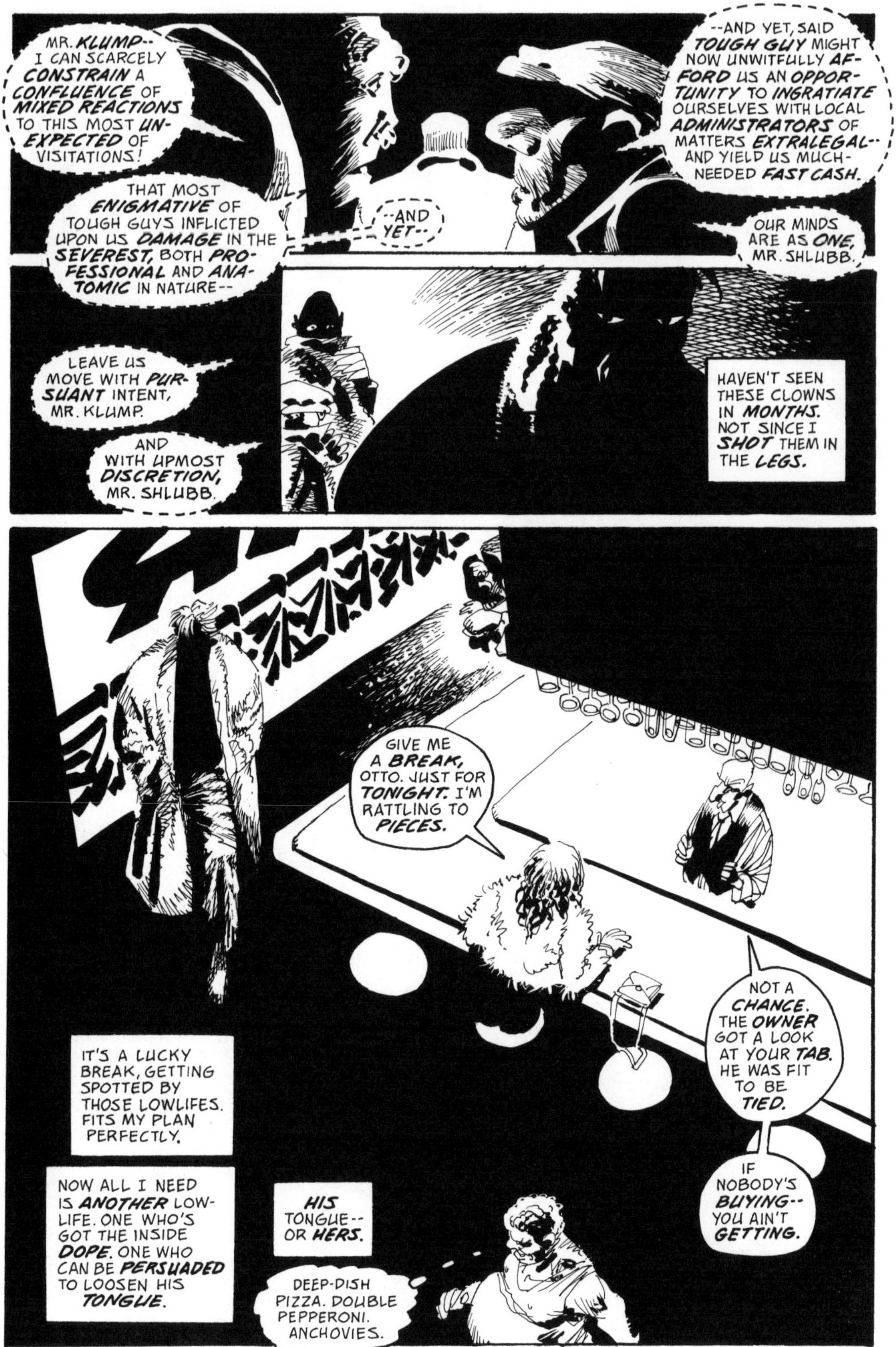
MR. KLUMP-- I CAN SCARCELY CONSTRAIN A CONFLUENCE OF MIXED REACTIONS TO THIS MOST UNEXPECTED OF VISITATIONS!
THAT MOST ENIGMATIVE OF TOUGH GUYS INFLICTED UPON US DAMAGE IN THE SEVEREST, BOTH PROFESSIONAL AND ANATOMIC IN NATURE--
--AND YET--
--AND YET, SAID TOUGH GUY MIGHT NOW UNWITFULLY AFFORD US AN OPPORTUNITY TO INGRATIATE OURSELVES WITH LOCAL ADMINISTRATORS OF MATTERS EXTRALEGAL-- AND YIELD US MUCH-NEEDED FAST CASH.
OUR MINDS ARE AS ONE, MR. SHLUBB.
LEAVE US MOVE WITH PURSUANT INTENT, MR. KLUMP.
AND WITH UPMOST DISCRETION, MR. SHLUBB.
HAVEN'T SEEN THESE CLOWNS IN MONTHS. NOT SINCE I SHOT THEM IN THE LEGS.
GIVE ME A BREAK, OTTO. JUST FOR TONIGHT. I'M RATTLING TO PIECES.
NOT A CHANCE. THE OWNER GOT A LOOK AT YOUR TAB. HE WAS FIT TO BE TIED.
IF NOBODY'S BUYING-- YOU AIN'T GETTING.
IT'S A LUCKY BREAK, GETTING SPOTTED BY THOSE LOWLIFES. FITS MY PLAN PERFECTLY.
NOW ALL I NEED IS ANOTHER LOWLIFE. ONE WHO'S GOT THE INSIDE DOPE. ONE WHO CAN BE PERSUADED TO LOOSEN HIS TONGUE.
HIS TONGUE-- OR HERS.
DEEP-DISH PIZZA. DOUBLE PEPPERONI. ANCHOVIES.

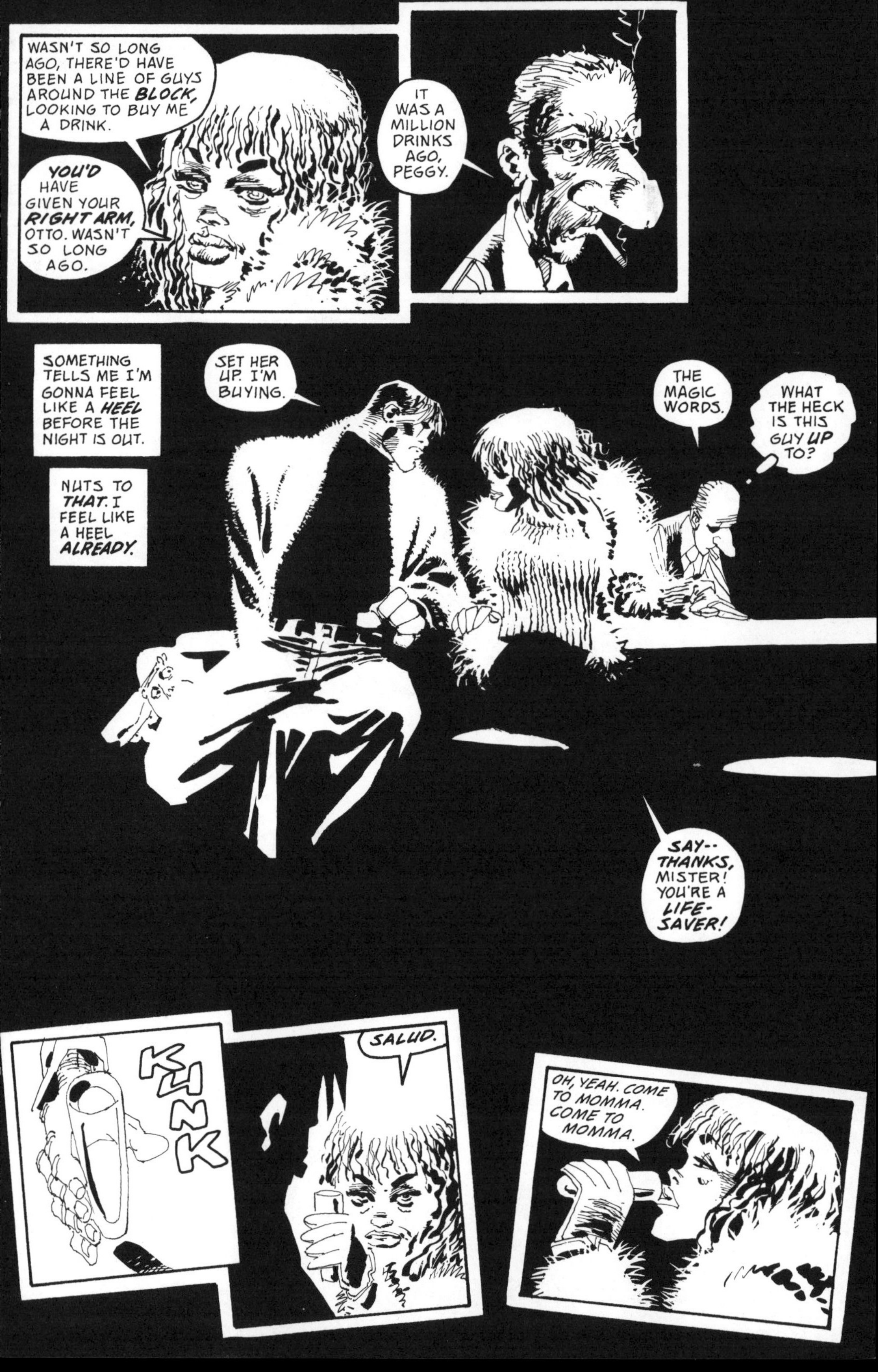
WASN'T SO LONG AGO, THERE'D HAVE BEEN A LINE OF GUYS AROUND THE BLOCK, LOOKING TO BUY ME A DRINK.
YOU'D HAVE GIVEN YOUR RIGHT ARM, OTTO. WASN'T SO LONG AGO.
IT WAS A MILLION DRINKS AGO, PEGGY.
SOMETHING TELLS ME I'M GONNA FEEL LIKE A HEEL BEFORE THE NIGHT IS OUT.
NUTS TO THAT. I FEEL LIKE A HEEL ALREADY.
SET HER UP. I'M BUYING.
THE MAGIC WORDS.
WHAT THE HECK IS THIS GUY UP TO?
SAY-- THANKS, MISTER! YOU'RE A LIFE-SAVER!
KLUNK
SALUD.
OH, YEAH. COME TO MOMMA. COME TO MOMMA.

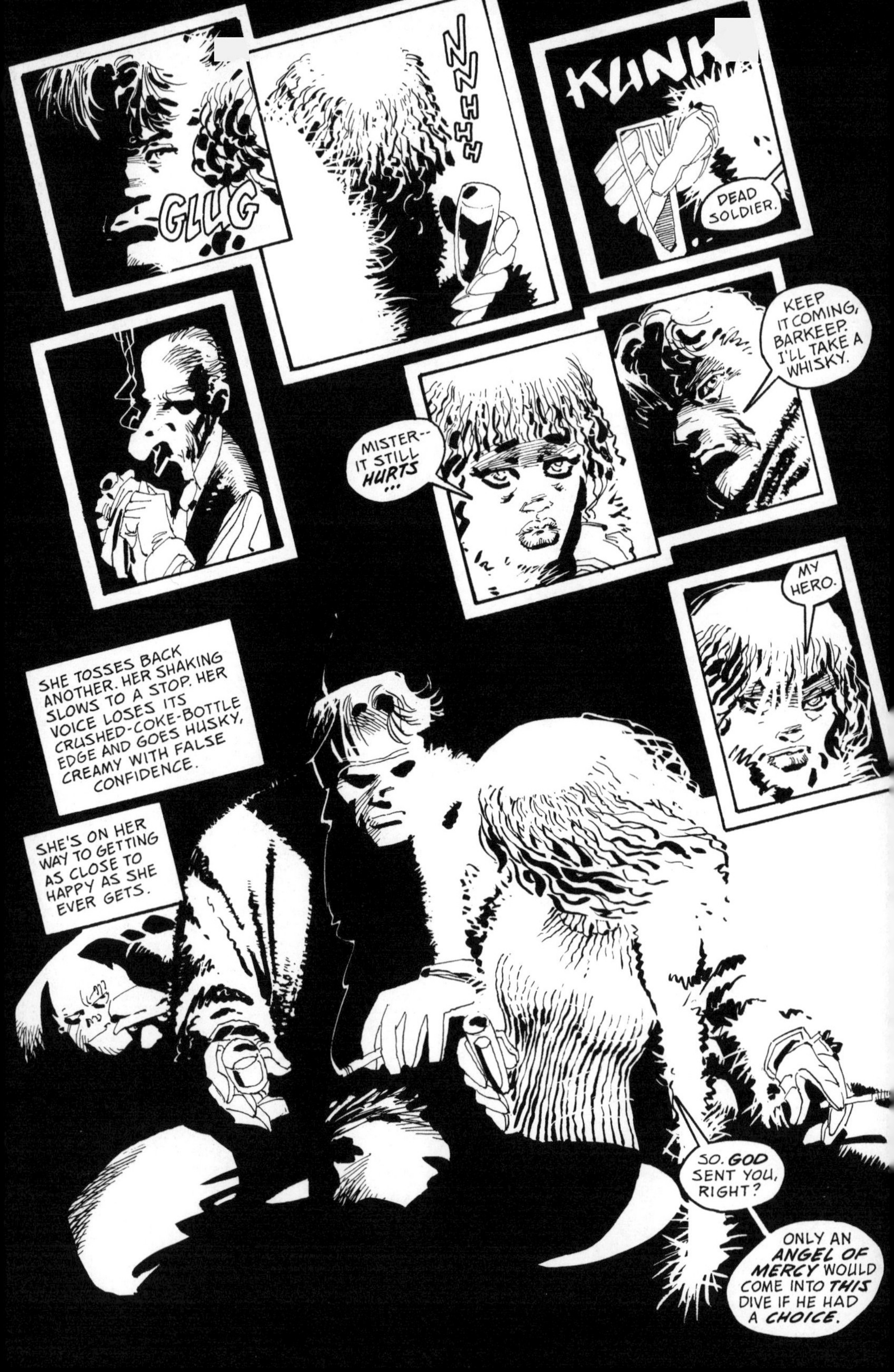
GLUG
NNHHHH
KUNK
DEAD SOLDIER.
MISTER-- IT STILL HURTS ...
KEEP IT COMING, BARKEEP. I'LL TAKE A WHISKY.
MY HERO.
SHE TOSSES BACK ANOTHER. HER SHAKING SLOWS TO A STOP. HER VOICE LOSES ITS CRUSHED-COKE-BOTTLE EDGE AND GOES HUSKY, CREAMY WITH FALSE CONFIDENCE.
SHE'S ON HER WAY TO GETTING AS CLOSE TO HAPPY AS SHE EVER GETS.
SO. GOD SENT YOU, RIGHT?
ONLY AN ANGEL OF MERCY WOULD COME INTO THIS DIVE IF HE HAD A CHOICE.

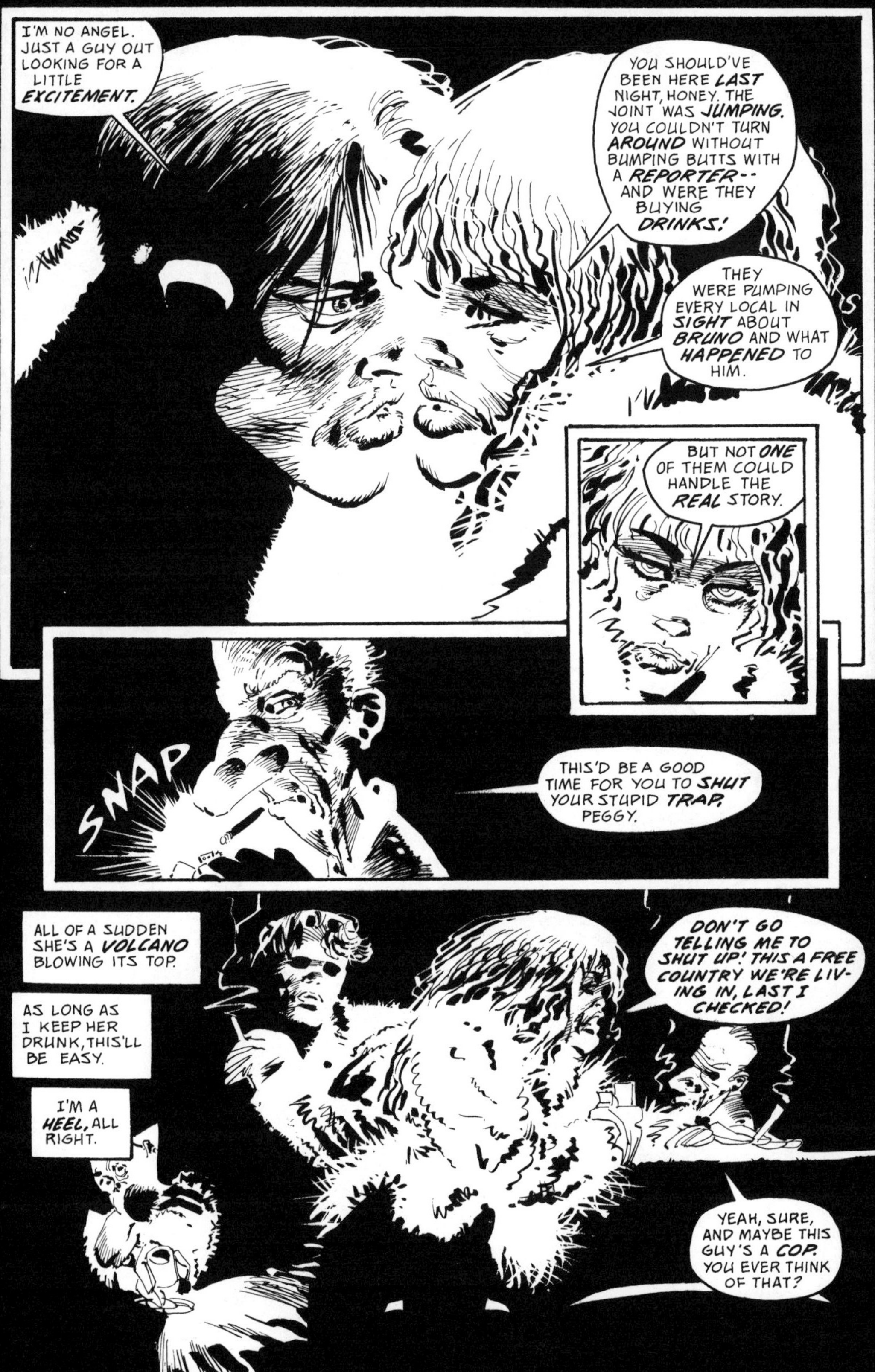
I'M NO ANGEL. JUST A GUY OUT LOOKING FOR A LITTLE EXCITEMENT.
YOU SHOULD'VE BEEN HERE LAST NIGHT, HONEY. THE JOINT WAS JUMPING. YOU COULDN'T TURN AROUND WITHOUT BUMPING BUTTS WITH A REPORTER-- AND WERE THEY BUYING DRINKS!
THEY WERE PUMPING EVERY LOCAL IN SIGHT ABOUT BRUNO AND WHAT HAPPENED TO HIM.
BUT NOT ONE OF THEM COULD HANDLE THE REAL STORY.
SNAP
THIS'D BE A GOOD TIME FOR YOU TO SHUT YOUR STUPID TRAP, PEGGY.
ALL OF A SUDDEN SHE'S A VOLCANO BLOWING ITS TOP.
DON'T GO TELLING ME TO SHUT UP! THIS A FREE COUNTRY WE'RE LIVING IN, LAST I CHECKED!
AS LONG AS I KEEP HER DRUNK, THIS'LL BE EASY.
I'M A HEEL, ALL RIGHT.
YEAH, SURE, AND MAYBE THIS GUY'S A COP. YOU EVER THINK OF THAT?

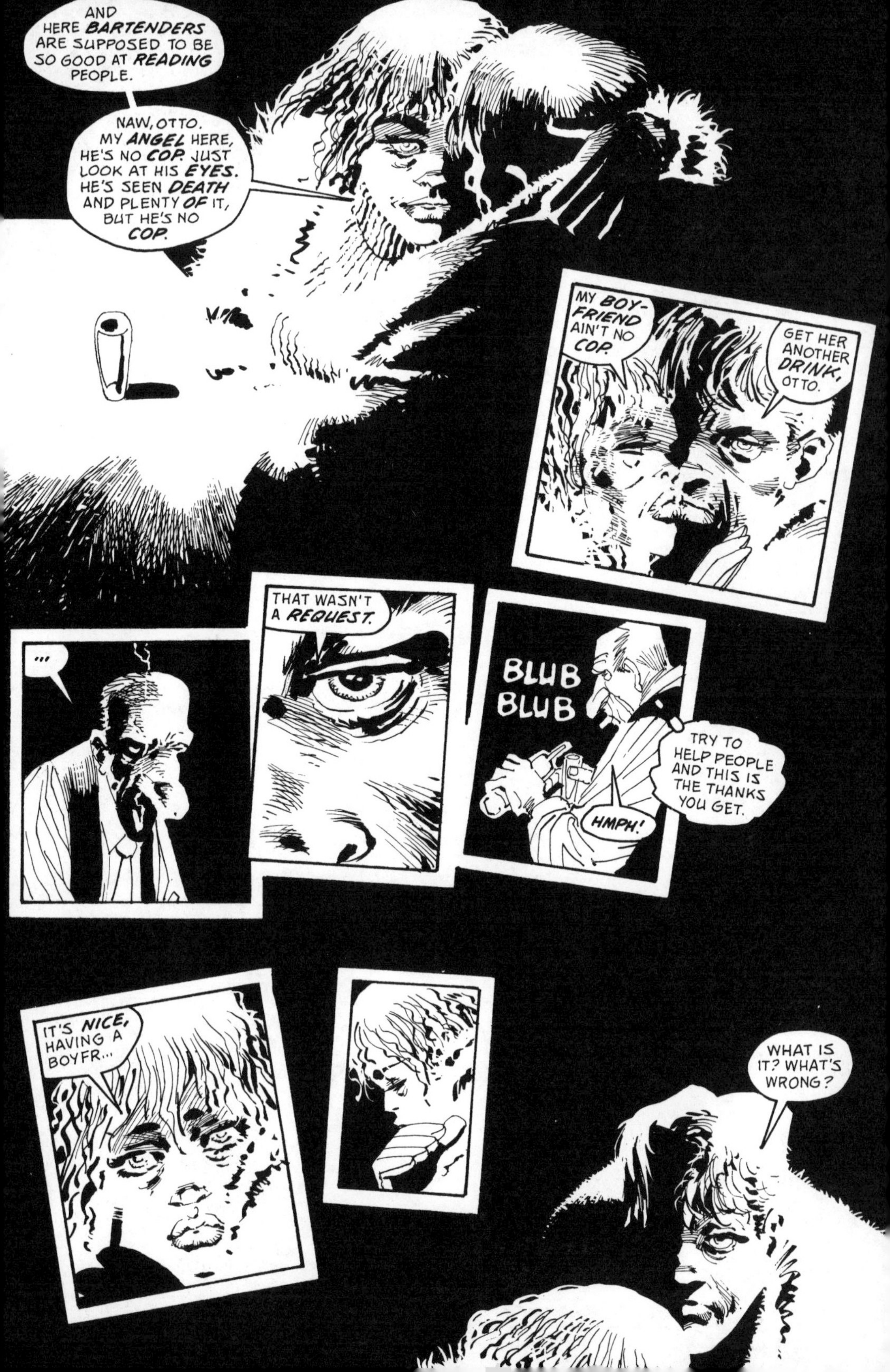
AND HERE BARTENDERS ARE SUPPOSED TO BE SO GOOD AT READING PEOPLE.
NAW, OTTO. MY ANGEL HERE, HE'S NO COP. JUST LOOK AT HIS EYES. HE'S SEEN DEATH AND PLENTY OF IT, BUT HE'S NO COP.
MY BOY-FRIEND AIN'T NO COP.
GET HER ANOTHER DRINK, OTTO.
...
THAT WASN'T A REQUEST.
BLUB BLUB
TRY TO HELP PEOPLE AND THIS IS THE THANKS YOU GET.
HMPH!
IT'S NICE, HAVING A BOYFR...
WHAT IS IT? WHAT'S WRONG?

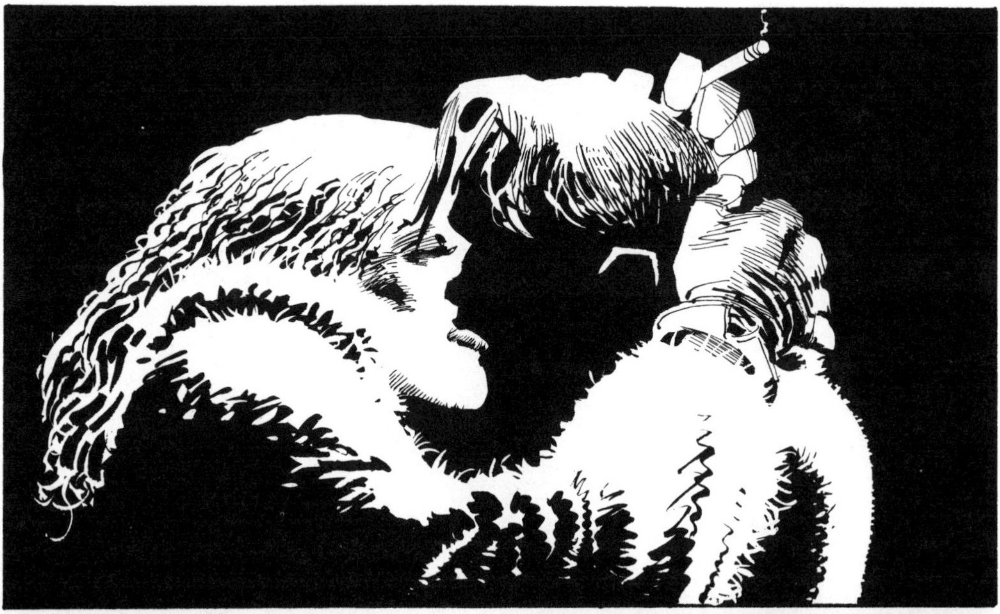

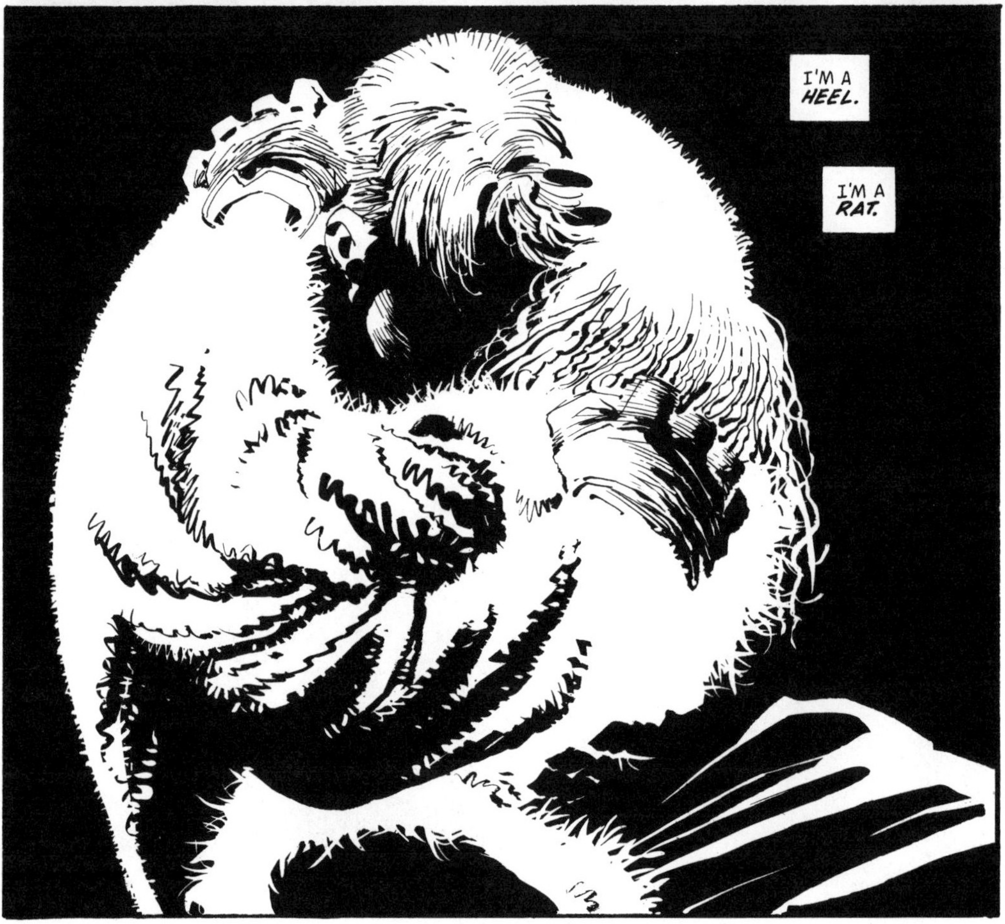
I'M A HEEL.
I'M A RAT.

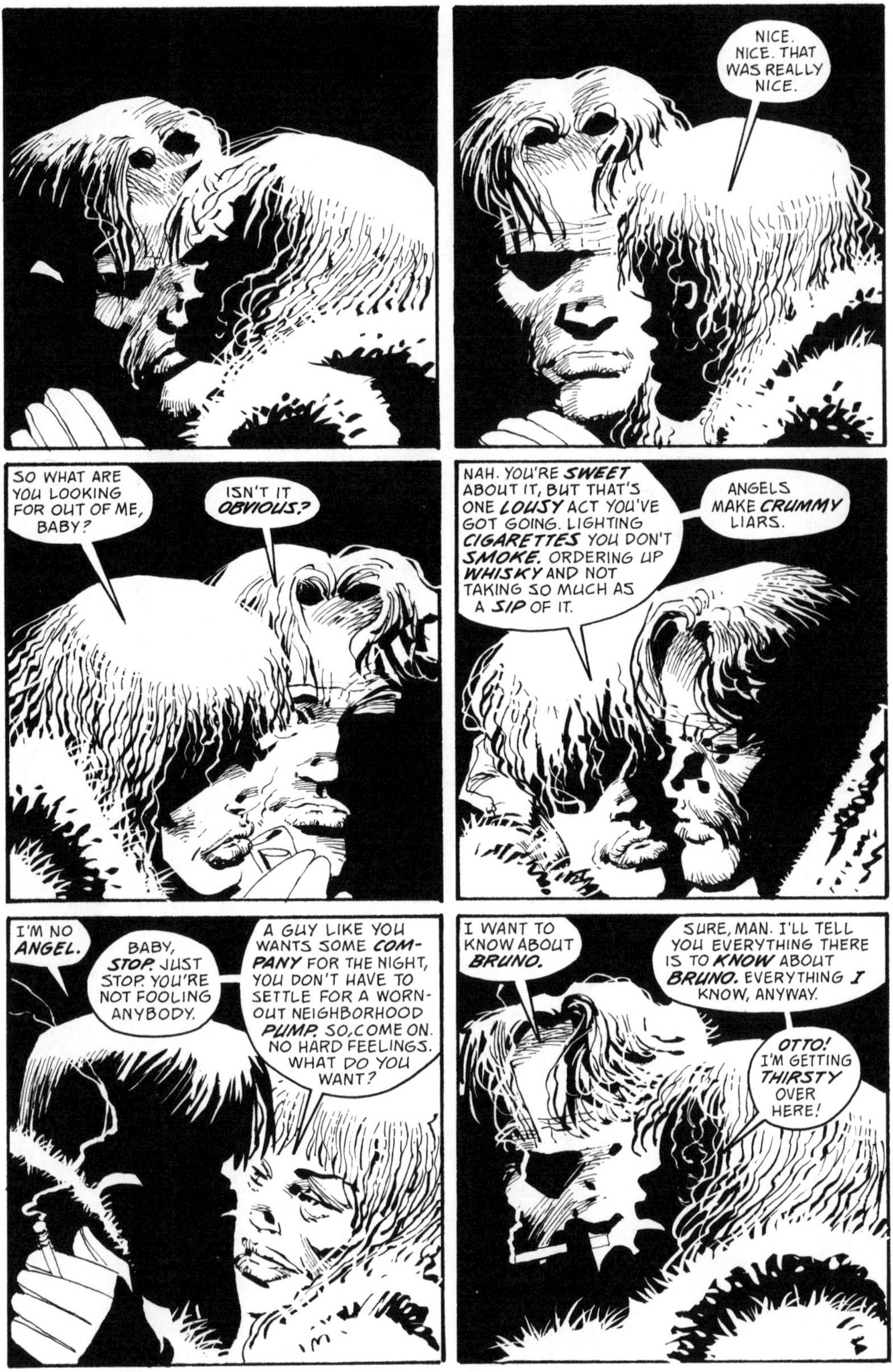
NICE. NICE. THAT WAS REALLY NICE.
SO WHAT ARE YOU LOOKING FOR OUT OF ME, BABY?
ISN'T IT OBVIOUS?
NAH. YOU'RE SWEET ABOUT IT, BUT THAT'S ONE LOUSY ACT YOU'VE GOT GOING. LIGHTING CIGARETTES YOU DON'T SMOKE. ORDERING UP WHISKY AND NOT TAKING SO MUCH AS A SIP OF IT.
ANGELS MAKE CRUMMY LIARS.
I'M NO ANGEL.
BABY, STOP. JUST STOP. YOU'RE NOT FOOLING ANYBODY.
A GUY LIKE YOU WANTS SOME COMPANY FOR THE NIGHT, YOU DON'T HAVE TO SETTLE FOR A WORN-OUT NEIGHBORHOOD PUMP. SO, COME ON. NO HARD FEELINGS. WHAT DO YOU WANT?
I WANT TO KNOW ABOUT BRUNO.
SURE, MAN. I'LL TELL YOU EVERYTHING THERE IS TO KNOW ABOUT BRUNO. EVERYTHING I KNOW, ANYWAY.
OTTO! I'M GETTING THIRSTY OVER HERE!

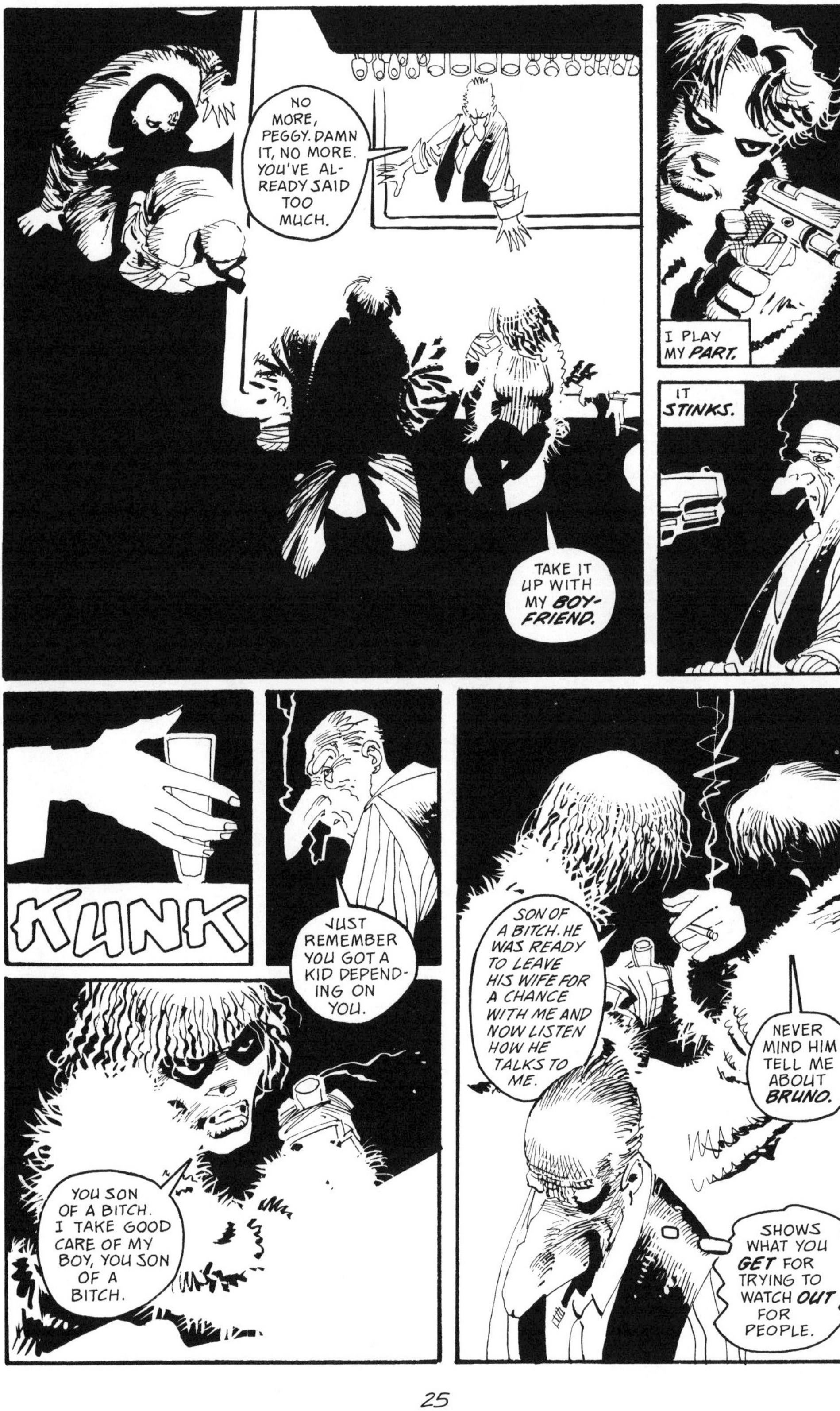

NO MORE, PEGGY. DAMN IT, NO MORE. YOU'VE ALREADY SAID TOO MUCH.
TAKE IT UP WITH MY BOYFRIEND.
I PLAY MY PART.
IT STINKS.
KUNK
JUST REMEMBER YOU GOT A KID DEPENDING ON YOU.
YOU SON OF A BITCH. I TAKE GOOD CARE OF MY BOY, YOU SON OF A BITCH.
SON OF A BITCH. HE WAS READY TO LEAVE HIS WIFE FOR A CHANCE WITH ME AND NOW LISTEN HOW HE TALKS TO ME.
NEVER MIND HIM. TELL ME ABOUT BRUNO.
SHOWS WHAT YOU GET FOR TRYING TO WATCH OUT FOR PEOPLE.

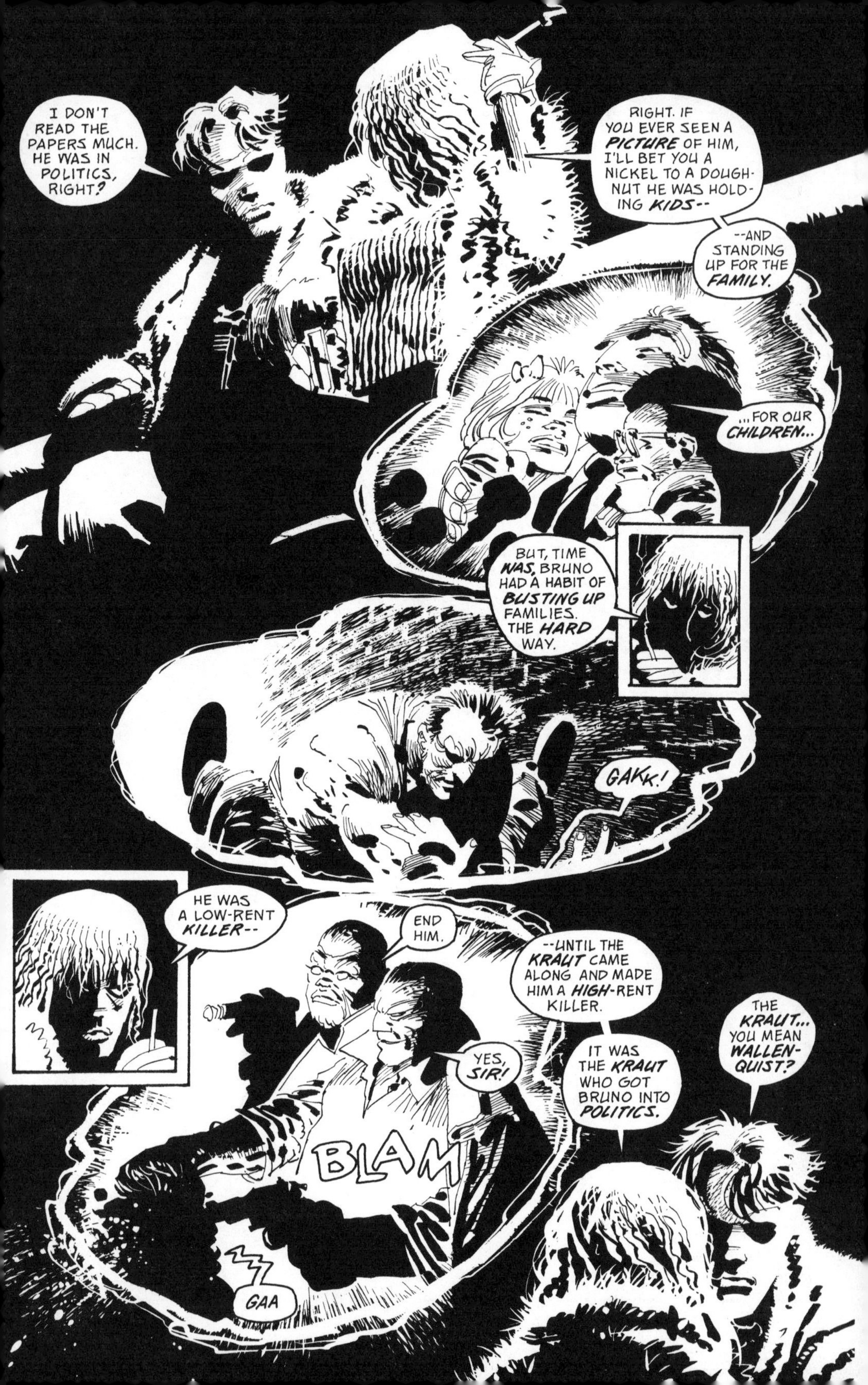
I DON'T READ THE PAPERS MUCH. HE WAS IN POLITICS, RIGHT?
RIGHT. IF YOU EVER SEEN A PICTURE OF HIM, I'LL BET YOU A NICKEL TO A DOUGHNUT HE WAS HOLDING KIDS--
--AND STANDING UP FOR THE FAMILY.
...FOR OUR CHILDREN...
BUT, TIME WAS, BRUNO HAD A HABIT OF BUSTING UP FAMILIES. THE HARD WAY.
GAKK!
HE WAS A LOW-RENT KILLER--
END HIM.
--UNTIL THE KRAUT CAME ALONG AND MADE HIM A HIGH-RENT KILLER.
YES, SIR!
IT WAS THE KRAUT WHO GOT BRUNO INTO POLITICS.
THE KRAUT... YOU MEAN WALLENQUIST?
BLAM
GAA

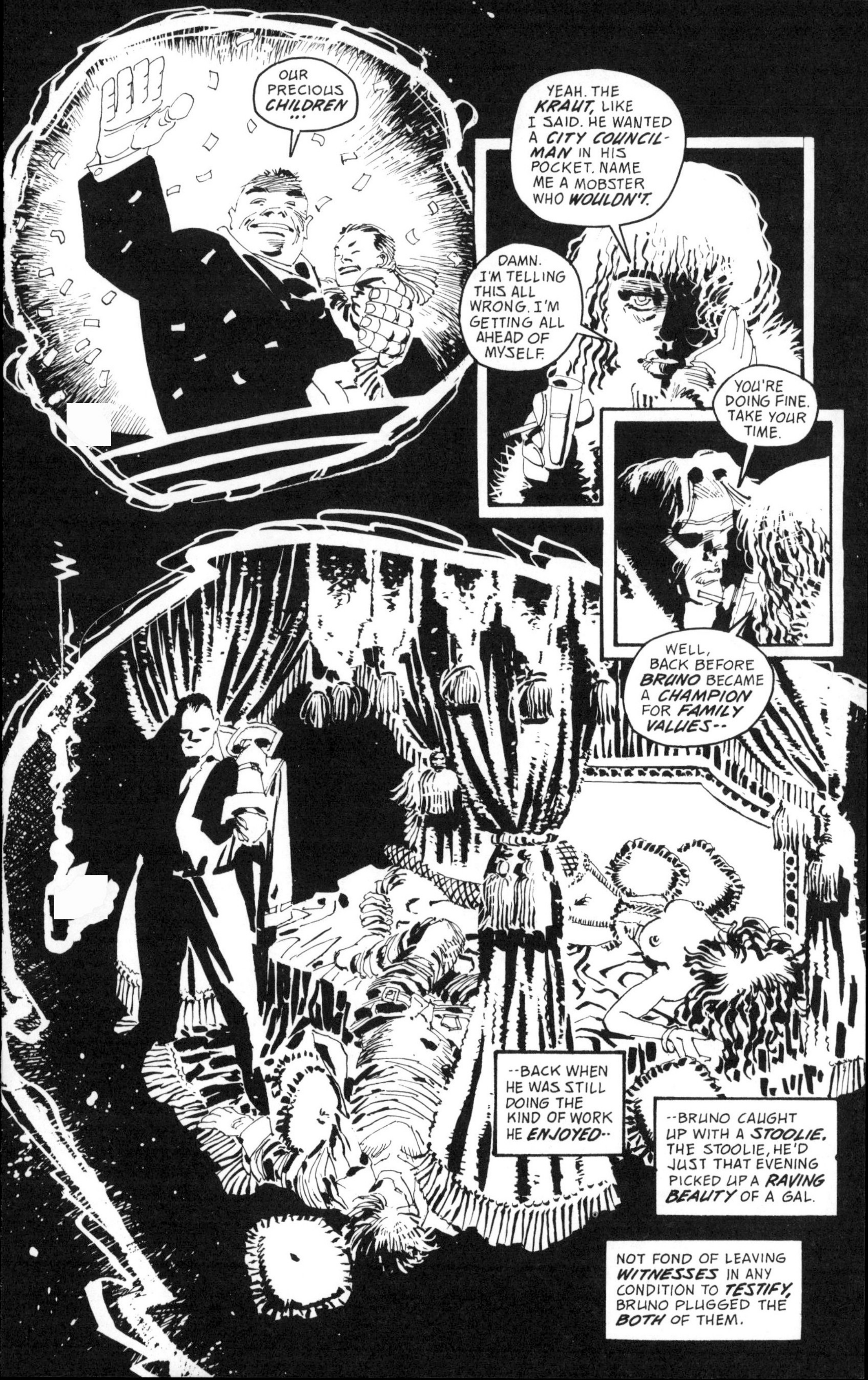
OUR PRECIOUS CHILDREN ...
YEAH. THE KRAUT, LIKE I SAID. HE WANTED A CITY COUNCILMAN IN HIS POCKET. NAME ME A MOBSTER WHO WOULDN'T.
DAMN. I'M TELLING THIS ALL WRONG. I'M GETTING ALL AHEAD OF MYSELF.
YOU'RE DOING FINE. TAKE YOUR TIME.
WELL, BACK BEFORE BRUNO BECAME A CHAMPION FOR FAMILY VALUES--
--BACK WHEN HE WAS STILL DOING THE KIND OF WORK HE ENJOYED--
--BRUNO CAUGHT UP WITH A STOOLIE. THE STOOLIE, HE'D JUST THAT EVENING PICKED UP A RAVING BEAUTY OF A GAL.
NOT FOND OF LEAVING WITNESSES IN ANY CONDITION TO TESTIFY, BRUNO PLUGGED THE BOTH OF THEM.

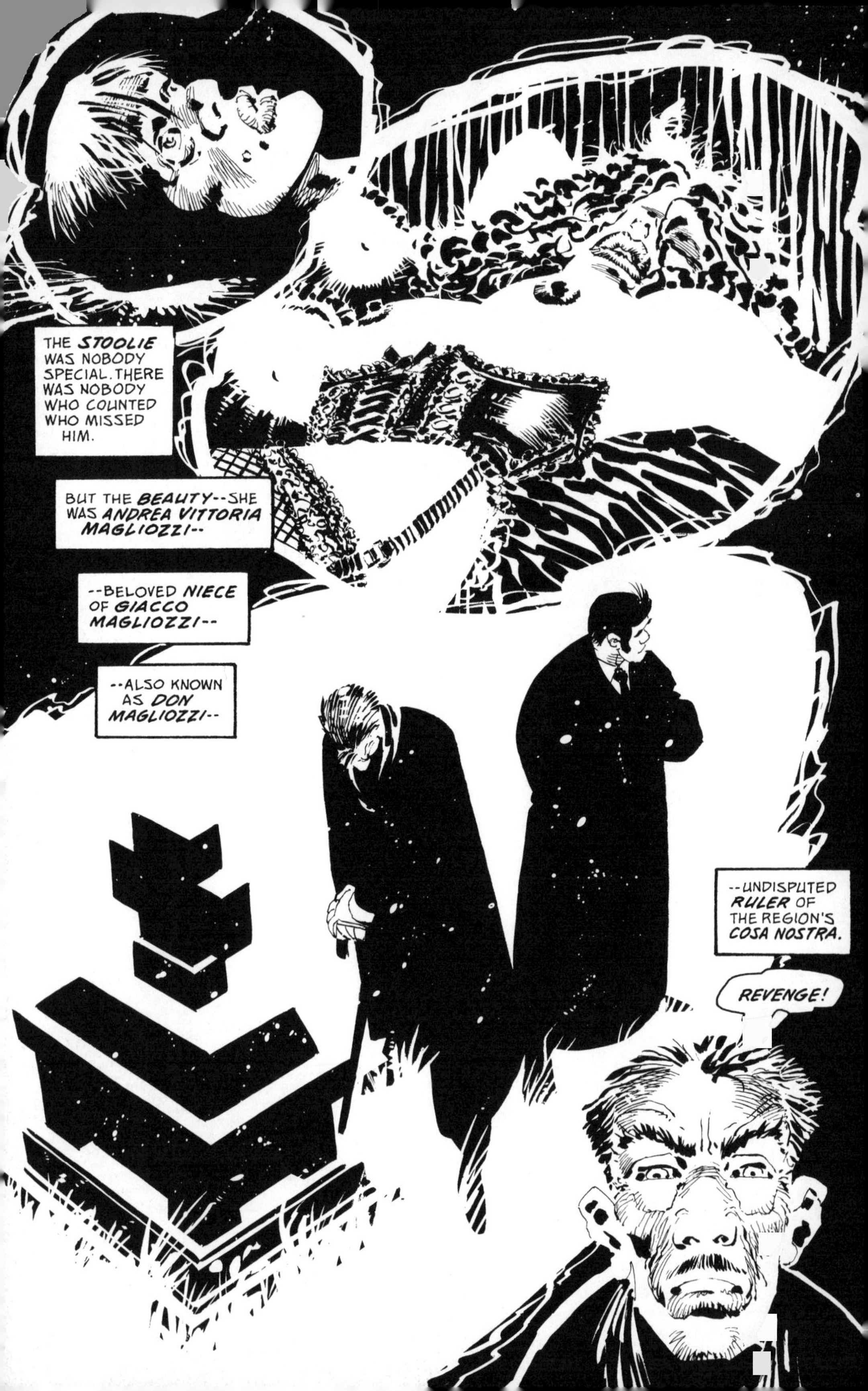
THE STOOLIE WAS NOBODY SPECIAL. THERE WAS NOBODY WHO COUNTED WHO MISSED HIM.
BUT THE BEAUTY--SHE WAS ANDREA VITTORIA MAGLIOZZI--
--BELOVED NIECE OF GIACCO MAGLIOZZI--
--ALSO KNOWN AS DON MAGLIOZZI--
--UNDISPUTED RULER OF THE REGION'S COSA NOSTRA.
REVENGE!

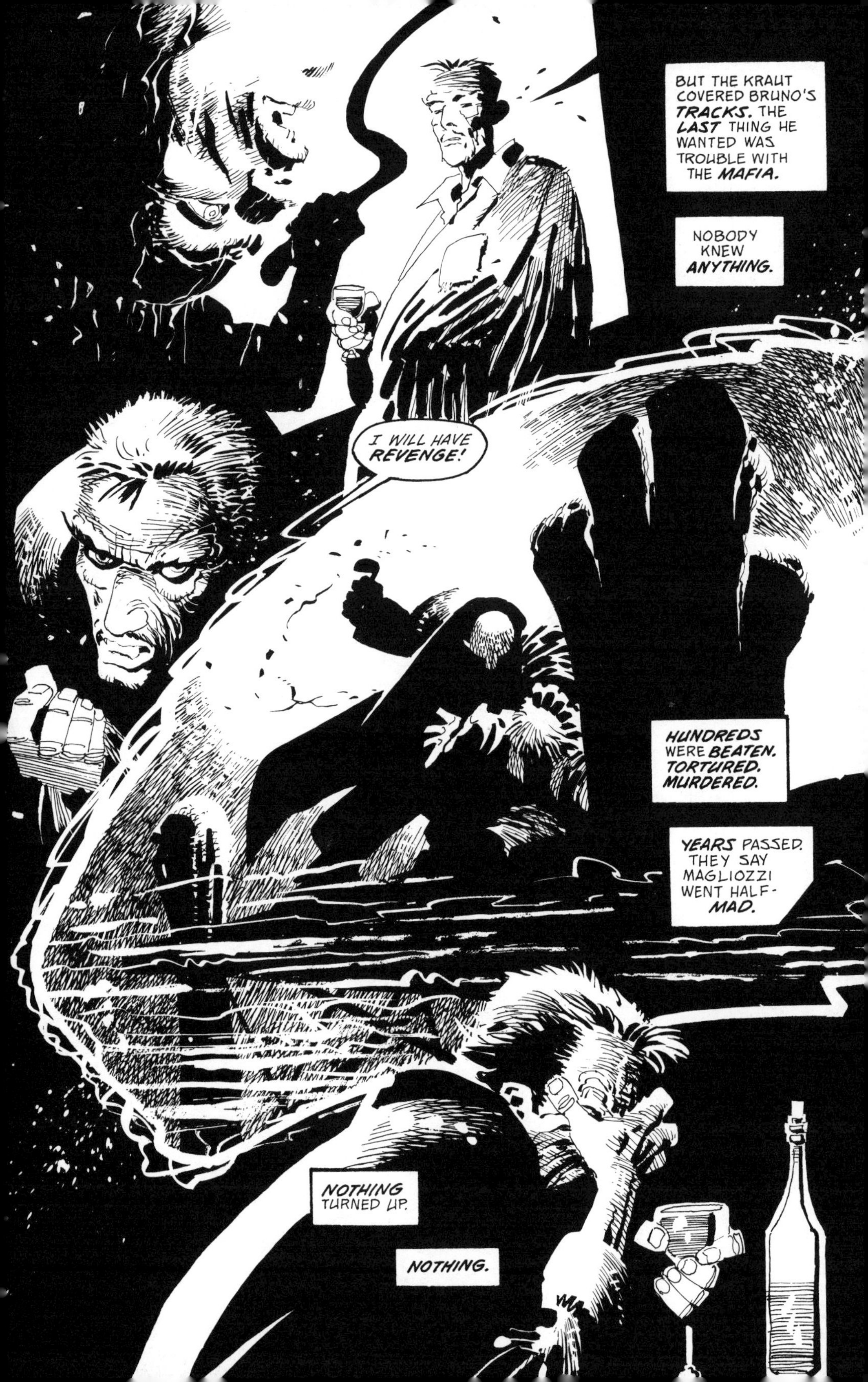
BUT THE KRAUT COVERED BRUNO'S **TRACKS.** THE **LAST** THING HE WANTED WAS TROUBLE WITH THE **MAFIA.**
NOBODY KNEW **ANYTHING.**
I WILL HAVE **REVENGE!**
HUNDREDS WERE **BEATEN. TORTURED. MURDERED.**
YEARS PASSED. THEY SAY MAGLIOZZI WENT HALF-**MAD.**
NOTHING TURNED UP.
NOTHING.

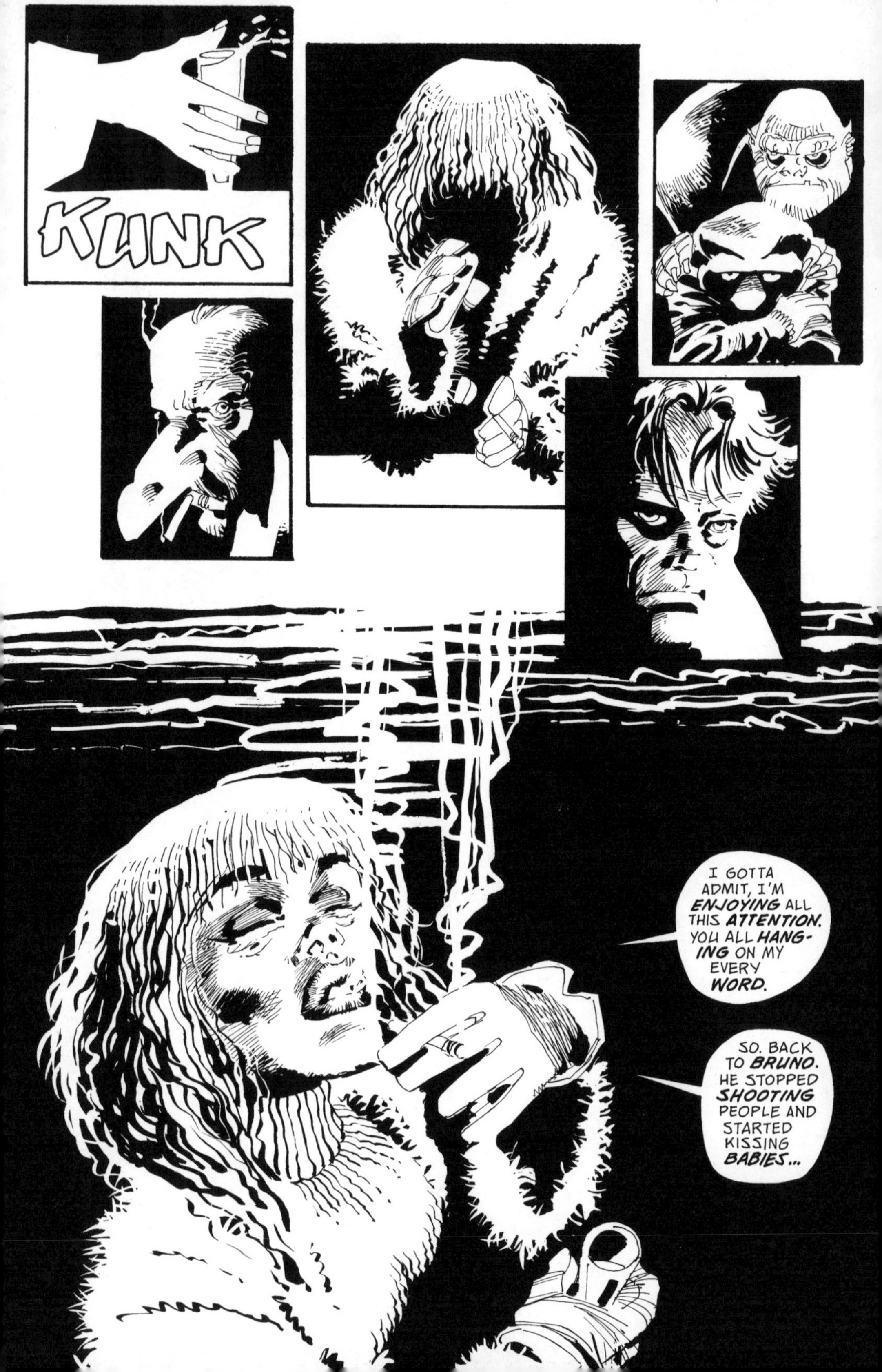
KUNK
I GOTTA ADMIT, I'M ENJOYING ALL THIS ATTENTION. YOU ALL HANG-ING ON MY EVERY WORD.
SO. BACK TO BRUNO. HE STOPPED SHOOTING PEOPLE AND STARTED KISSING BABIES...

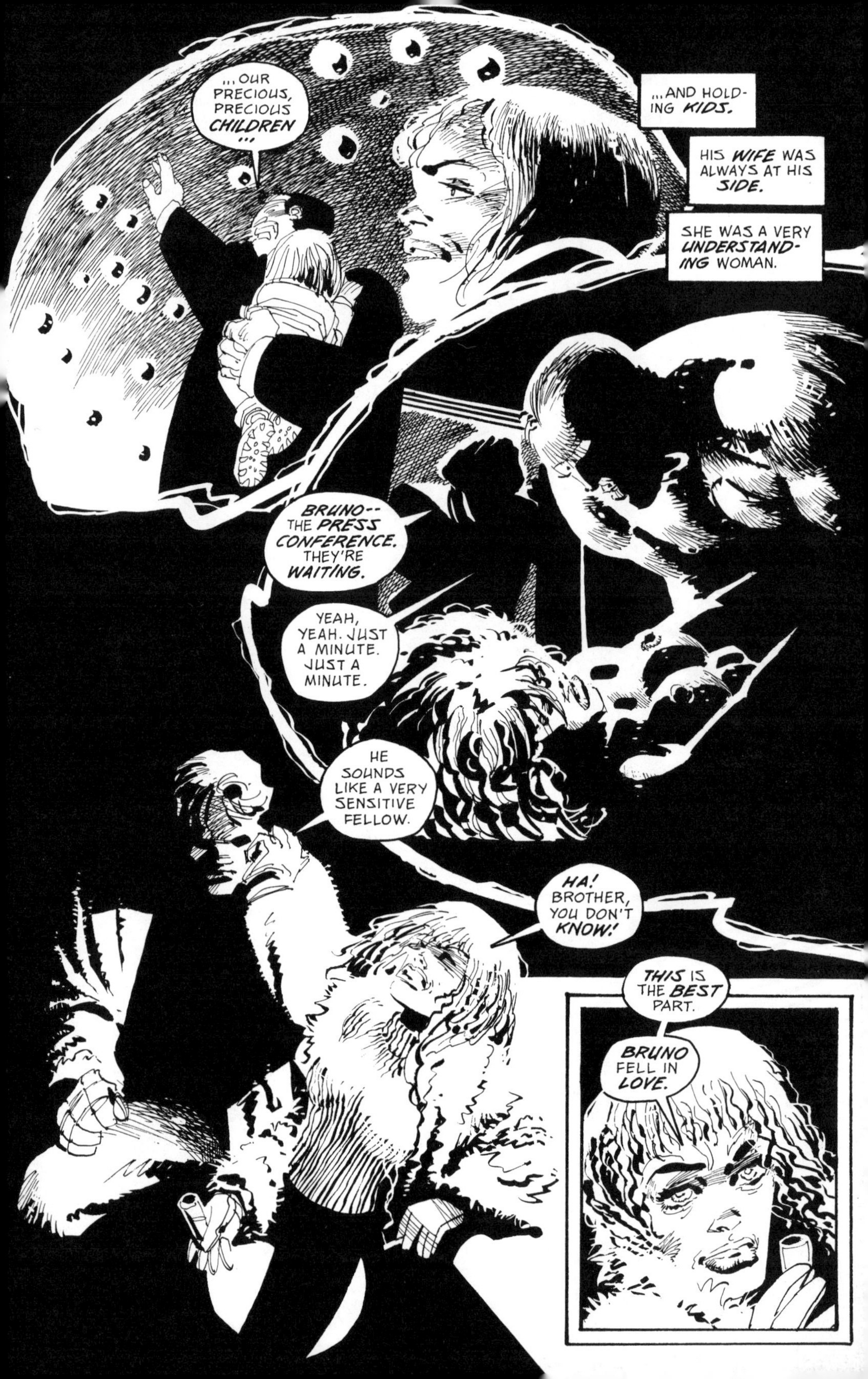
...OUR PRECIOUS, PRECIOUS CHILDREN ...
...AND HOLDING KIDS.
HIS WIFE WAS ALWAYS AT HIS SIDE.
SHE WAS A VERY UNDERSTANDING WOMAN.
BRUNO-- THE PRESS CONFERENCE. THEY'RE WAITING.
YEAH, YEAH. JUST A MINUTE. JUST A MINUTE.
HE SOUNDS LIKE A VERY SENSITIVE FELLOW.
HA! BROTHER, YOU DON'T KNOW!
THIS IS THE BEST PART.
BRUNO FELL IN LOVE.

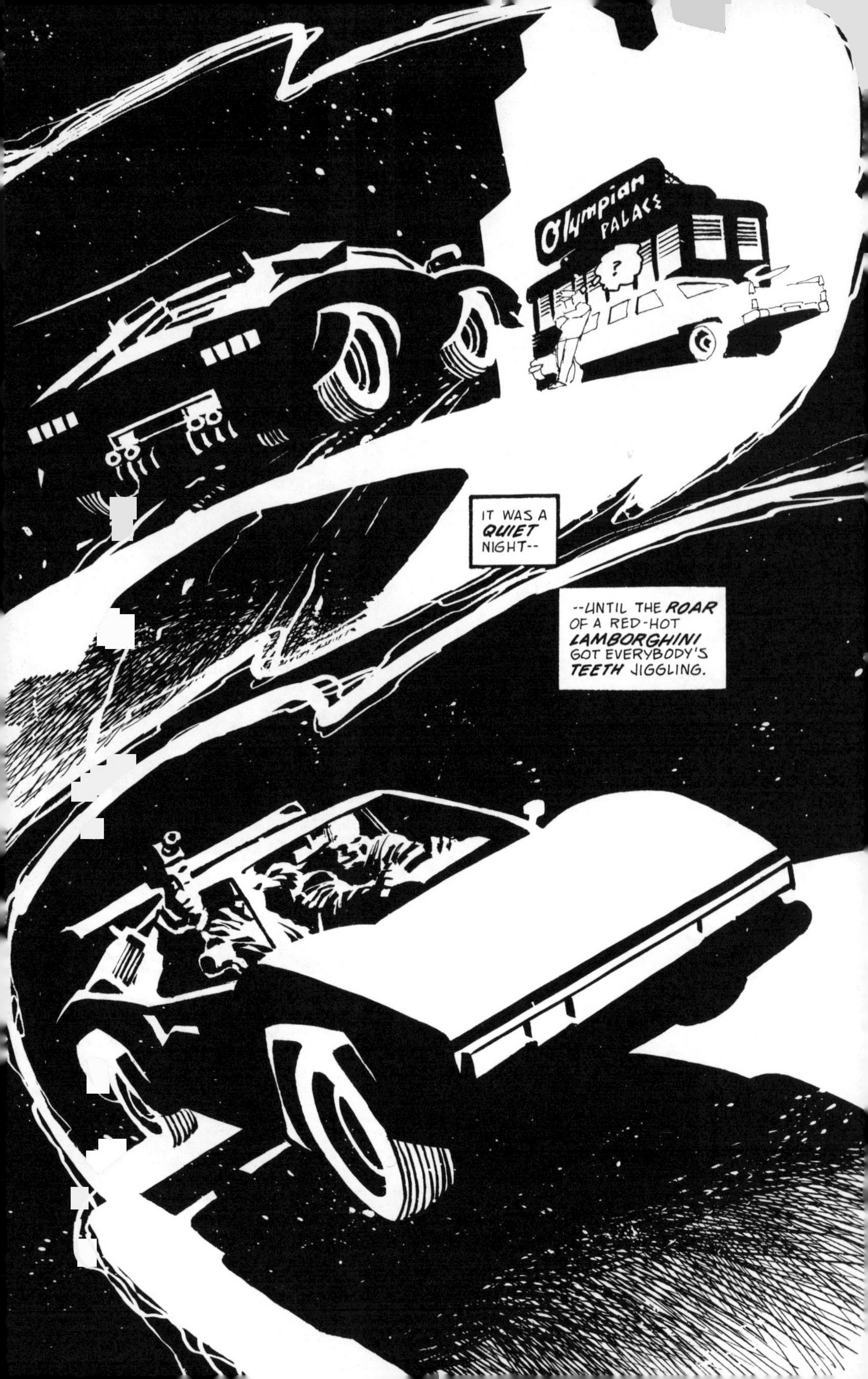

Olympian PALACE
IT WAS A QUIET NIGHT--
--UNTIL THE ROAR OF A RED-HOT LAMBORGHINI GOT EVERYBODY'S TEETH JIGGLING.

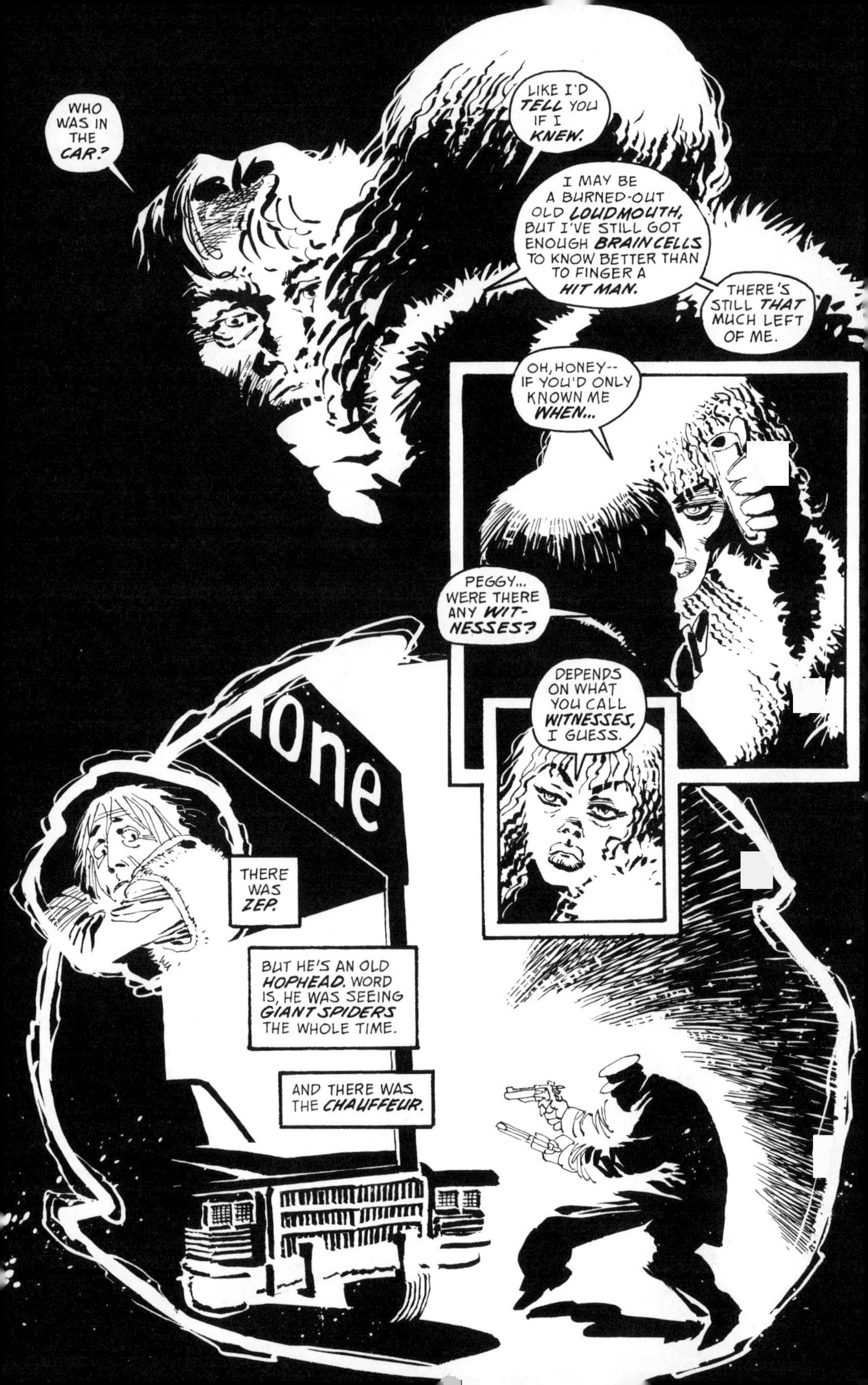
WHO WAS IN THE CAR?
LIKE I'D TELL YOU IF I KNEW.
I MAY BE A BURNED-OUT OLD LOUDMOUTH, BUT I'VE STILL GOT ENOUGH BRAIN CELLS TO KNOW BETTER THAN TO FINGER A HIT MAN.
THERE'S STILL THAT MUCH LEFT OF ME.
OH, HONEY-- IF YOU'D ONLY KNOWN ME WHEN...
PEGGY... WERE THERE ANY WIT-NESSES?
DEPENDS ON WHAT YOU CALL WITNESSES, I GUESS.
THERE WAS ZEP.
BUT HE'S AN OLD HOPHEAD. WORD IS, HE WAS SEEING GIANT SPIDERS THE WHOLE TIME.
AND THERE WAS THE CHAUFFEUR.

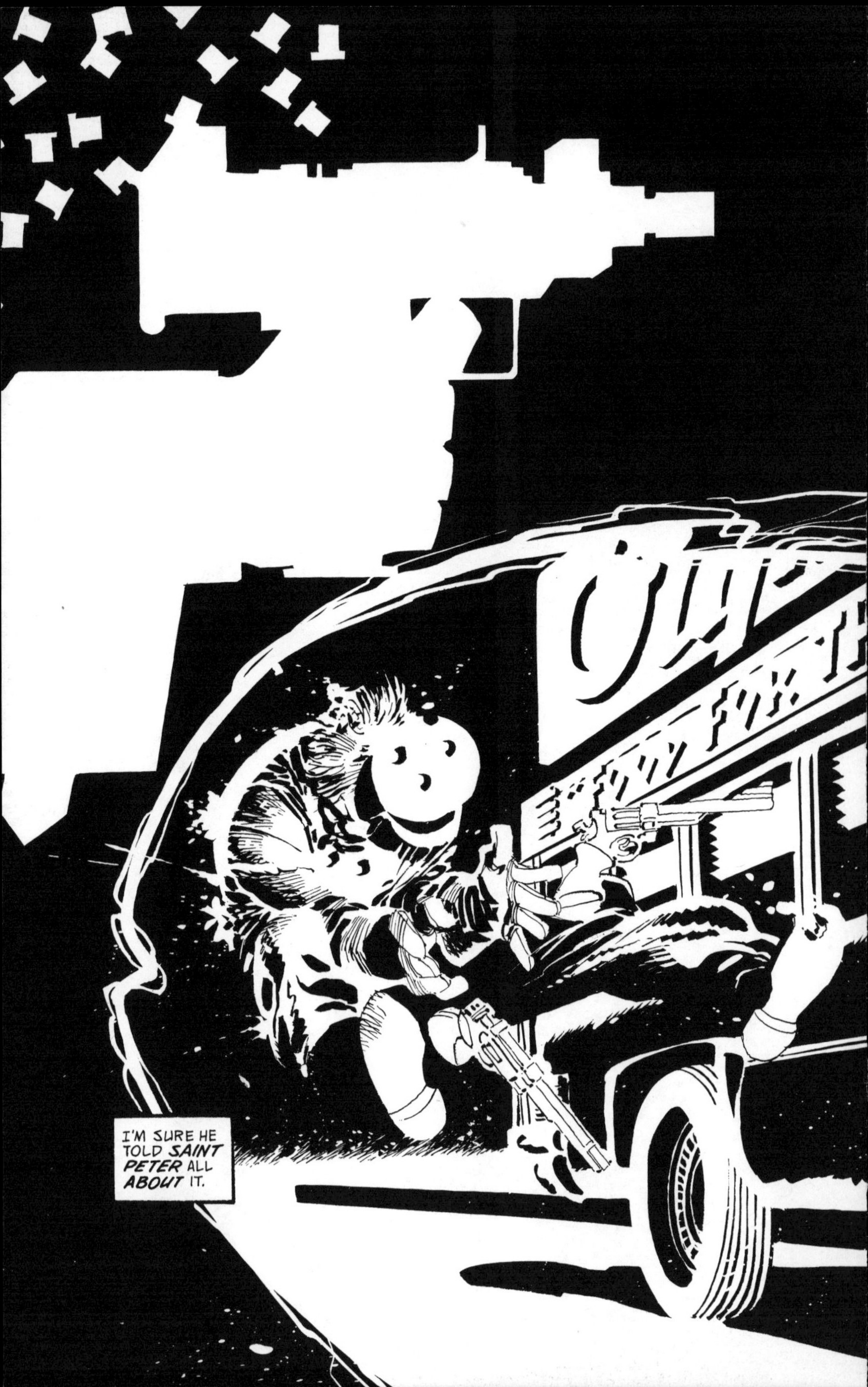
I'M SURE HE TOLD *SAINT PETER* ALL *ABOUT* IT.

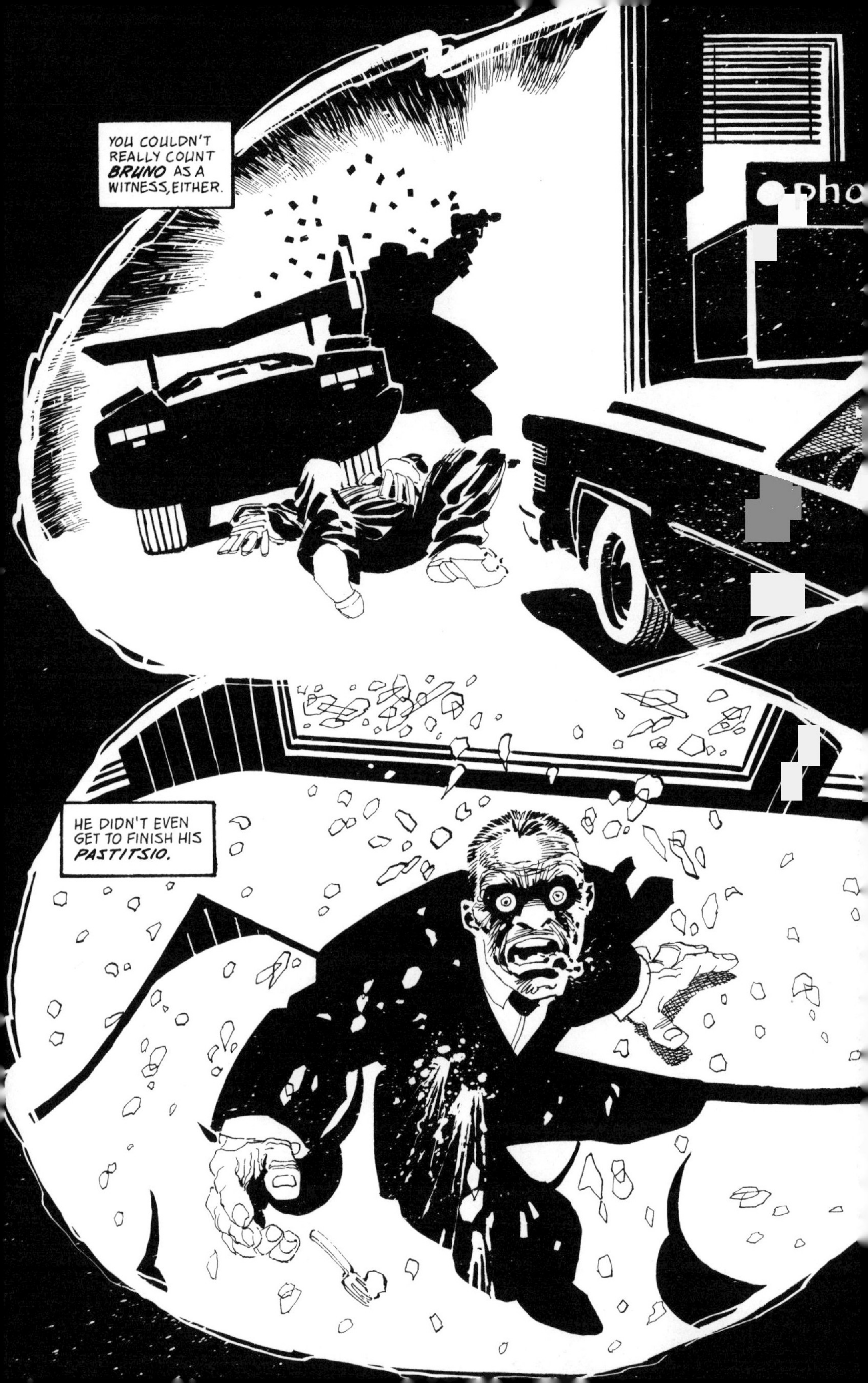
YOU COULDN'T REALLY COUNT *BRUNO* AS A WITNESS, EITHER.
HE DIDN'T EVEN GET TO FINISH HIS *PASTITSIO.*

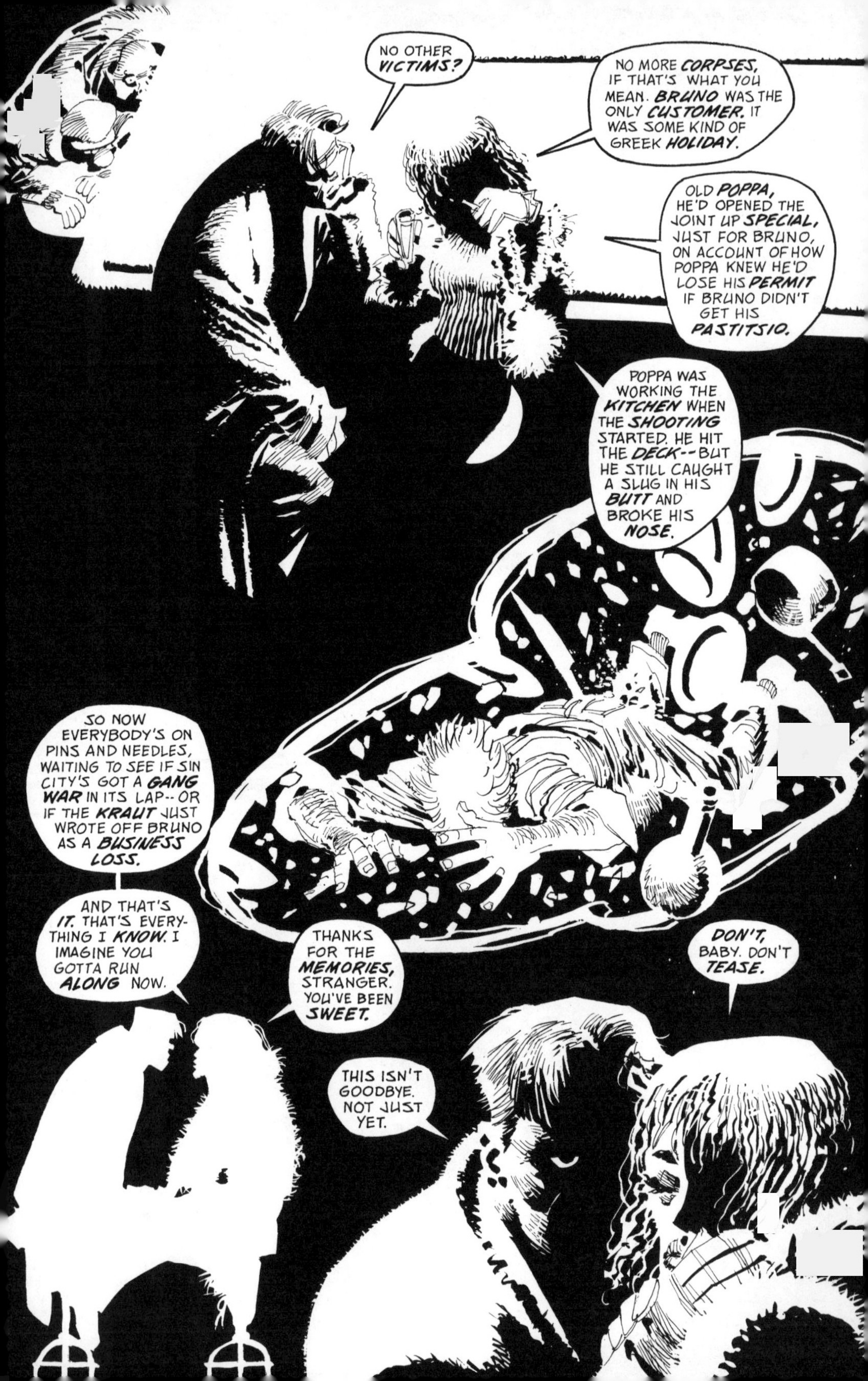
NO OTHER VICTIMS?
NO MORE CORPSES, IF THAT'S WHAT YOU MEAN. BRUNO WAS THE ONLY CUSTOMER. IT WAS SOME KIND OF GREEK HOLIDAY.
OLD POPPA, HE'D OPENED THE JOINT UP SPECIAL, JUST FOR BRUNO, ON ACCOUNT OF HOW POPPA KNEW HE'D LOSE HIS PERMIT IF BRUNO DIDN'T GET HIS PASTITSIO.
POPPA WAS WORKING THE KITCHEN WHEN THE SHOOTING STARTED. HE HIT THE DECK--BUT HE STILL CAUGHT A SLUG IN HIS BUTT AND BROKE HIS NOSE.
SO NOW EVERYBODY'S ON PINS AND NEEDLES, WAITING TO SEE IF SIN CITY'S GOT A GANG WAR IN ITS LAP--OR IF THE KRAUT JUST WROTE OFF BRUNO AS A BUSINESS LOSS.
AND THAT'S IT. THAT'S EVERYTHING I KNOW. I IMAGINE YOU GOTTA RUN ALONG NOW.
THANKS FOR THE MEMORIES, STRANGER. YOU'VE BEEN SWEET.
DON'T, BABY. DON'T TEASE.
THIS ISN'T GOODBYE. NOT JUST YET.

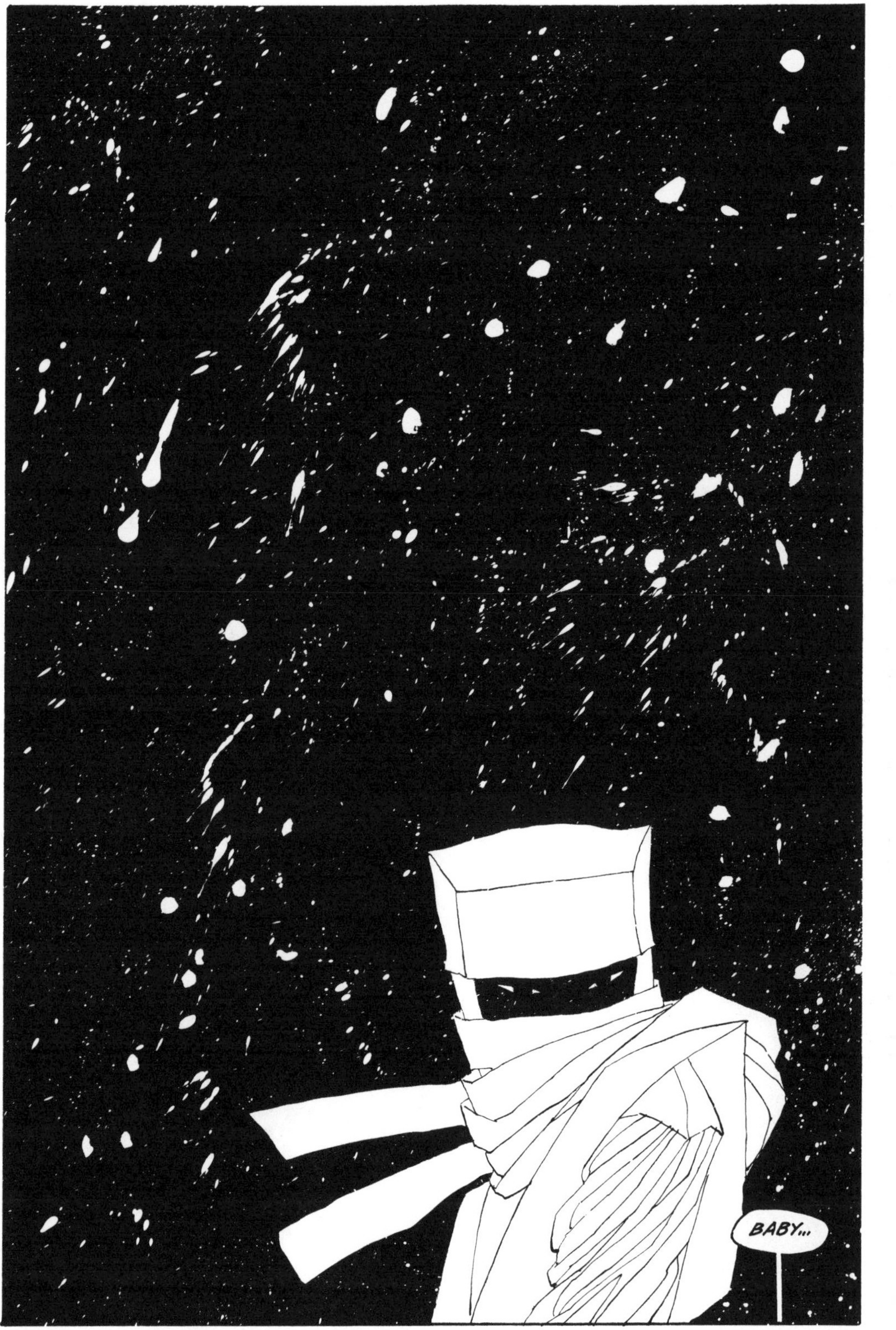
BABY...

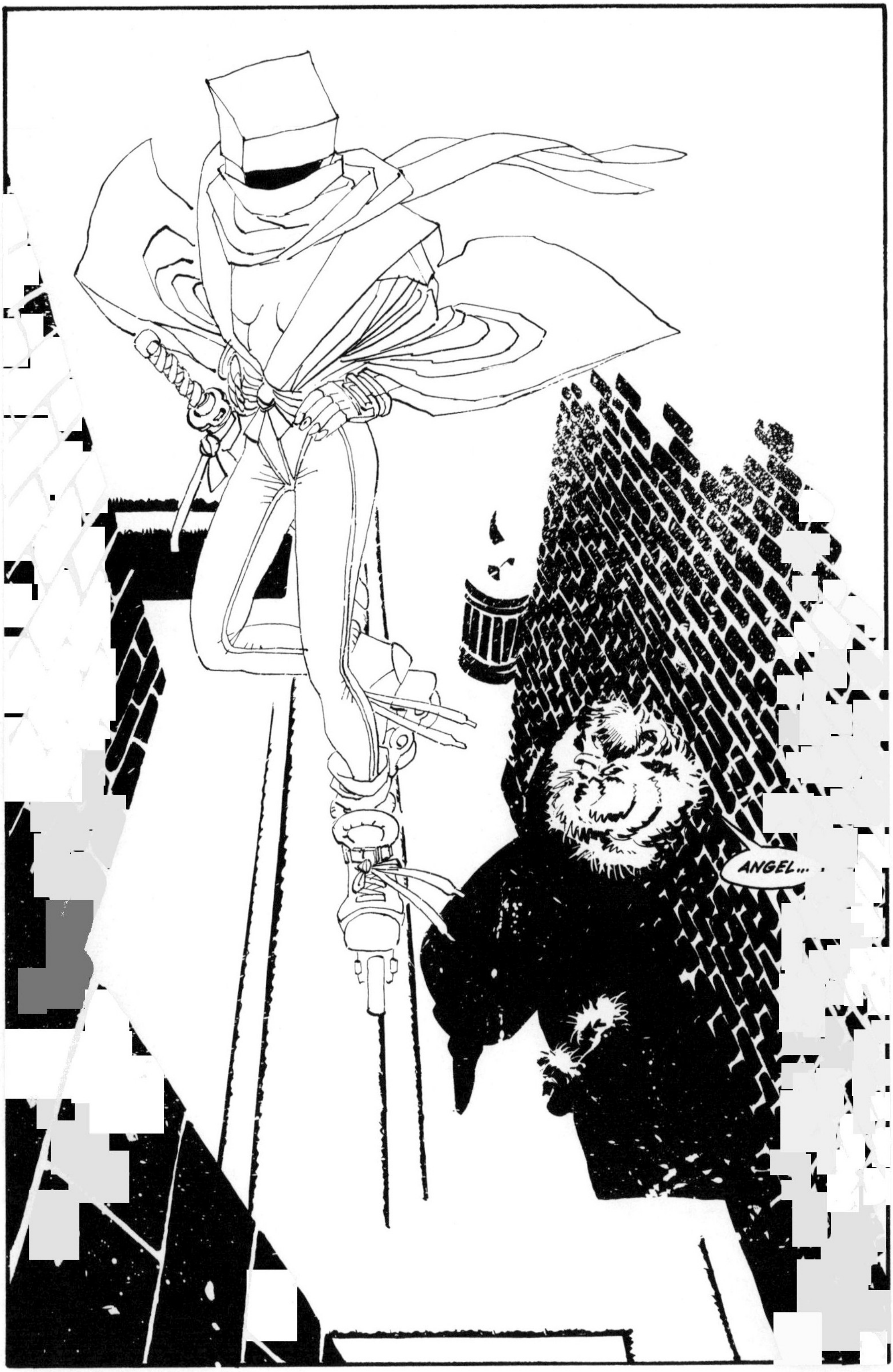
ANGEL...

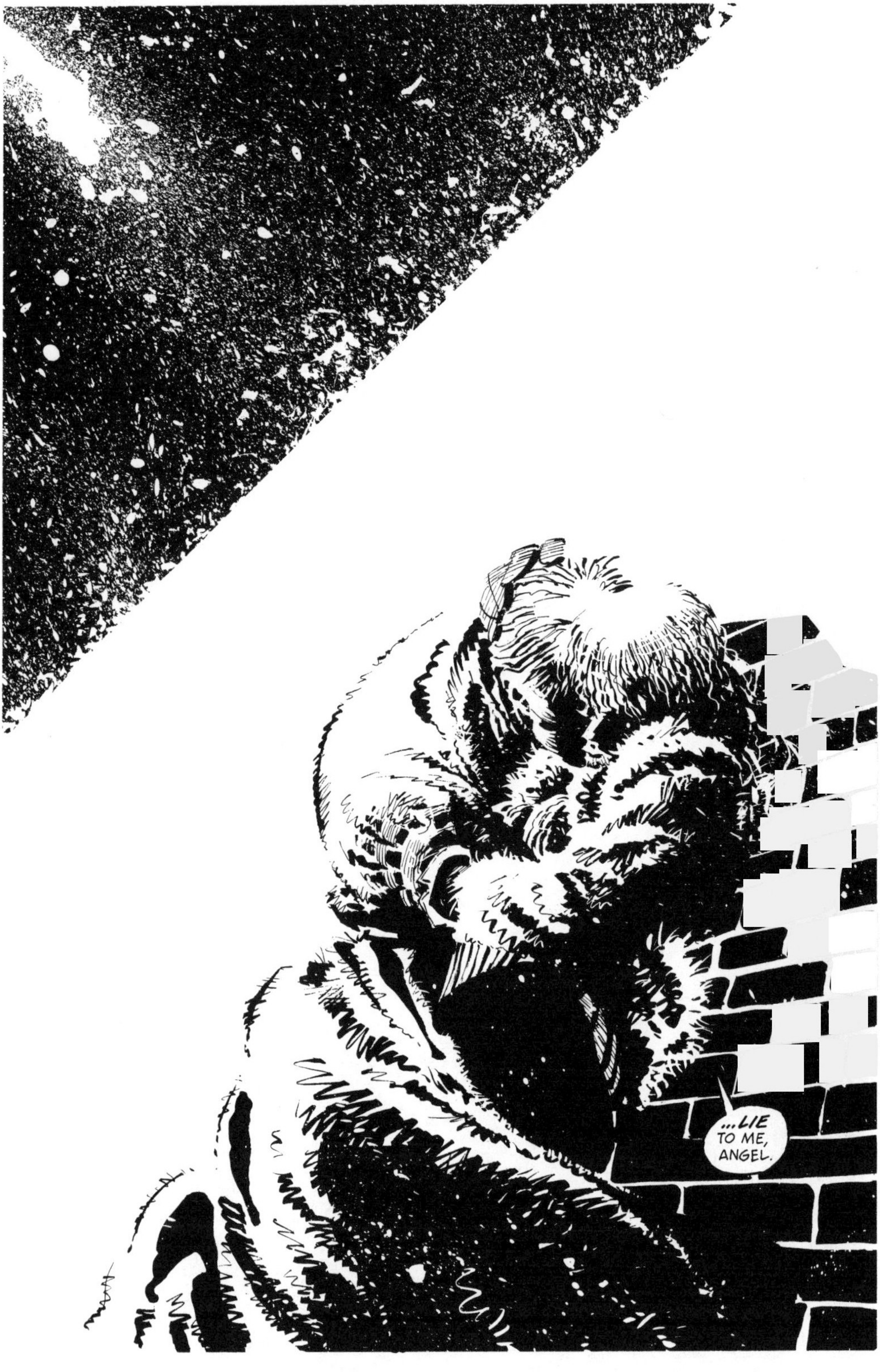
...LIE TO ME, ANGEL.

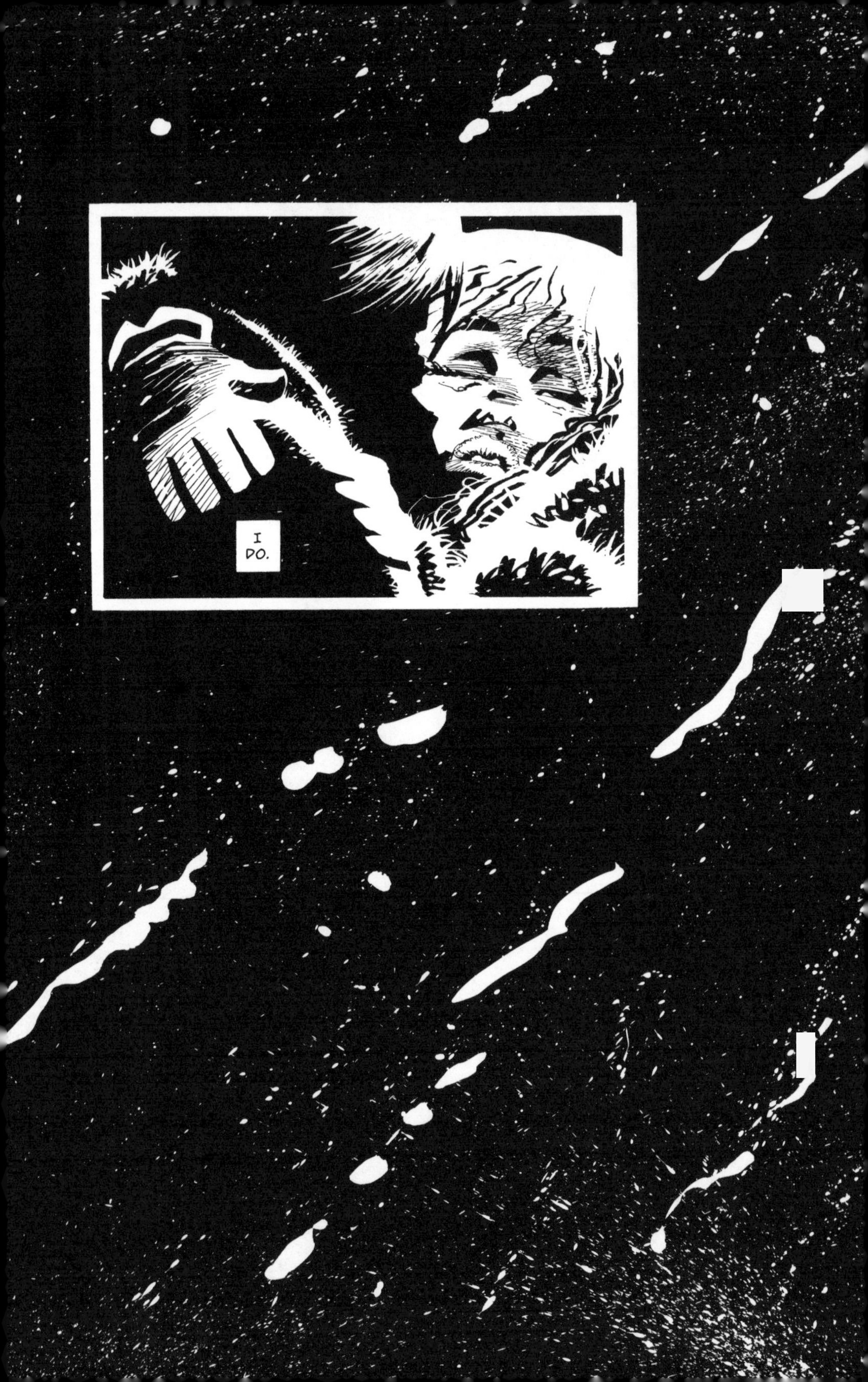
I DO.

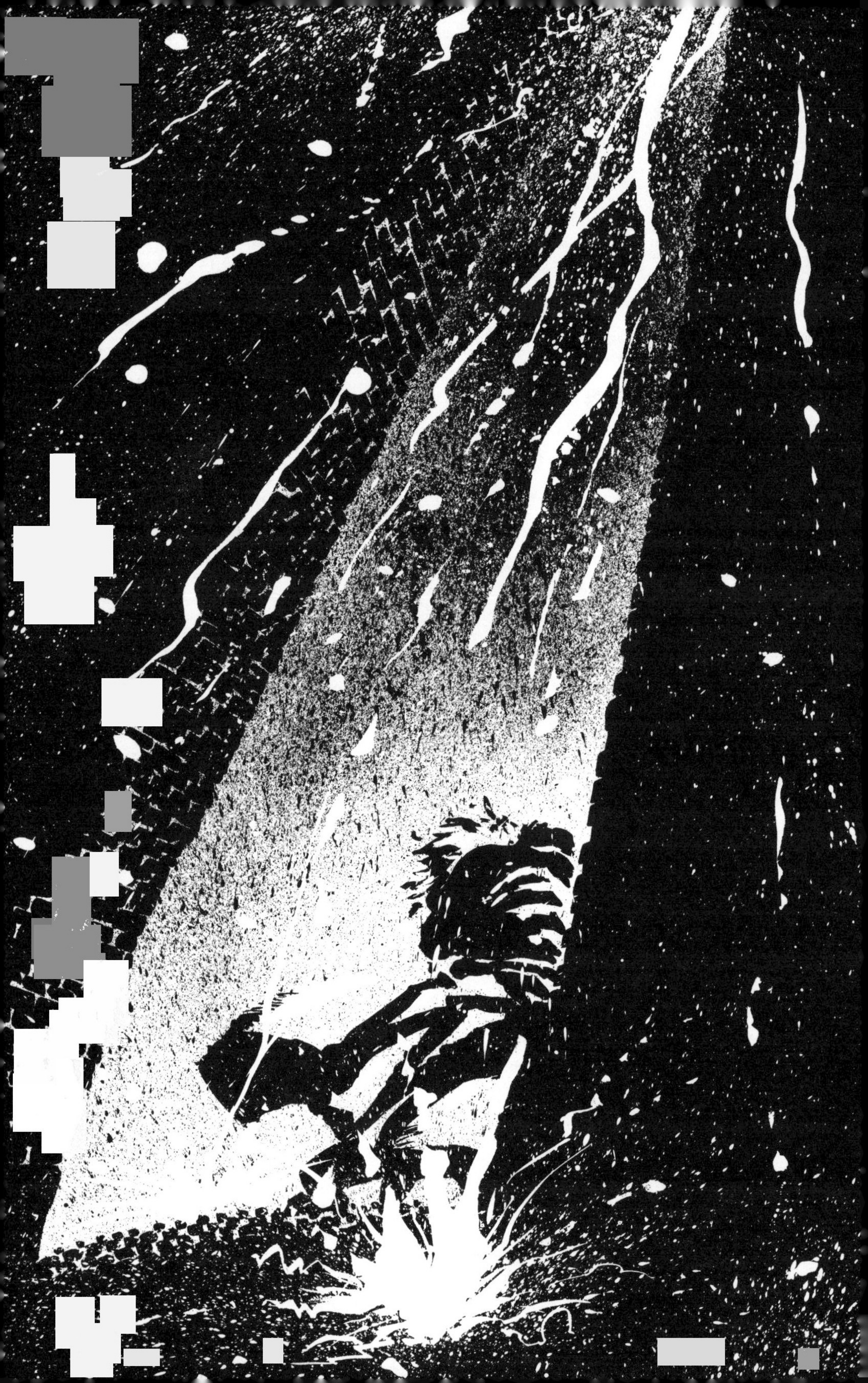

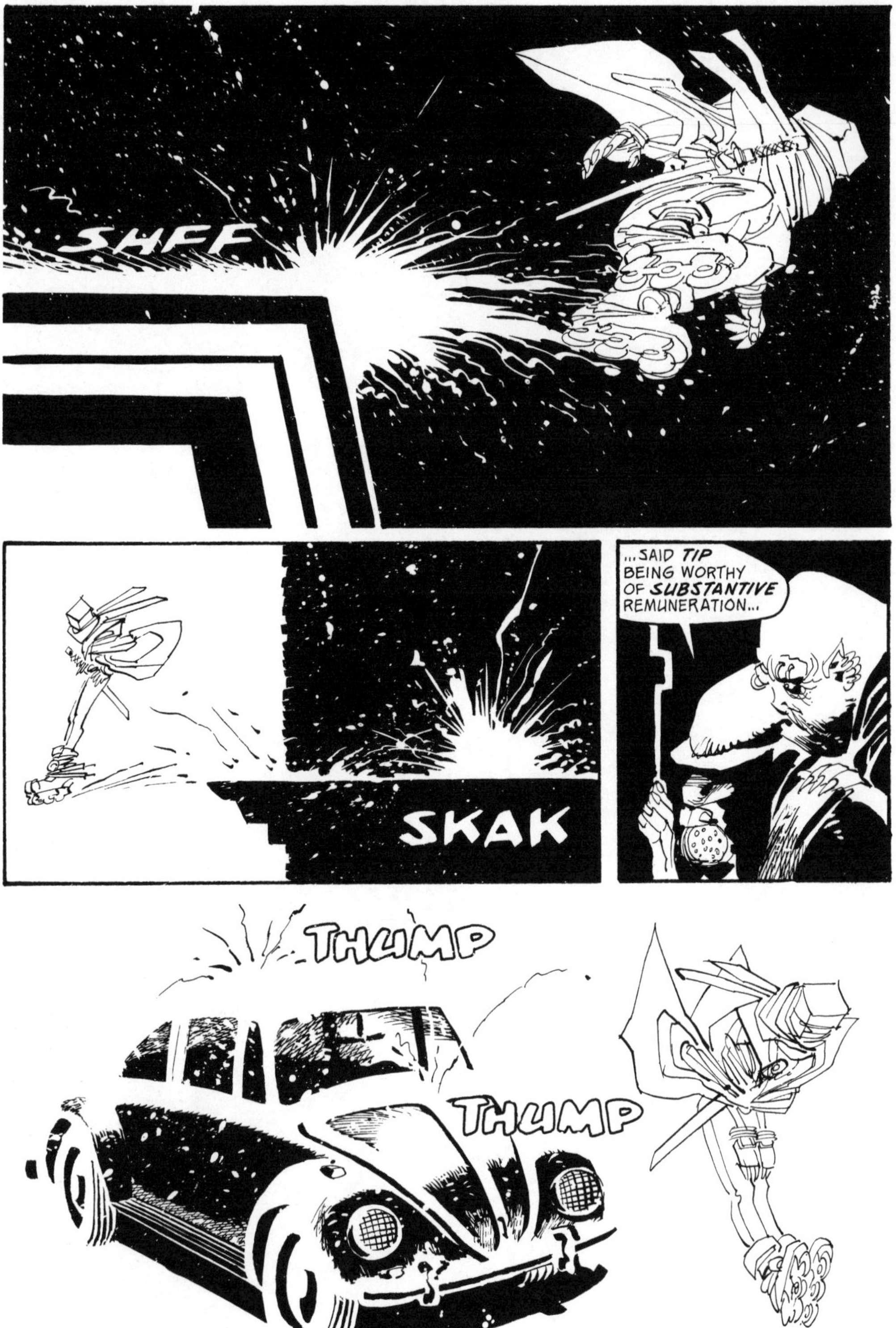
SHFF
SKAK
...SAID TIP BEING WORTHY OF SUBSTANTIVE REMUNERATION...
THUMP
THUMP

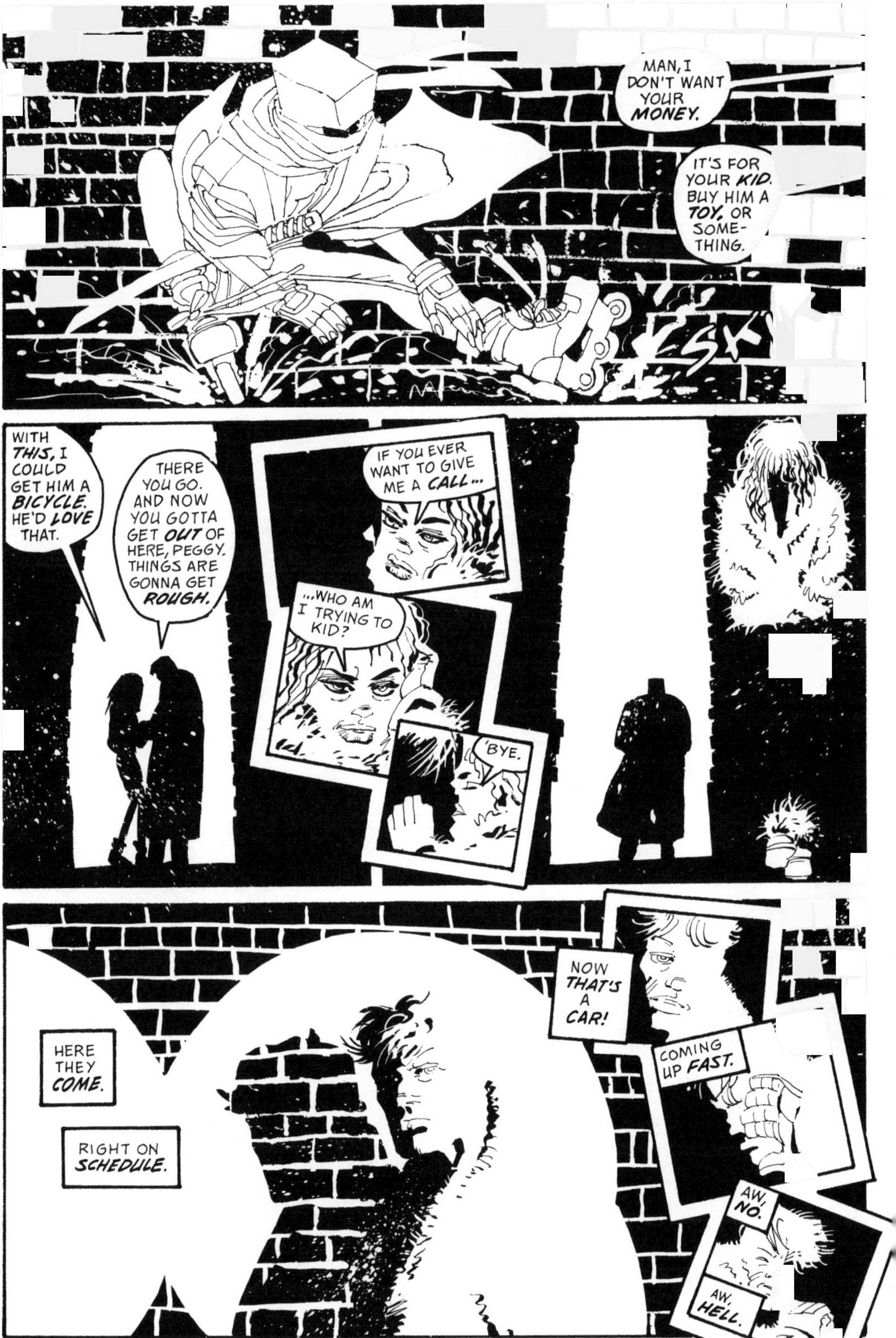
MAN, I DON'T WANT YOUR MONEY.
IT'S FOR YOUR KID. BUY HIM A TOY, OR SOME-THING.
WITH THIS, I COULD GET HIM A BICYCLE. HE'D LOVE THAT.
THERE YOU GO. AND NOW YOU GOTTA GET OUT OF HERE, PEGGY. THINGS ARE GONNA GET ROUGH.
IF YOU EVER WANT TO GIVE ME A CALL...
...WHO AM I TRYING TO KID?
'BYE.
HERE THEY COME.
RIGHT ON SCHEDULE.
NOW THAT'S A CAR!
COMING UP FAST.
AW, NO.
AW. HELL.

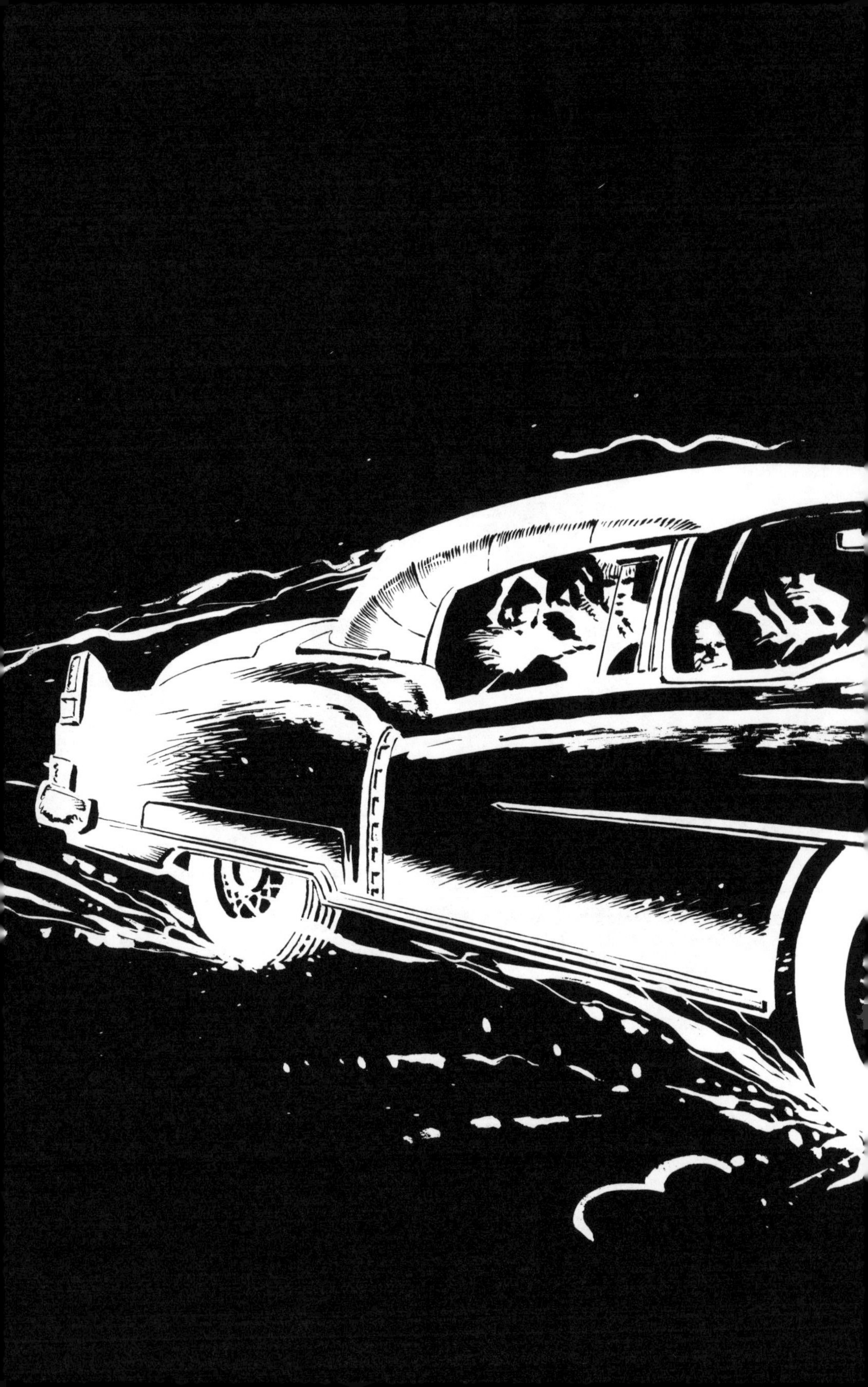

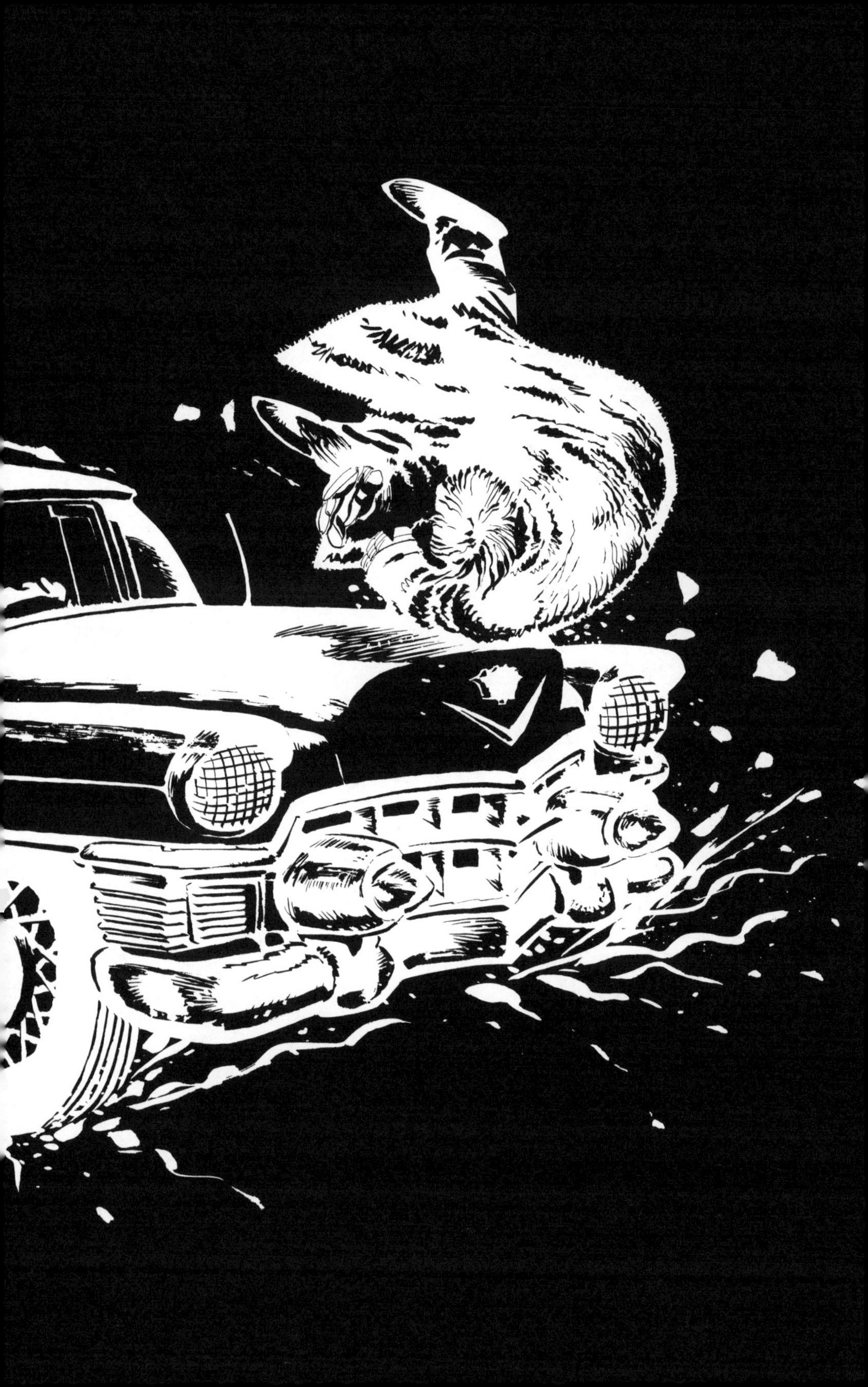

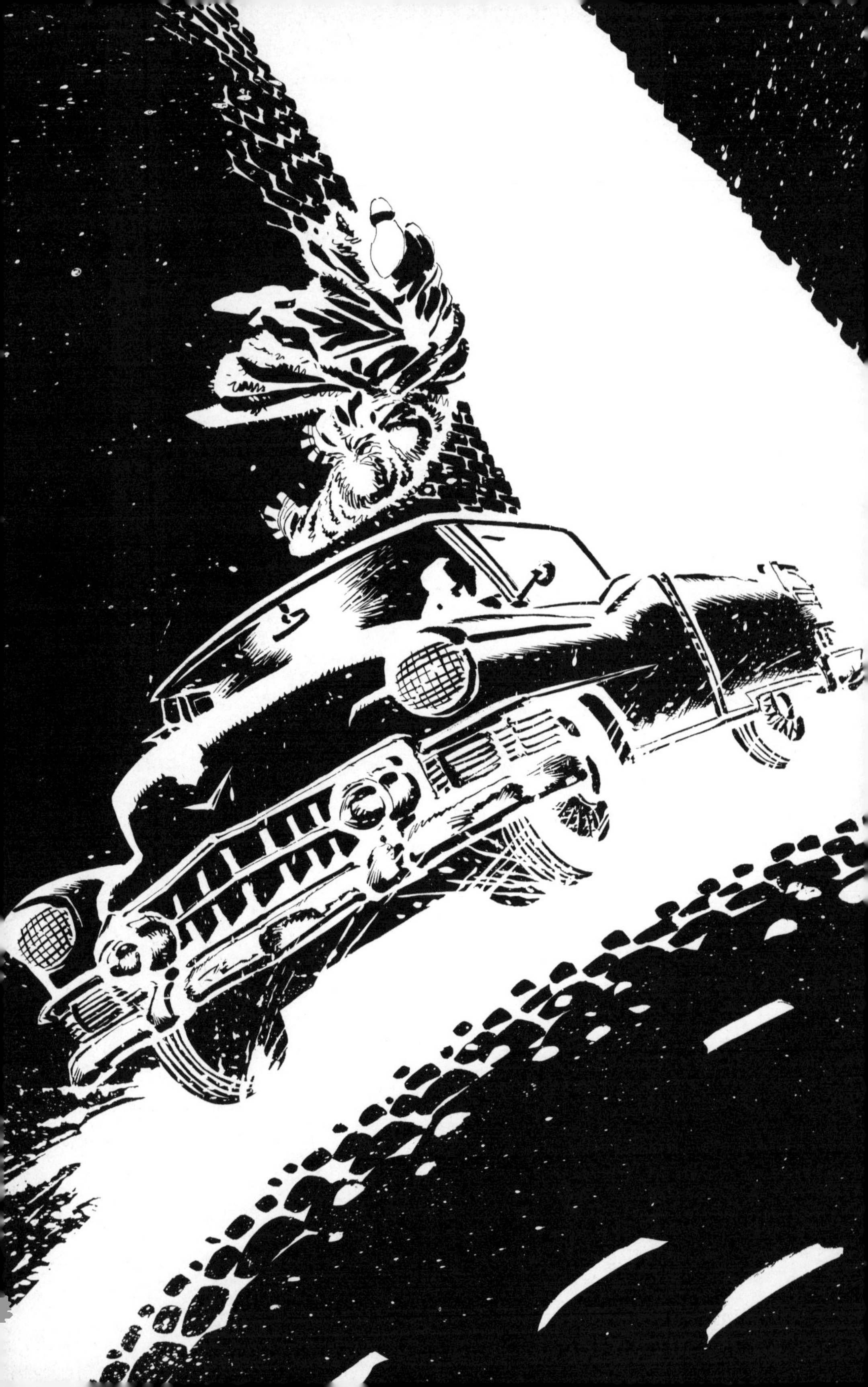

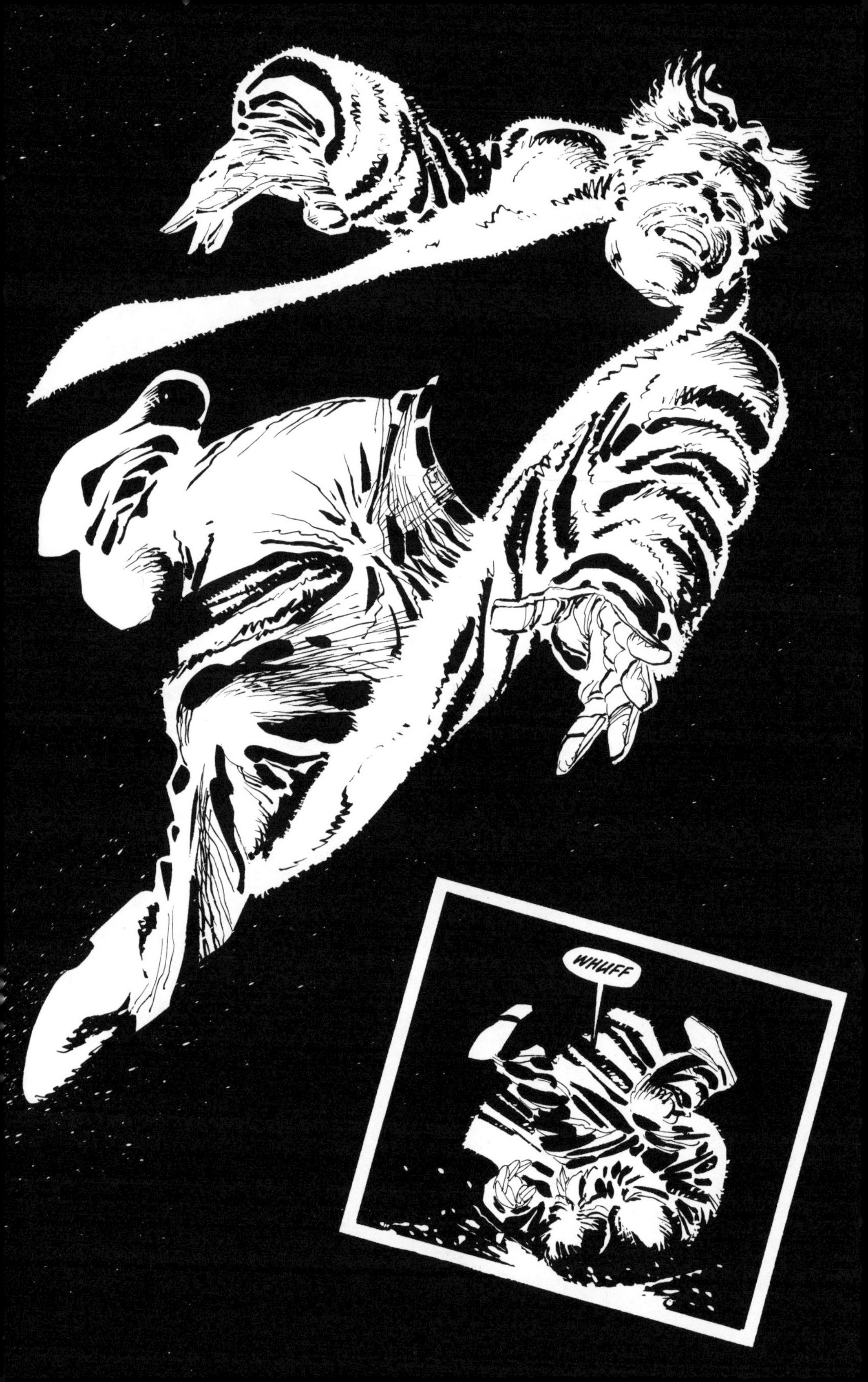
WHUFF

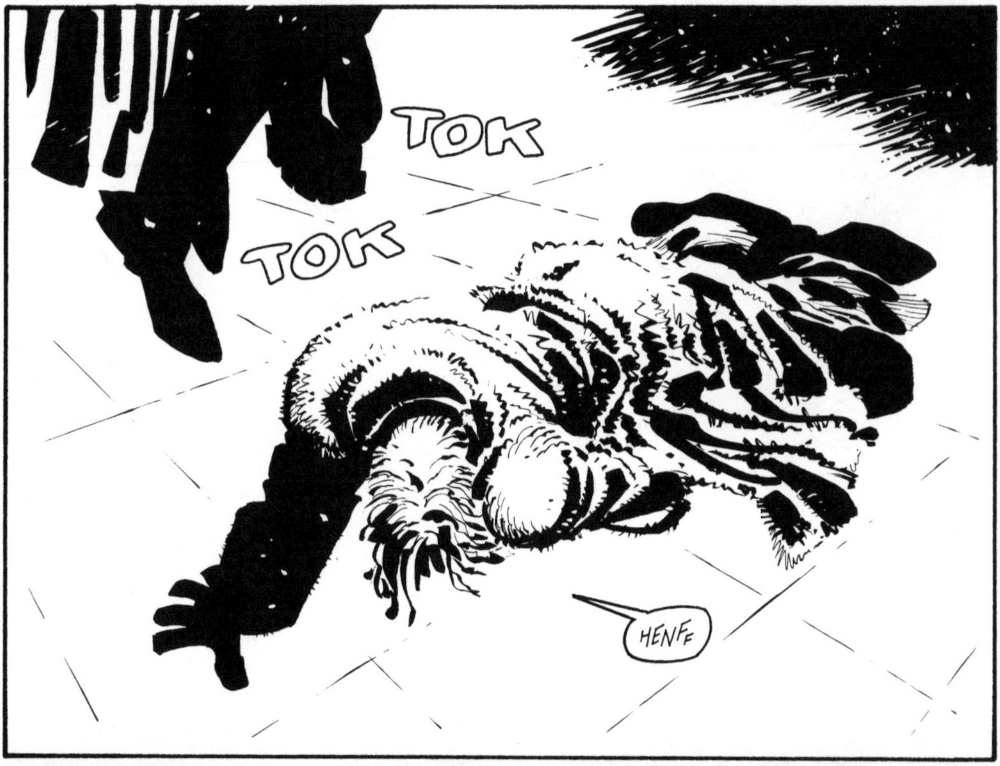
TOK
TOK
HENFF

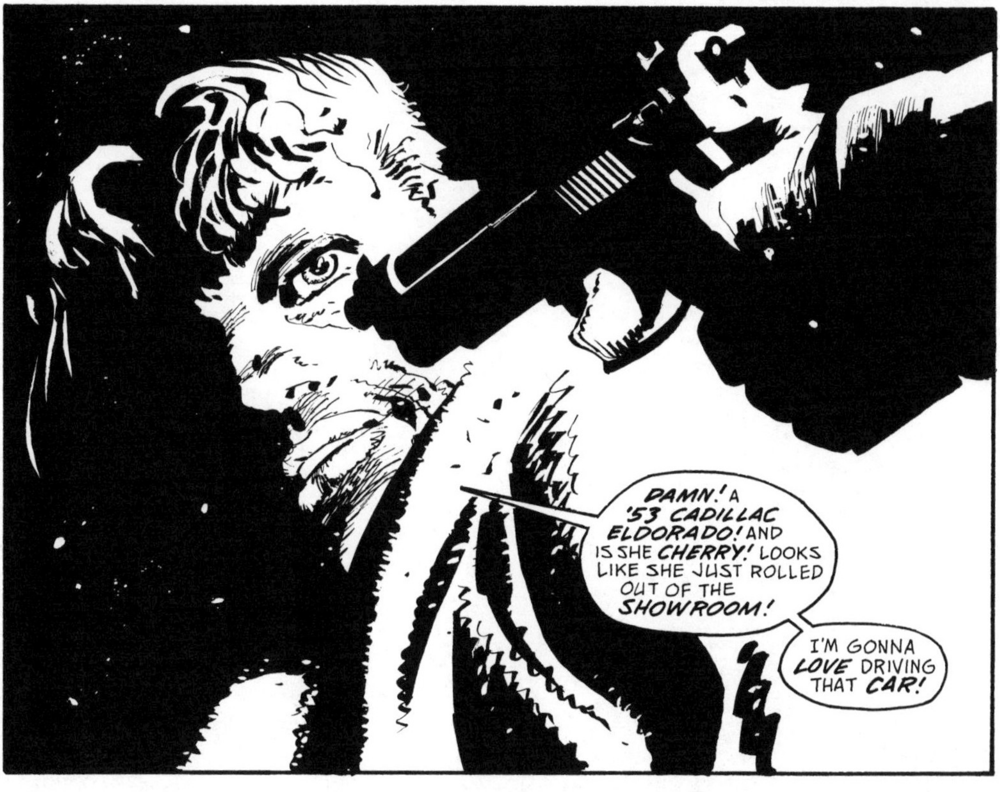
DAMN! A '53 CADILLAC ELDORADO! AND IS SHE CHERRY! LOOKS LIKE SHE JUST ROLLED OUT OF THE SHOWROOM!
I'M GONNA LOVE DRIVING THAT CAR!

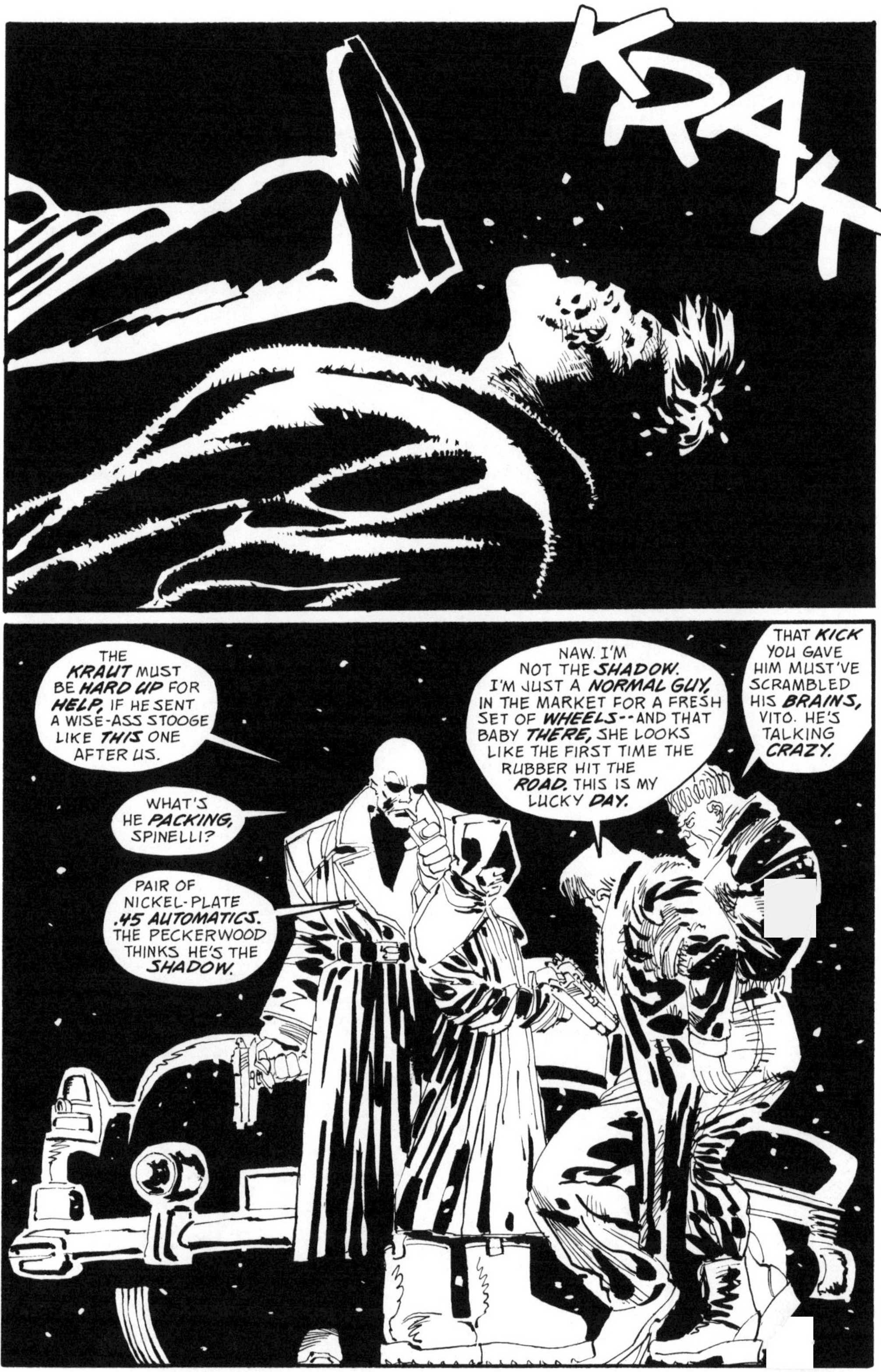
KRAK
THE KRAUT MUST BE HARD UP FOR HELP, IF HE SENT A WISE-ASS STOOGE LIKE THIS ONE AFTER US.
WHAT'S HE PACKING, SPINELLI?
PAIR OF NICKEL-PLATE .45 AUTOMATICS. THE PECKERWOOD THINKS HE'S THE SHADOW.
NAW. I'M NOT THE SHADOW. I'M JUST A NORMAL GUY, IN THE MARKET FOR A FRESH SET OF WHEELS--AND THAT BABY THERE, SHE LOOKS LIKE THE FIRST TIME THE RUBBER HIT THE ROAD. THIS IS MY LUCKY DAY.
THAT KICK YOU GAVE HIM MUST'VE SCRAMBLED HIS BRAINS, VITO. HE'S TALKING CRAZY.

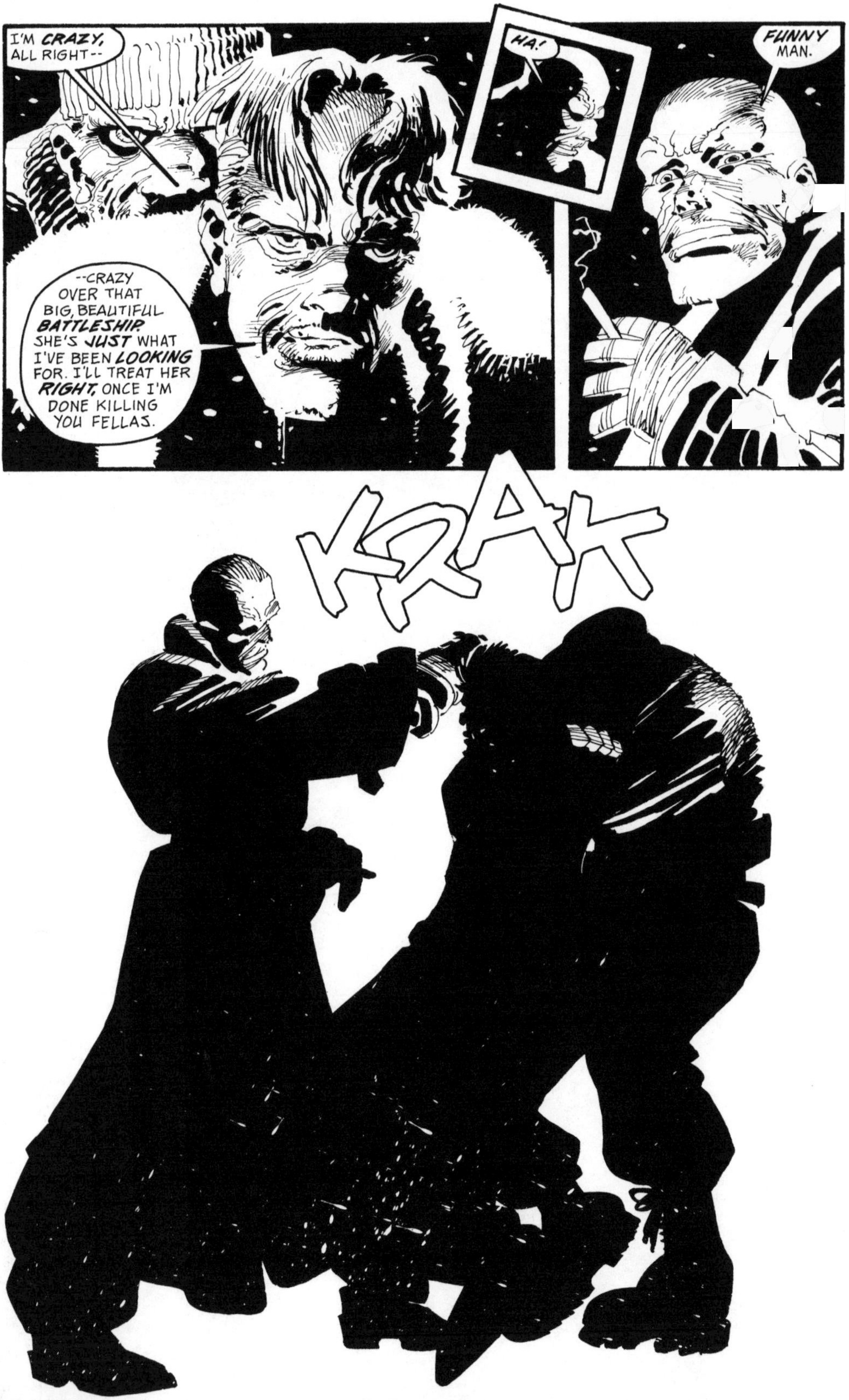
I'M CRAZY, ALL RIGHT--
--CRAZY OVER THAT BIG, BEAUTIFUL BATTLESHIP. SHE'S JUST WHAT I'VE BEEN LOOKING FOR. I'LL TREAT HER RIGHT, ONCE I'M DONE KILLING YOU FELLAS.
HA!
FUNNY MAN.
KRAK

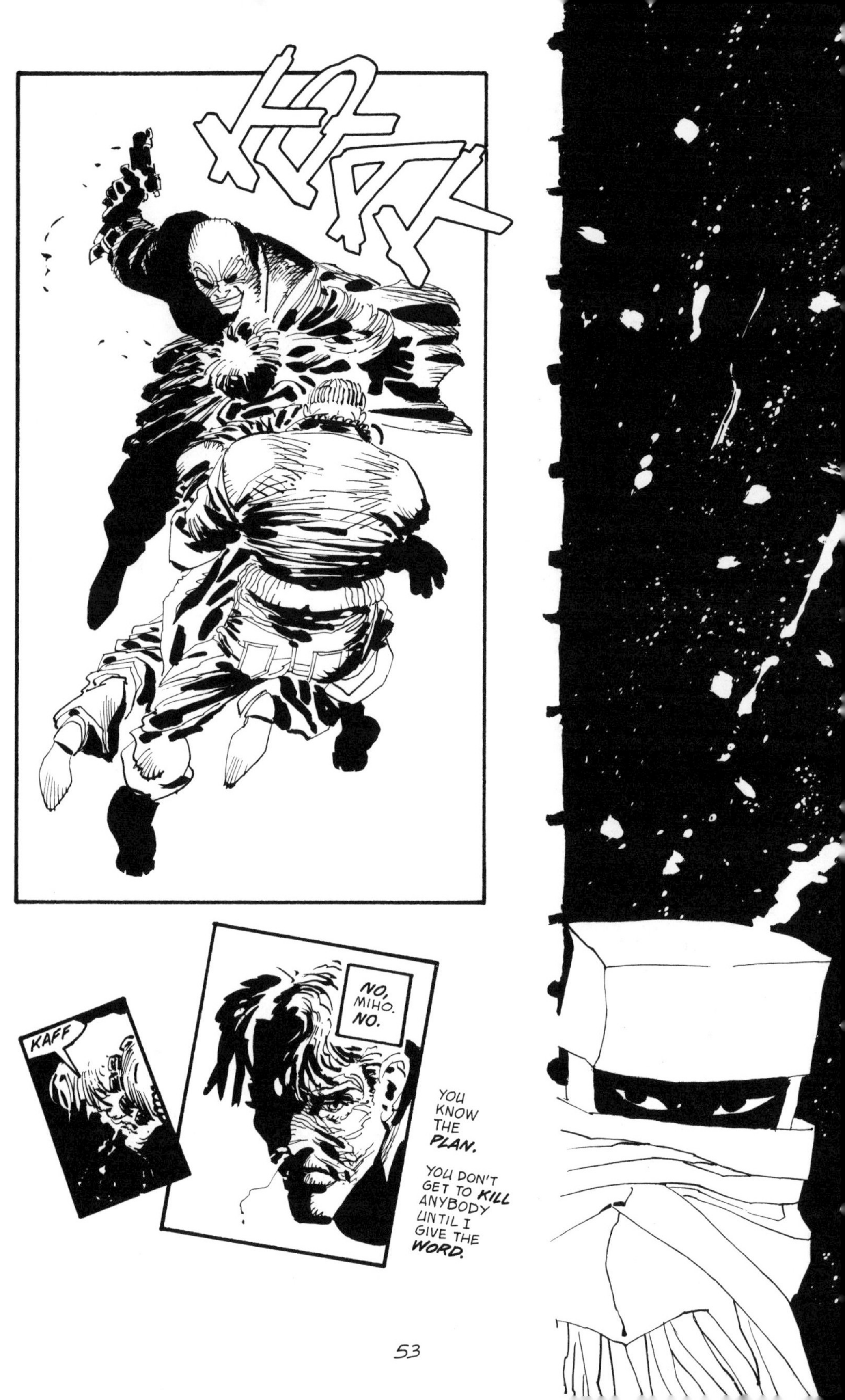
KAFF
NO, MIHO. NO.
YOU KNOW THE PLAN.
YOU DON'T GET TO KILL ANYBODY UNTIL I GIVE THE WORD.

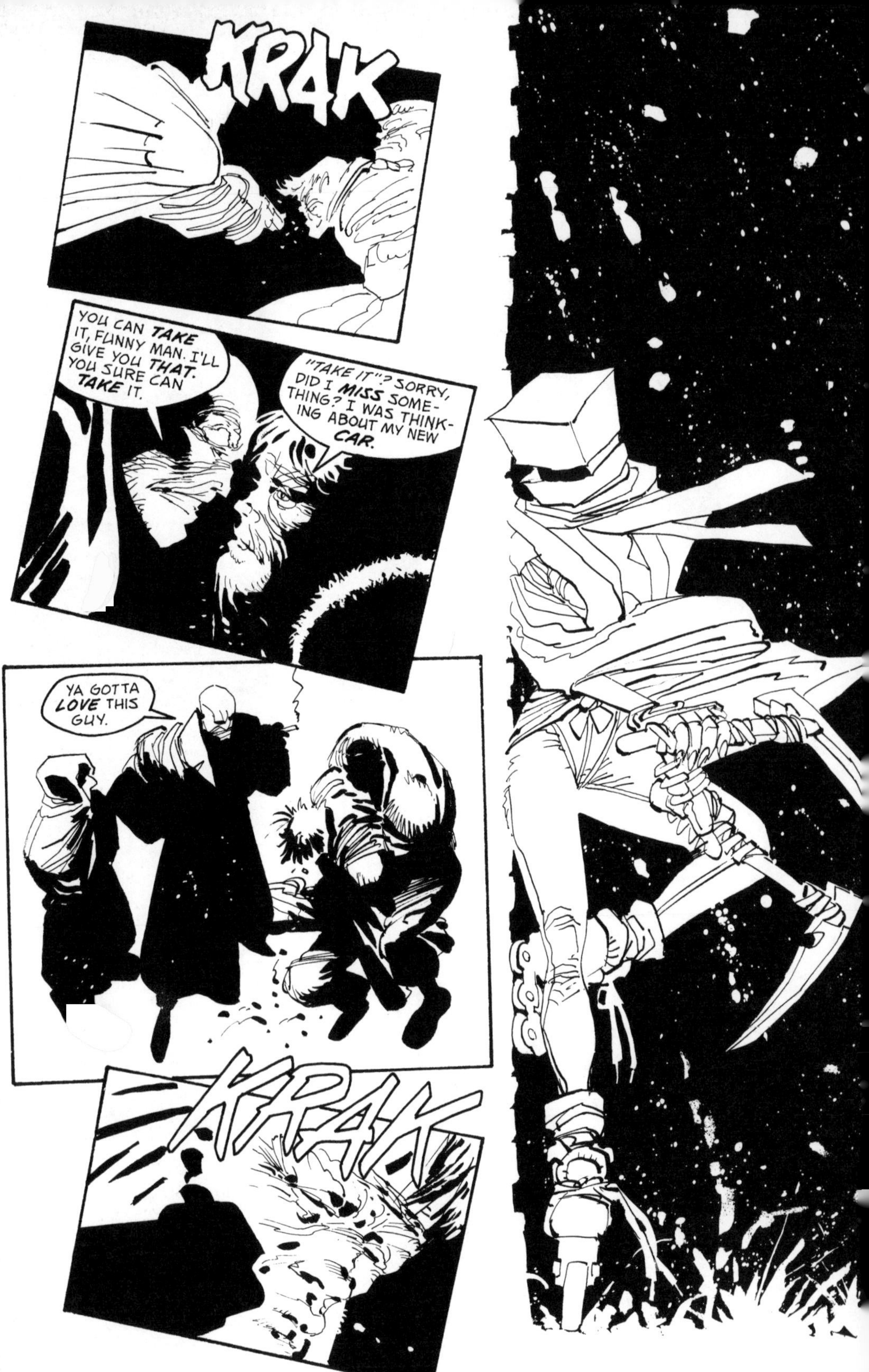
KRAK
YOU CAN TAKE IT, FUNNY MAN. I'LL GIVE YOU THAT. YOU SURE CAN TAKE IT.
"TAKE IT"? SORRY, DID I MISS SOMETHING? I WAS THINKING ABOUT MY NEW CAR.
YA GOTTA LOVE THIS GUY.
KRAK

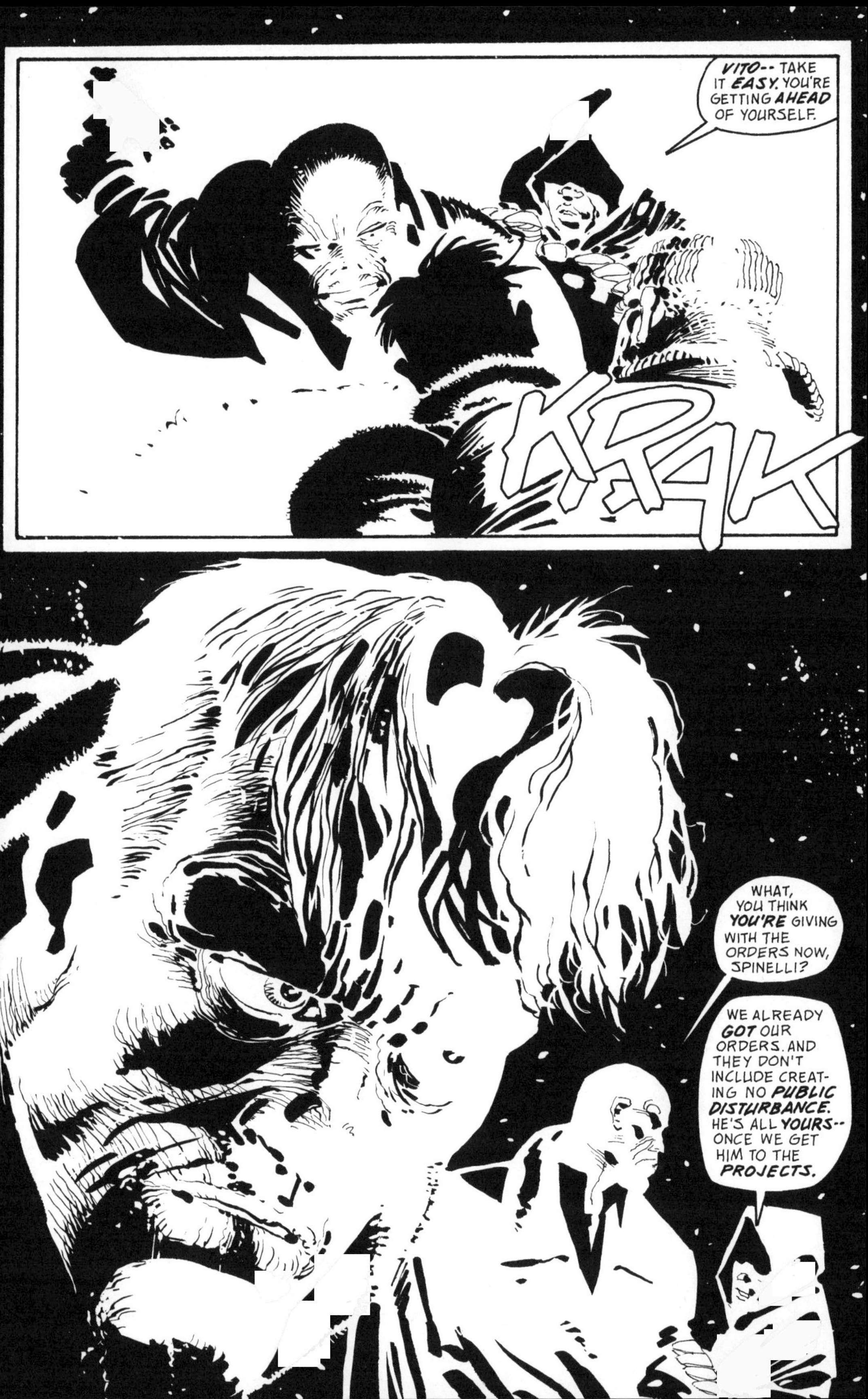
VITO-- TAKE IT EASY. YOU'RE GETTING AHEAD OF YOURSELF.
KRAK
WHAT, YOU THINK YOU'RE GIVING WITH THE ORDERS NOW, SPINELLI?
WE ALREADY GOT OUR ORDERS. AND THEY DON'T INCLUDE CREATING NO PUBLIC DISTURBANCE. HE'S ALL YOURS-- ONCE WE GET HIM TO THE PROJECTS.

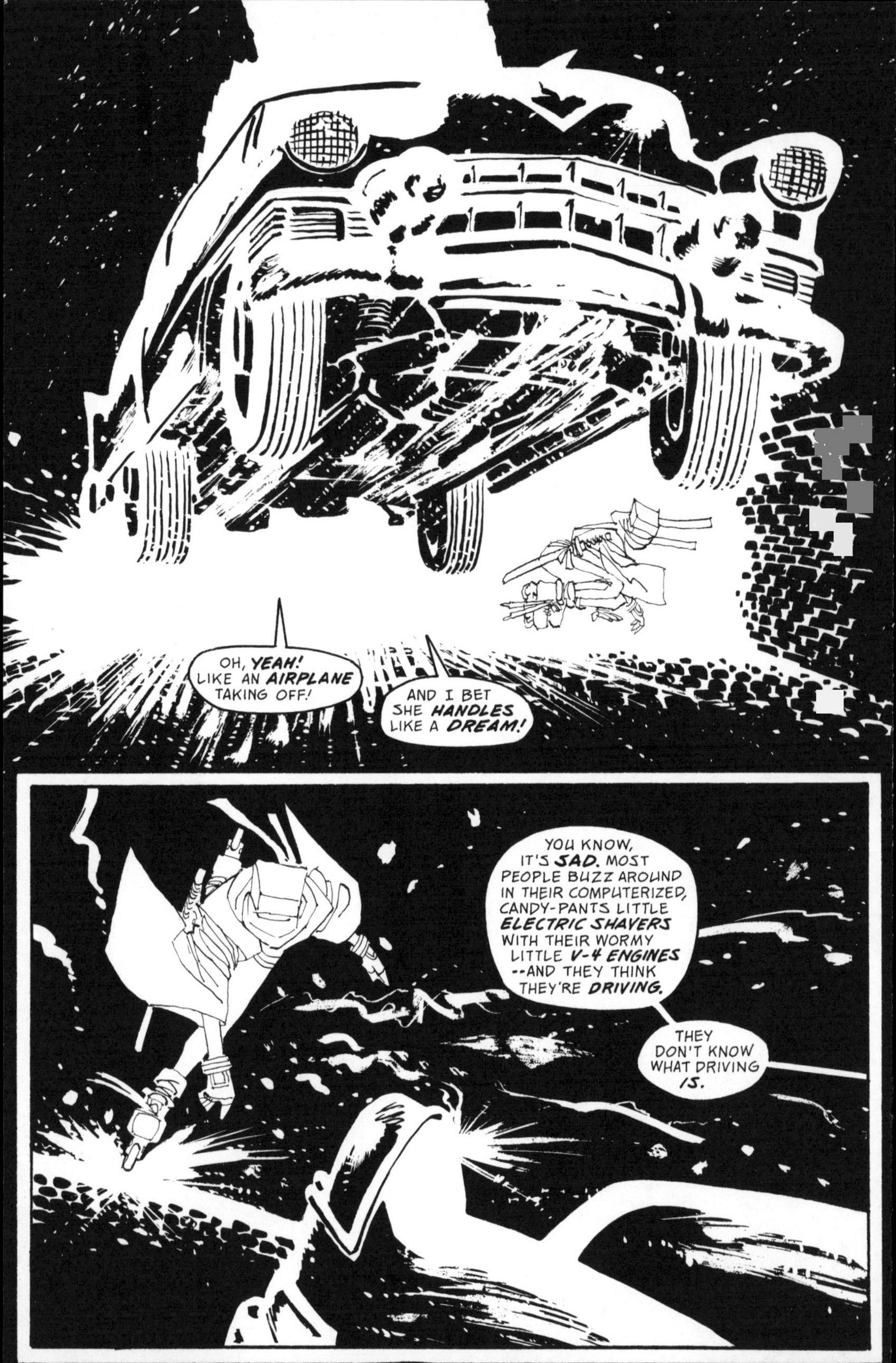
OH, YEAH! LIKE AN AIRPLANE TAKING OFF!
AND I BET SHE HANDLES LIKE A DREAM!
YOU KNOW, IT'S SAD. MOST PEOPLE BUZZ AROUND IN THEIR COMPUTERIZED, CANDY-PANTS LITTLE ELECTRIC SHAVERS WITH THEIR WORMY LITTLE V-4 ENGINES --AND THEY THINK THEY'RE DRIVING.
THEY DON'T KNOW WHAT DRIVING IS.

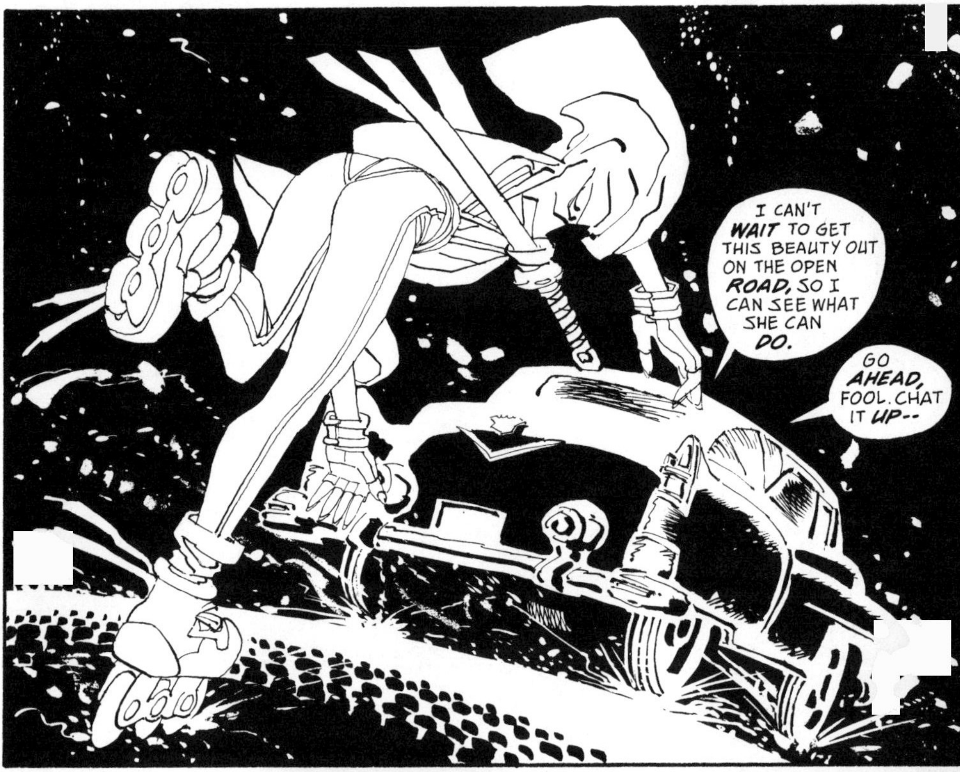
I CAN'T WAIT TO GET THIS BEAUTY OUT ON THE OPEN ROAD, SO I CAN SEE WHAT SHE CAN DO.
GO AHEAD, FOOL. CHAT IT UP--

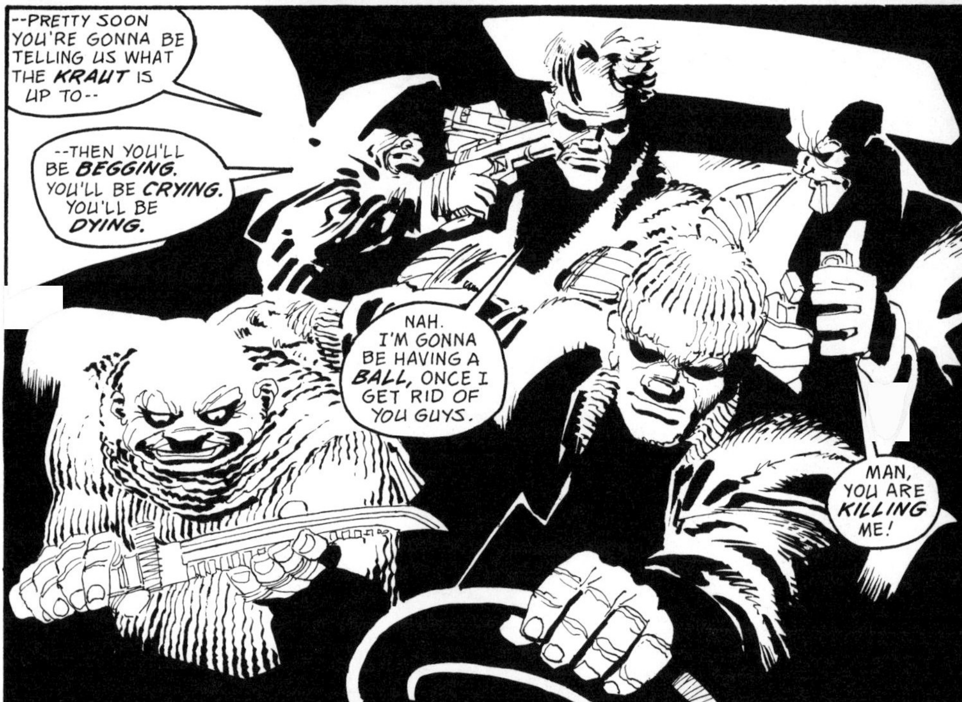
--PRETTY SOON YOU'RE GONNA BE TELLING US WHAT THE KRAUT IS UP TO--
--THEN YOU'LL BE BEGGING. YOU'LL BE CRYING. YOU'LL BE DYING.
NAH. I'M GONNA BE HAVING A BALL, ONCE I GET RID OF YOU GUYS.
MAN, YOU ARE KILLING ME!

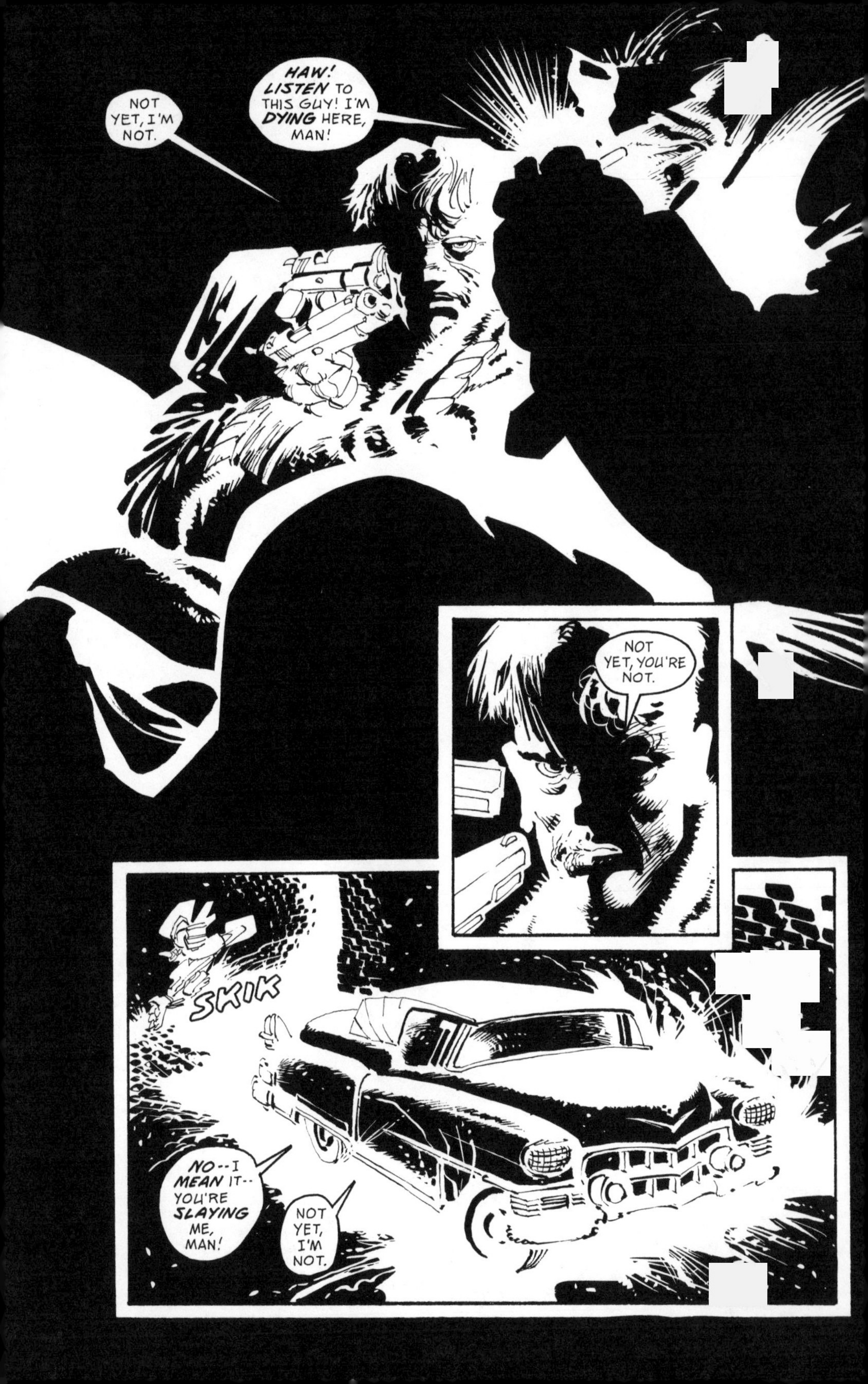

NOT YET, I'M NOT.
HAW! LISTEN TO THIS GUY! I'M DYING HERE, MAN!
NOT YET, YOU'RE NOT.
SKIK
NO--I MEAN IT--YOU'RE SLAYING ME, MAN!
NOT YET, I'M NOT.

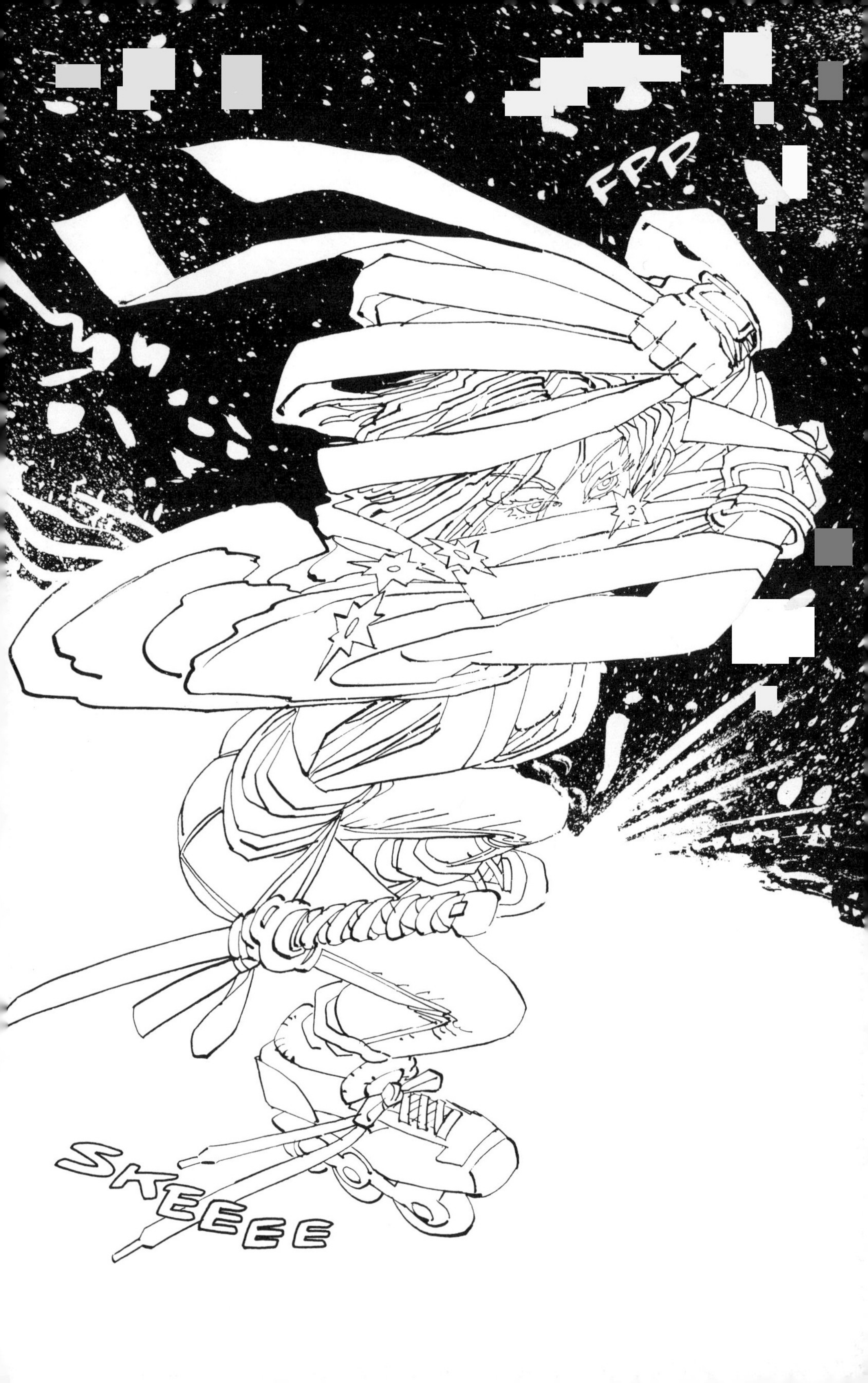
FPP
SKEEEE

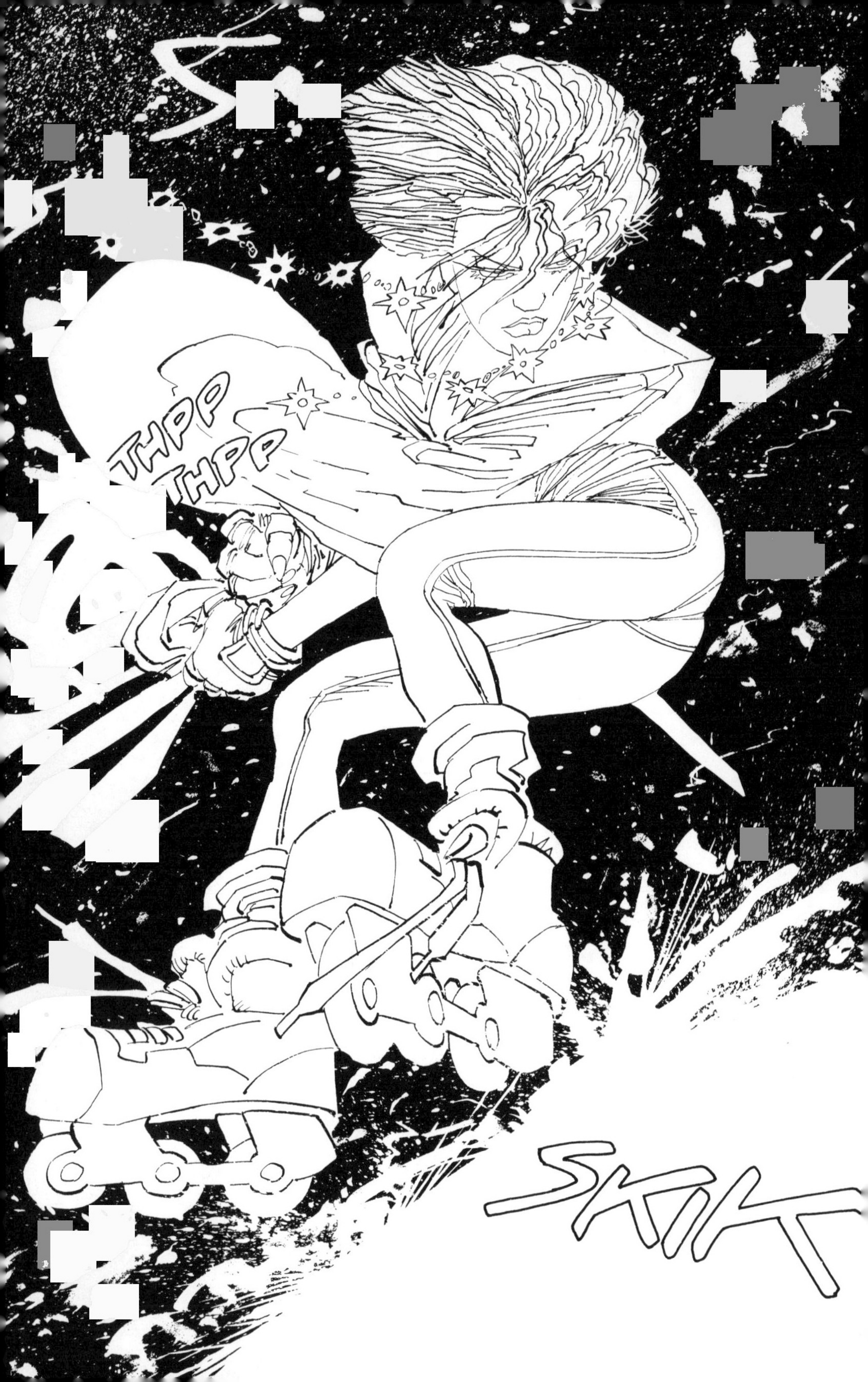
THPP
THPP
SKKT

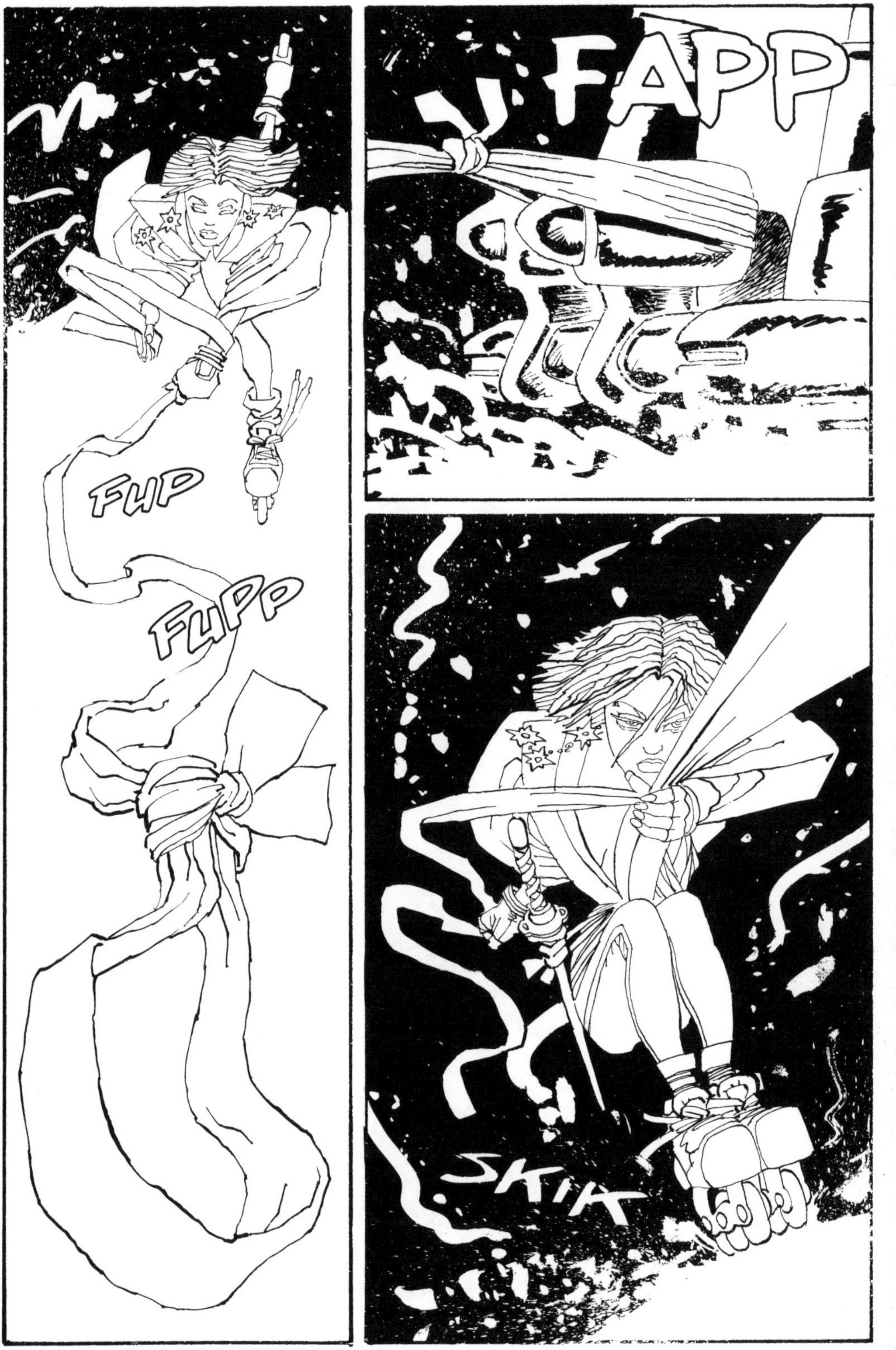
FUP
FUPP
FAPP
SKIK

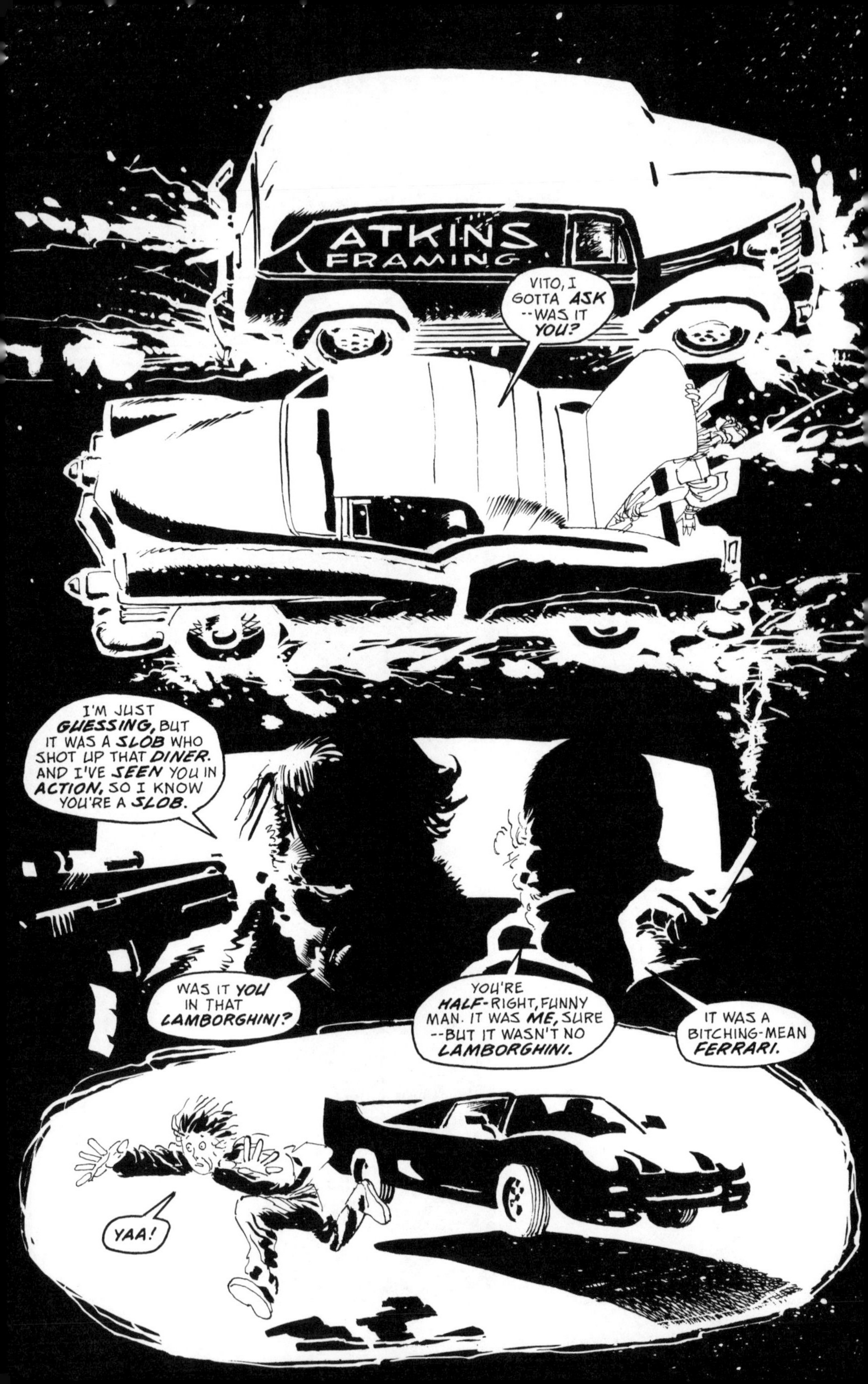
ATKINS FRAMING
VITO, I GOTTA ASK --WAS IT YOU?
I'M JUST GUESSING, BUT IT WAS A SLOB WHO SHOT UP THAT DINER. AND I'VE SEEN YOU IN ACTION, SO I KNOW YOU'RE A SLOB.
WAS IT YOU IN THAT LAMBORGHINI?
YOU'RE HALF-RIGHT, FUNNY MAN. IT WAS ME, SURE --BUT IT WASN'T NO LAMBORGHINI.
IT WAS A BITCHING-MEAN FERRARI.
YAA!

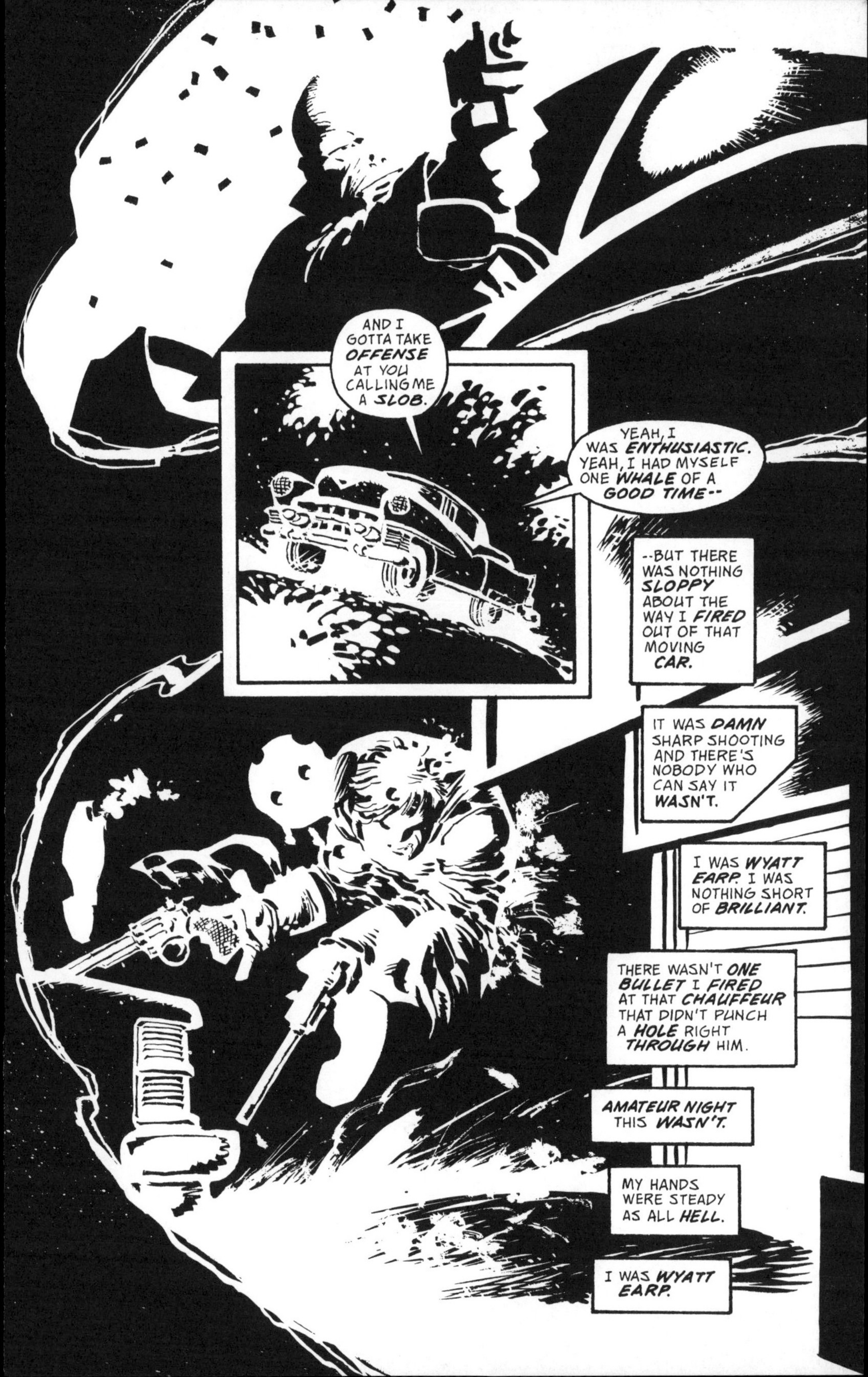
AND I GOTTA TAKE OFFENSE AT YOU CALLING ME A SLOB.
YEAH, I WAS ENTHUSIASTIC. YEAH, I HAD MYSELF ONE WHALE OF A GOOD TIME--
--BUT THERE WAS NOTHING SLOPPY ABOUT THE WAY I FIRED OUT OF THAT MOVING CAR.
IT WAS DAMN SHARP SHOOTING AND THERE'S NOBODY WHO CAN SAY IT WASN'T.
I WAS WYATT EARP. I WAS NOTHING SHORT OF BRILLIANT.
THERE WASN'T ONE BULLET I FIRED AT THAT CHAUFFEUR THAT DIDN'T PUNCH A HOLE RIGHT THROUGH HIM.
AMATEUR NIGHT THIS WASN'T.
MY HANDS WERE STEADY AS ALL HELL.
I WAS WYATT EARP.

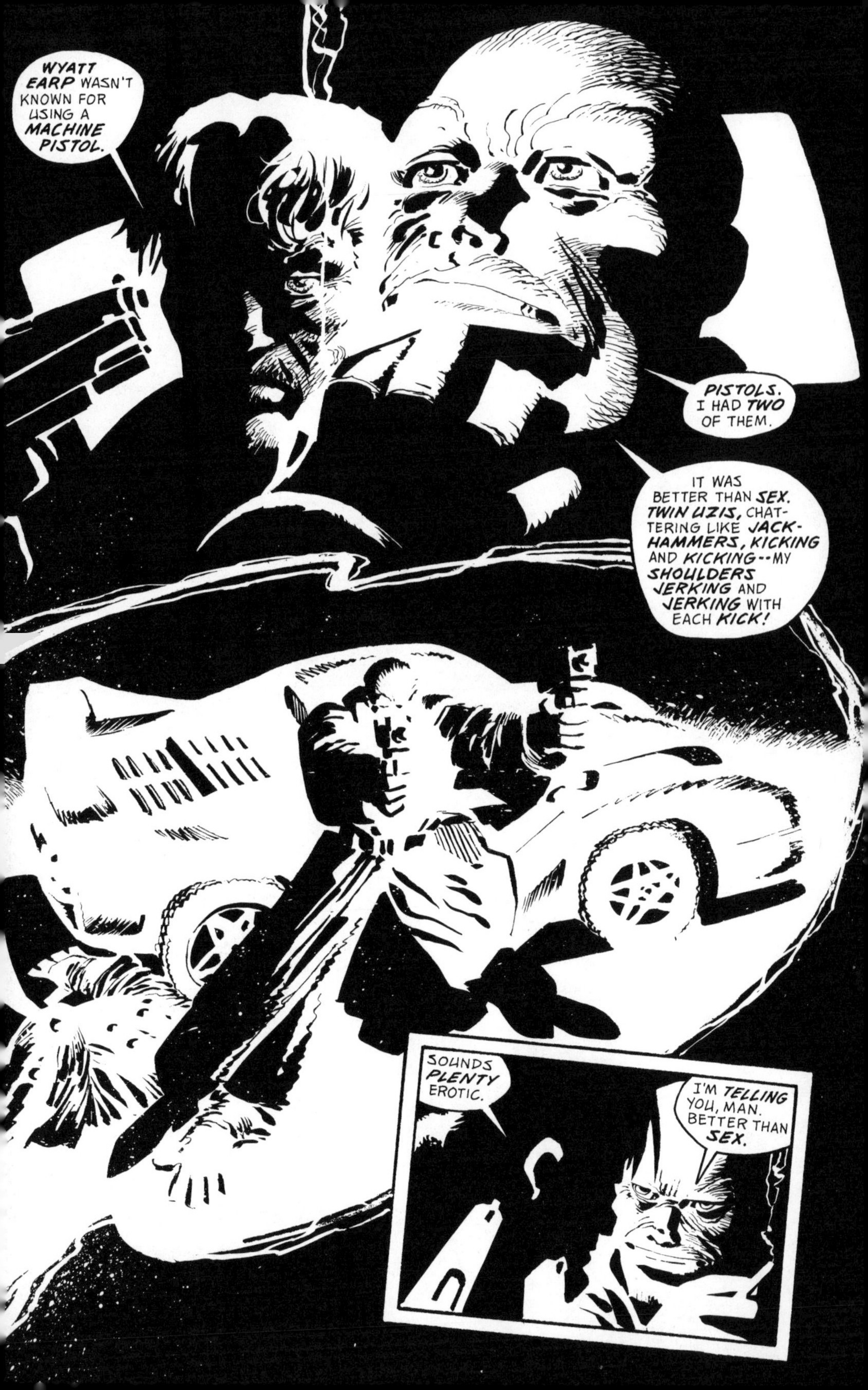
WYATT EARP WASN'T KNOWN FOR USING A MACHINE PISTOL.
PISTOLS. I HAD TWO OF THEM.
IT WAS BETTER THAN SEX. TWIN UZIS, CHATTERING LIKE JACKHAMMERS, KICKING AND KICKING--MY SHOULDERS JERKING AND JERKING WITH EACH KICK!
SOUNDS PLENTY EROTIC.
I'M TELLING YOU, MAN. BETTER THAN SEX.

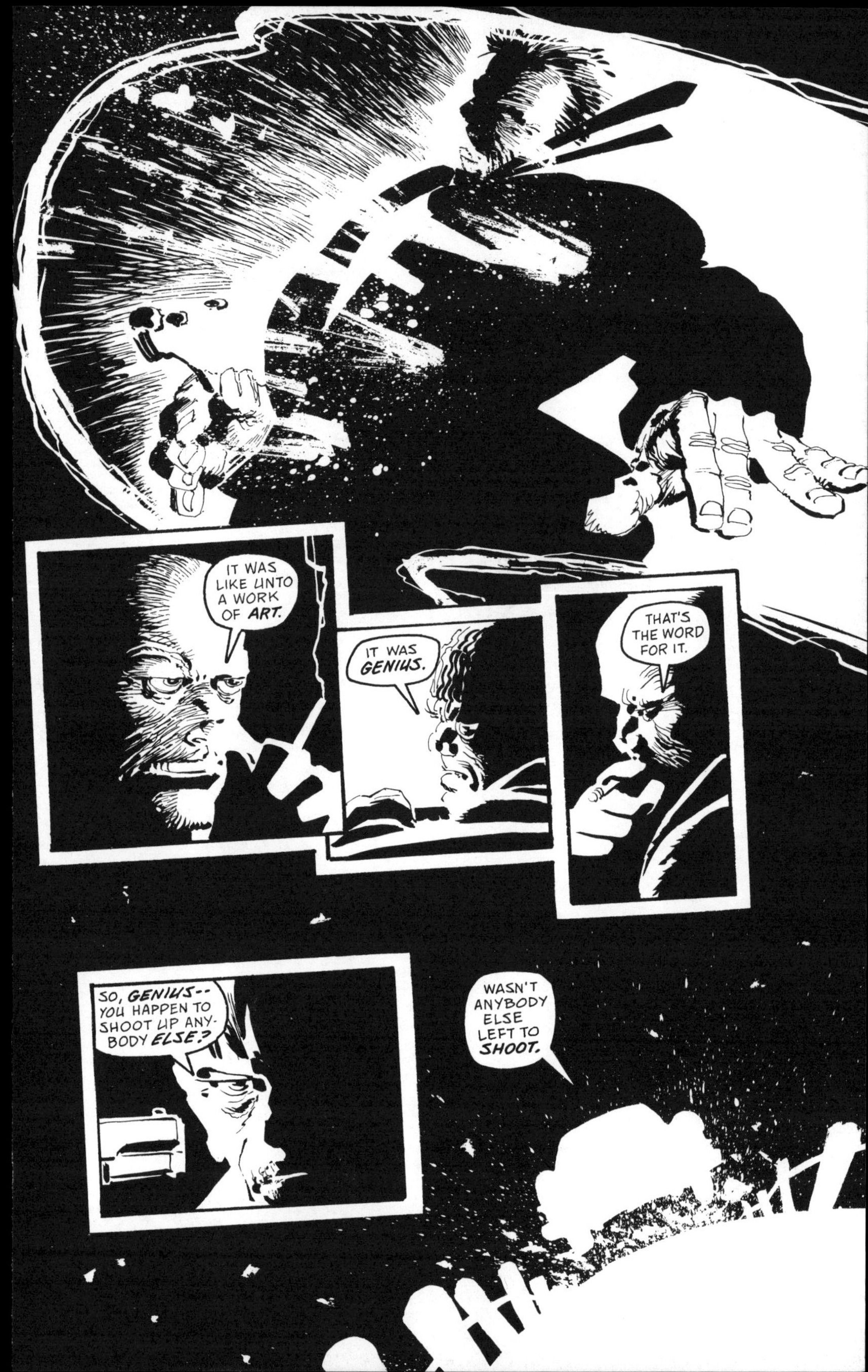
IT WAS LIKE UNTO A WORK OF ART.
IT WAS GENIUS.
THAT'S THE WORD FOR IT.
SO, GENIUS-- YOU HAPPEN TO SHOOT UP ANYBODY ELSE?
WASN'T ANYBODY ELSE LEFT TO SHOOT.

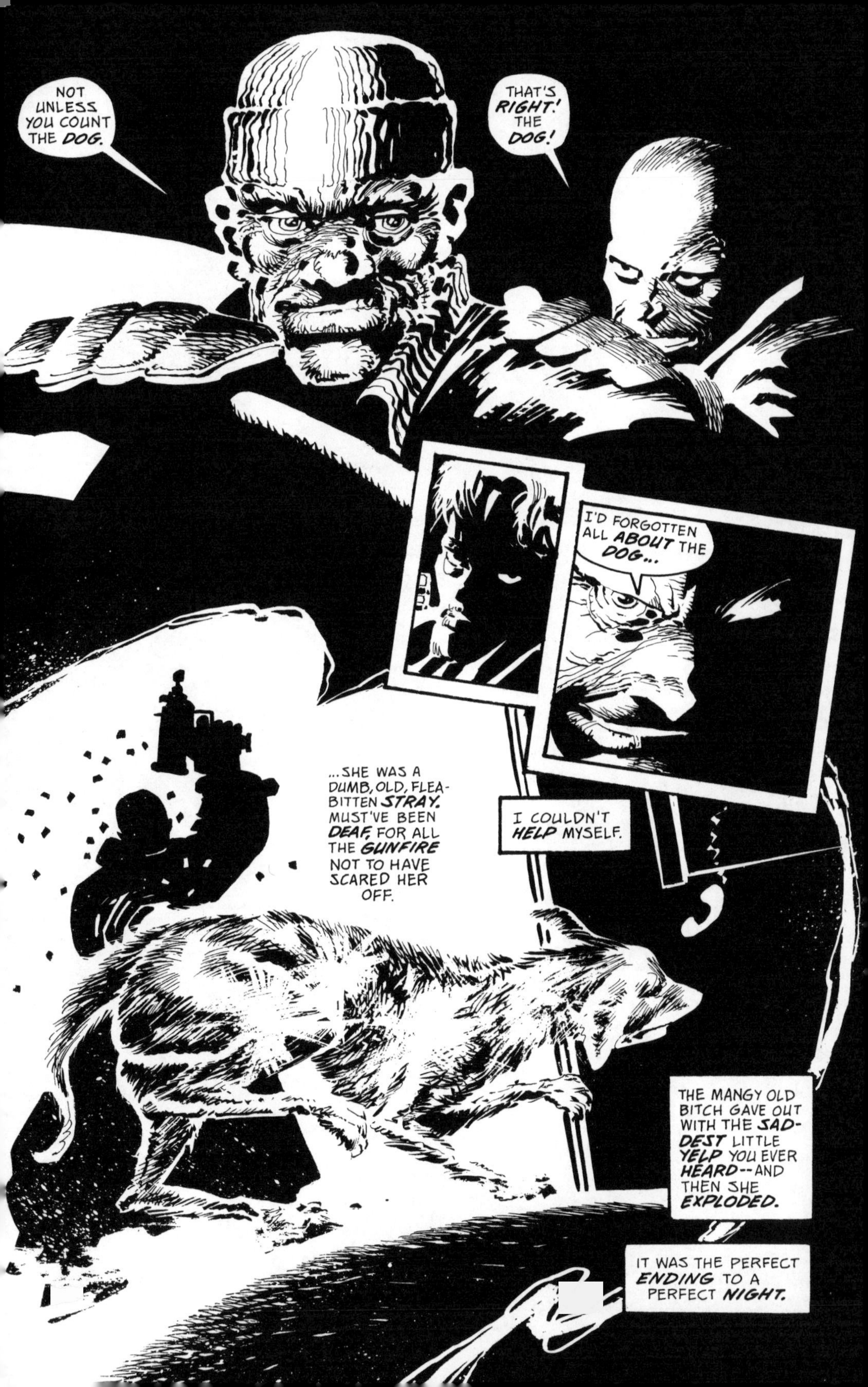
NOT UNLESS YOU COUNT THE DOG.
THAT'S RIGHT! THE DOG!
I'D FORGOTTEN ALL ABOUT THE DOG...
...SHE WAS A DUMB, OLD, FLEA-BITTEN STRAY. MUST'VE BEEN DEAF, FOR ALL THE GUNFIRE NOT TO HAVE SCARED HER OFF.
I COULDN'T HELP MYSELF.
THE MANGY OLD BITCH GAVE OUT WITH THE SAD-DEST LITTLE YELP YOU EVER HEARD--AND THEN SHE EXPLODED.
IT WAS THE PERFECT ENDING TO A PERFECT NIGHT.

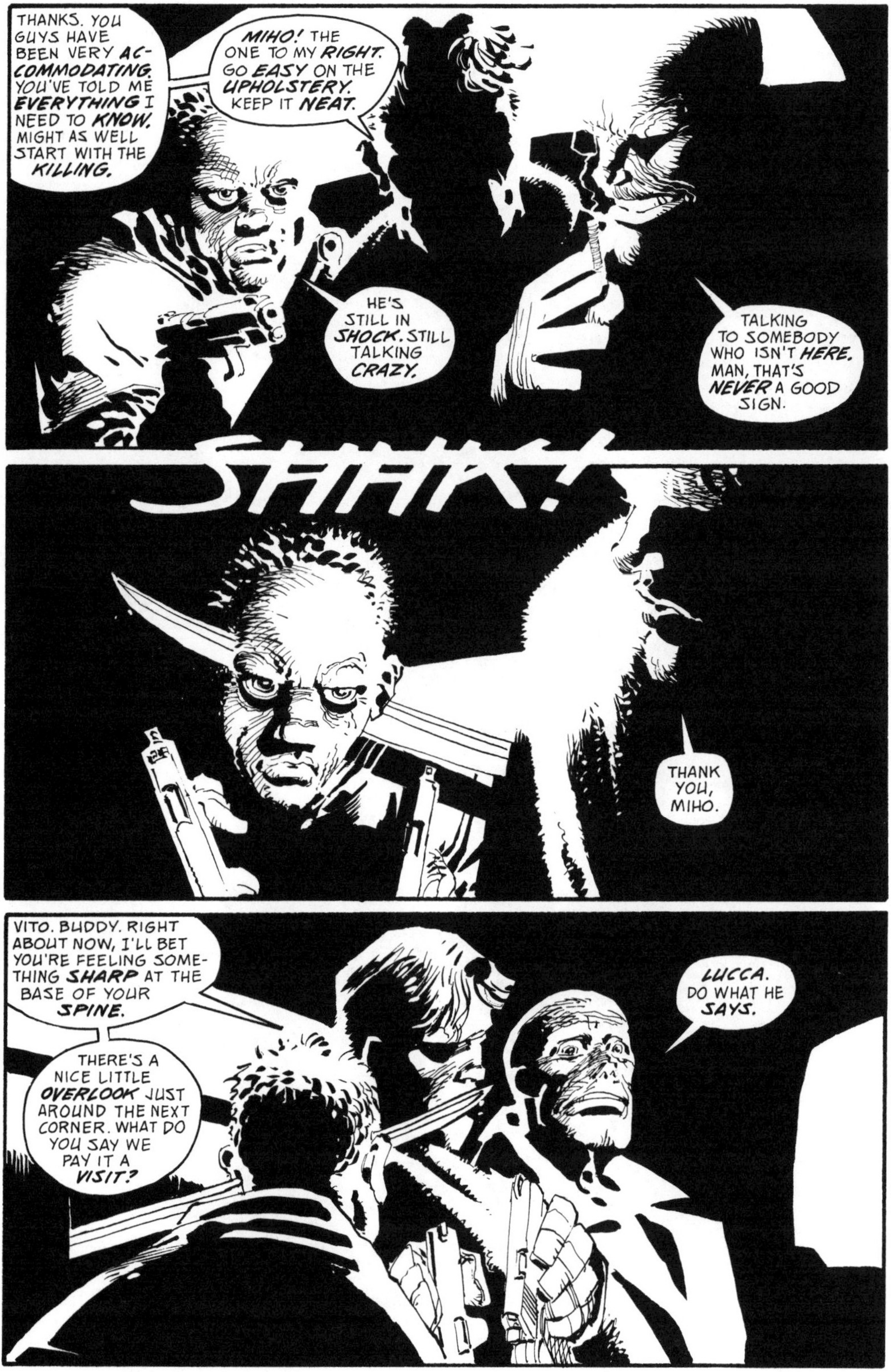
THANKS. YOU GUYS HAVE BEEN VERY AC-COMMODATING. YOU'VE TOLD ME EVERYTHING I NEED TO KNOW. MIGHT AS WELL START WITH THE KILLING.
MIHO! THE ONE TO MY RIGHT. GO EASY ON THE UPHOLSTERY. KEEP IT NEAT.
HE'S STILL IN SHOCK. STILL TALKING CRAZY.
TALKING TO SOMEBODY WHO ISN'T HERE. MAN, THAT'S NEVER A GOOD SIGN.
SHHK!
THANK YOU, MIHO.
VITO. BUDDY. RIGHT ABOUT NOW, I'LL BET YOU'RE FEELING SOME-THING SHARP AT THE BASE OF YOUR SPINE.
THERE'S A NICE LITTLE OVERLOOK JUST AROUND THE NEXT CORNER. WHAT DO YOU SAY WE PAY IT A VISIT?
LUCCA. DO WHAT HE SAYS.

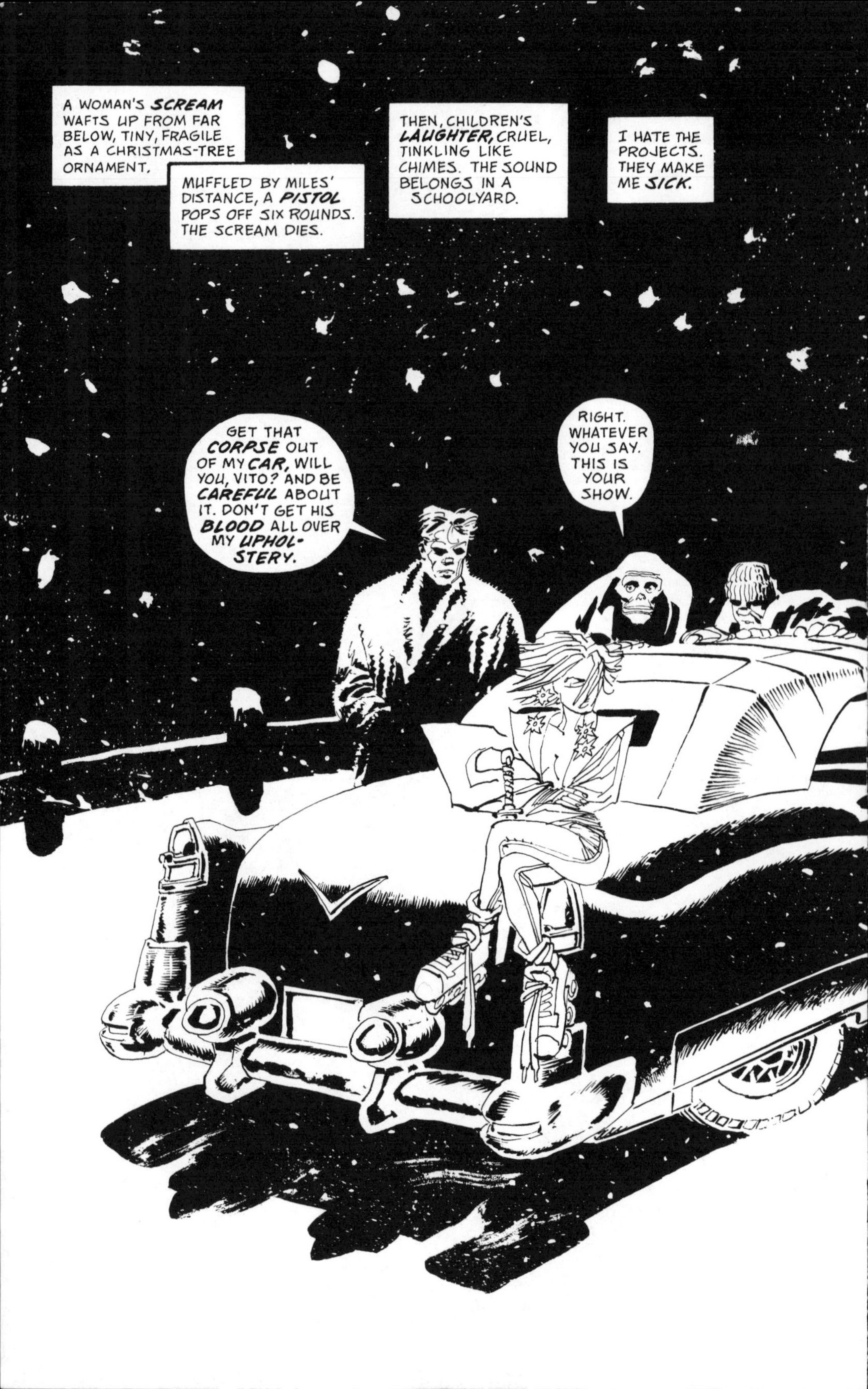
A WOMAN'S SCREAM WAFTS UP FROM FAR BELOW, TINY, FRAGILE AS A CHRISTMAS-TREE ORNAMENT.
MUFFLED BY MILES' DISTANCE, A PISTOL POPS OFF SIX ROUNDS. THE SCREAM DIES.
THEN, CHILDREN'S LAUGHTER, CRUEL, TINKLING LIKE CHIMES. THE SOUND BELONGS IN A SCHOOLYARD.
I HATE THE PROJECTS. THEY MAKE ME SICK.
GET THAT CORPSE OUT OF MY CAR, WILL YOU, VITO? AND BE CAREFUL ABOUT IT. DON'T GET HIS BLOOD ALL OVER MY UPHOLSTERY.
RIGHT. WHATEVER YOU SAY. THIS IS YOUR SHOW.

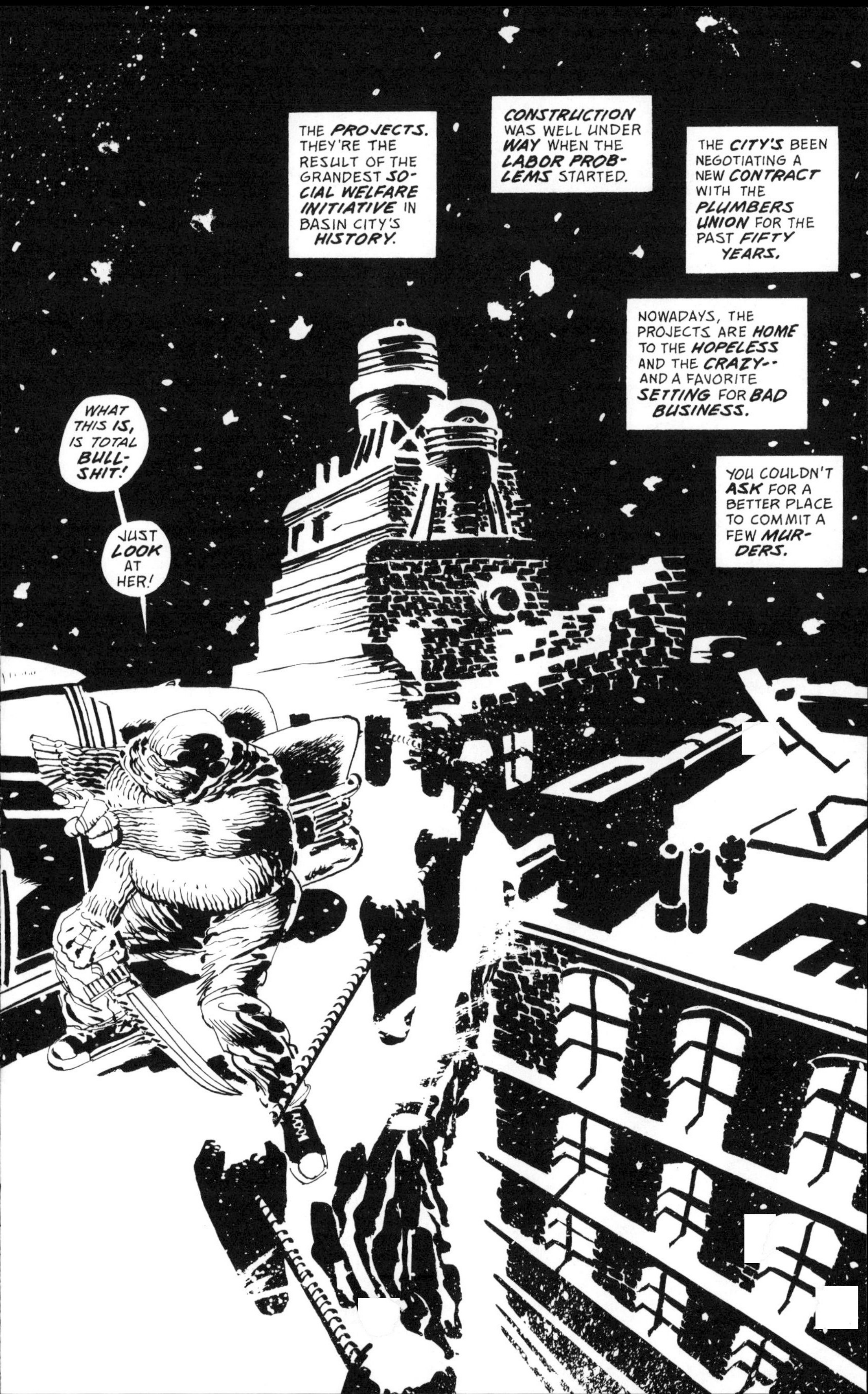

THE PROJECTS. THEY'RE THE RESULT OF THE GRANDEST SOCIAL WELFARE INITIATIVE IN BASIN CITY'S HISTORY.
CONSTRUCTION WAS WELL UNDER WAY WHEN THE LABOR PROBLEMS STARTED.
THE CITY'S BEEN NEGOTIATING A NEW CONTRACT WITH THE PLUMBERS UNION FOR THE PAST FIFTY YEARS.
NOWADAYS, THE PROJECTS ARE HOME TO THE HOPELESS AND THE CRAZY-- AND A FAVORITE SETTING FOR BAD BUSINESS.
WHAT THIS IS, IS TOTAL BULL-SHIT!
JUST LOOK AT HER!
YOU COULDN'T ASK FOR A BETTER PLACE TO COMMIT A FEW MURDERS.

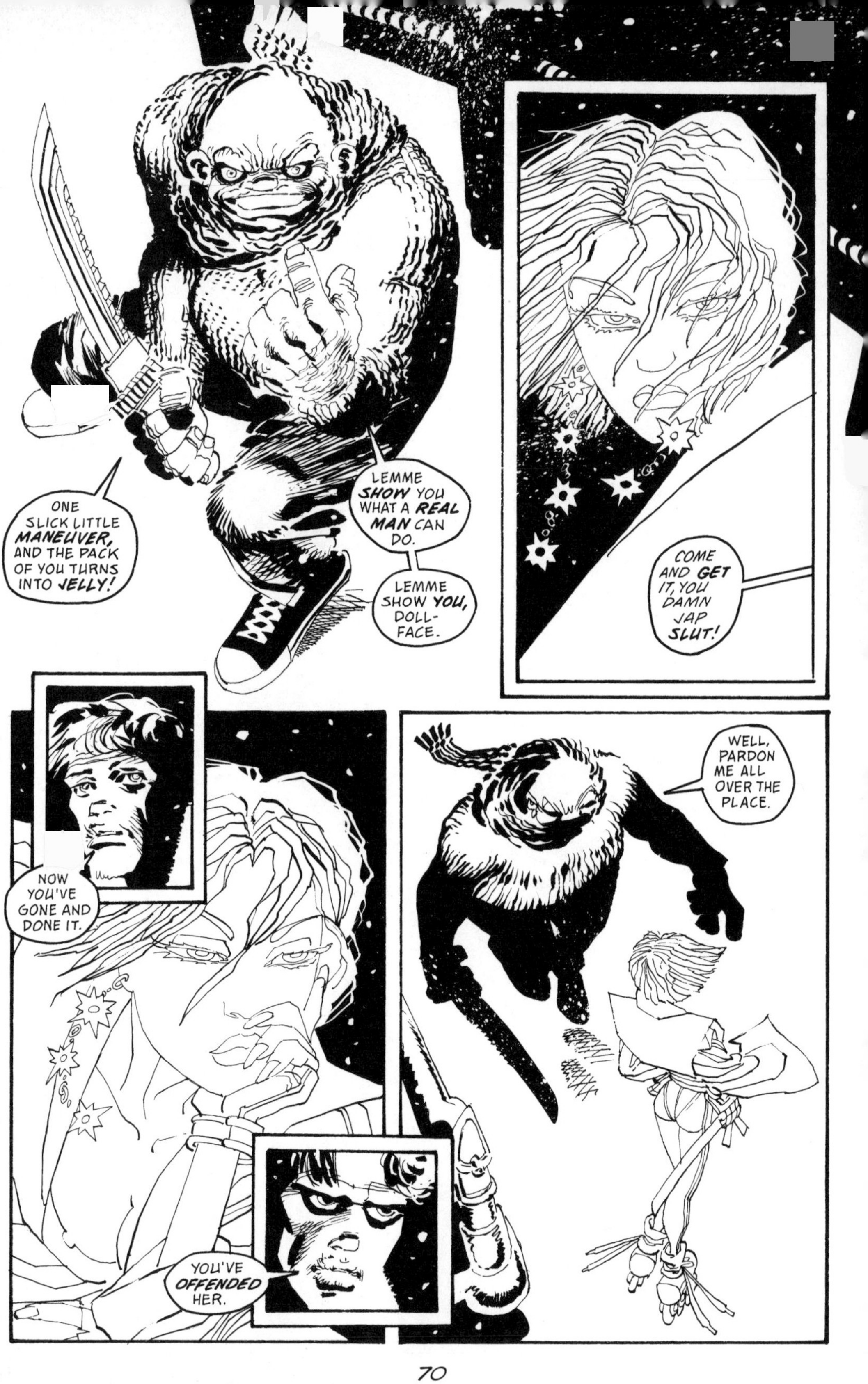
ONE SLICK LITTLE MANEUVER, AND THE PACK OF YOU TURNS INTO JELLY!
LEMME SHOW YOU WHAT A REAL MAN CAN DO.
LEMME SHOW YOU, DOLL-FACE.
COME AND GET IT, YOU DAMN JAP SLUT!
NOW YOU'VE GONE AND DONE IT.
YOU'VE OFFENDED HER.
WELL, PARDON ME ALL OVER THE PLACE.

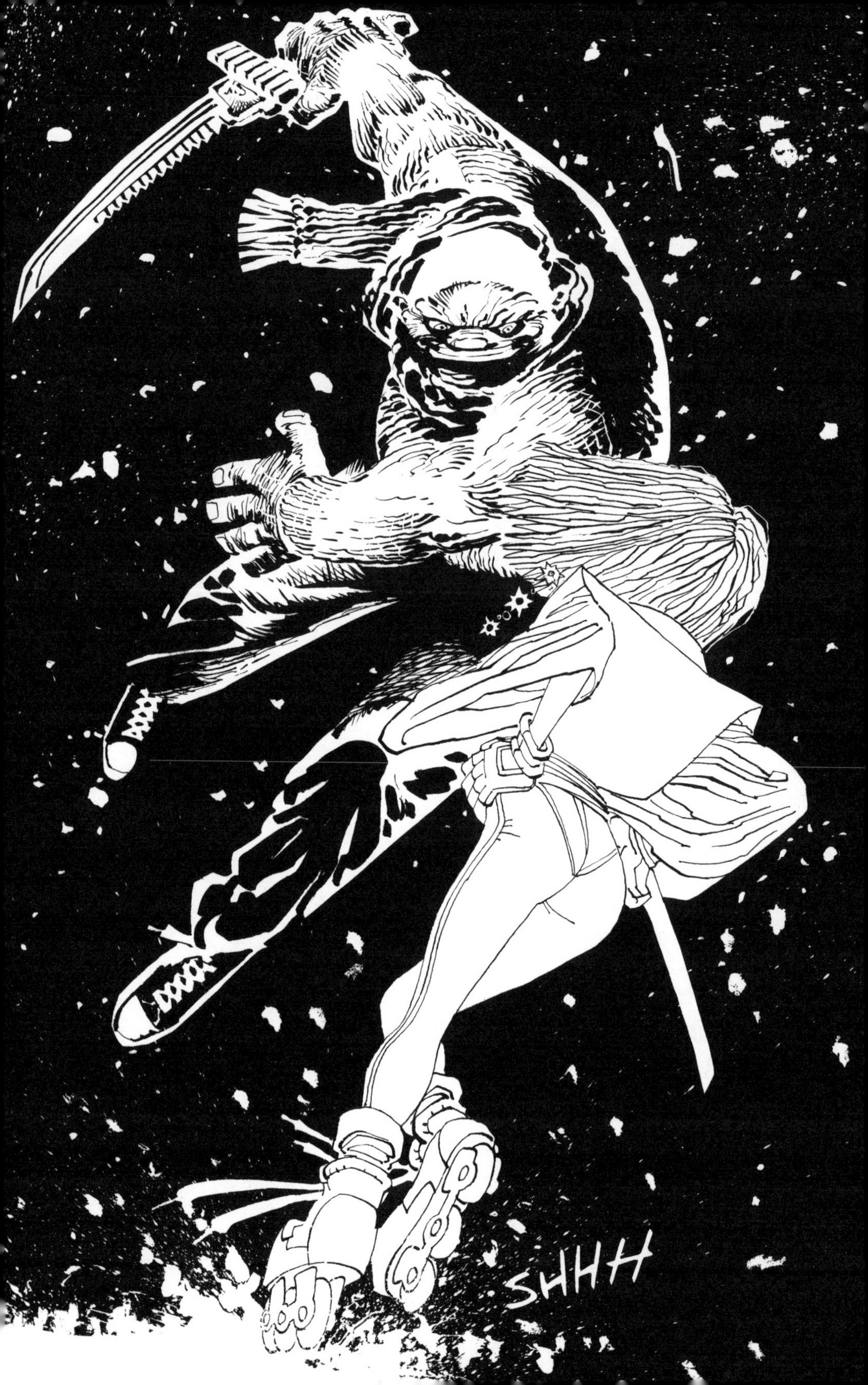
SHHH

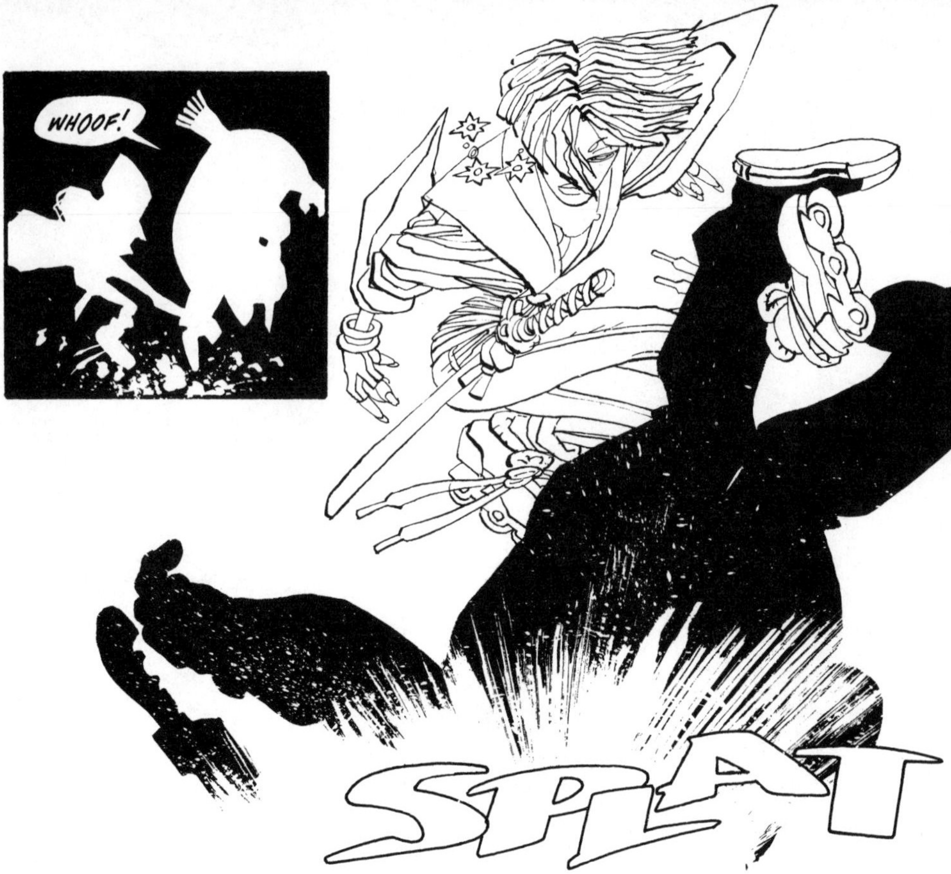
WHOOF!
SPLAT

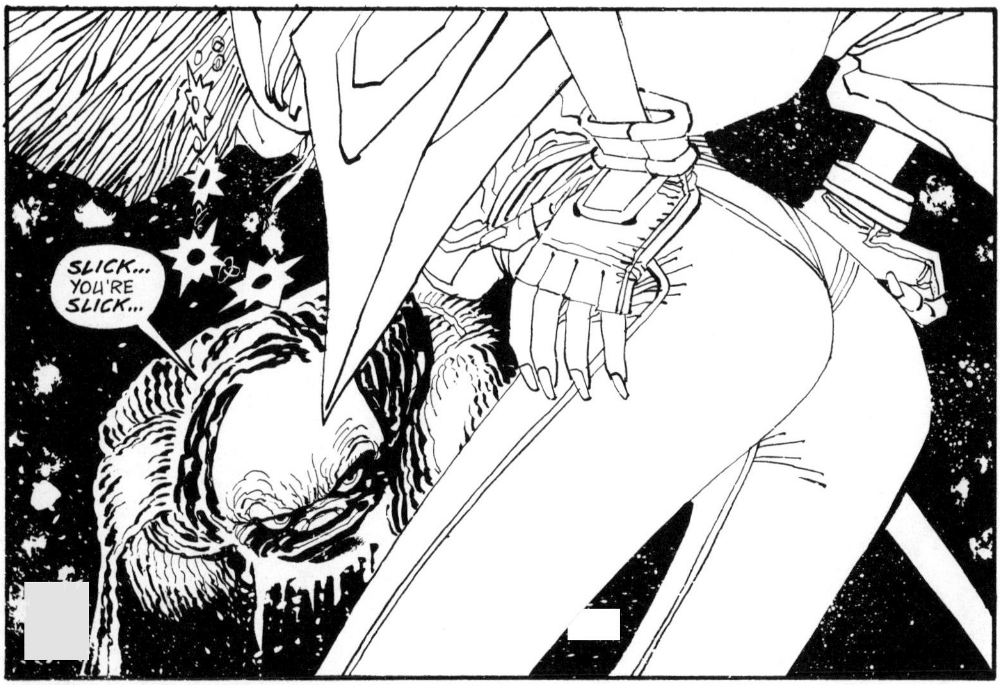
SLICK... YOU'RE SLICK...

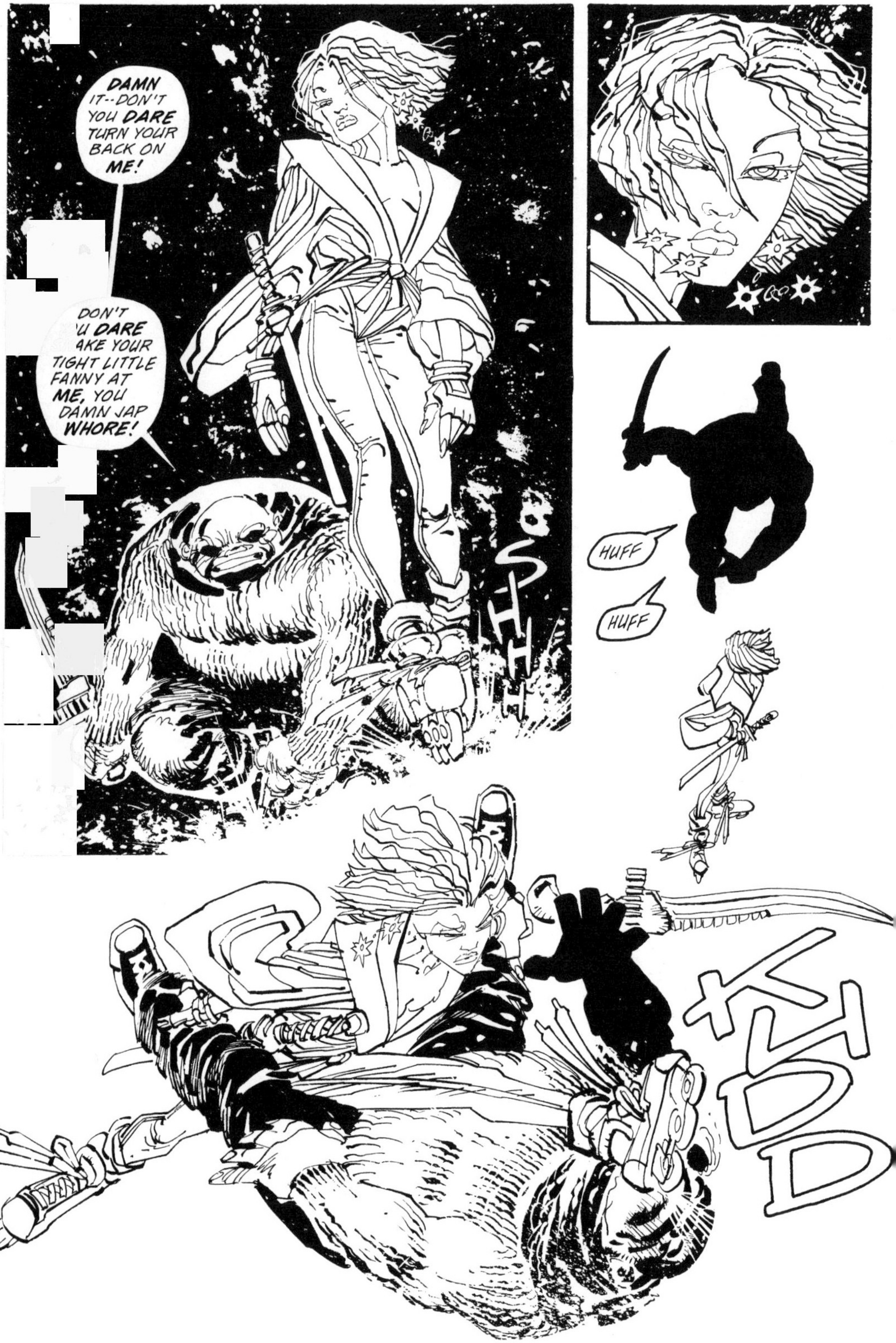
DAMN IT--DON'T YOU DARE TURN YOUR BACK ON ME!
DON'T U DARE AKE YOUR TIGHT LITTLE FANNY AT ME, YOU DAMN JAP WHORE!
HUFF
HUFF

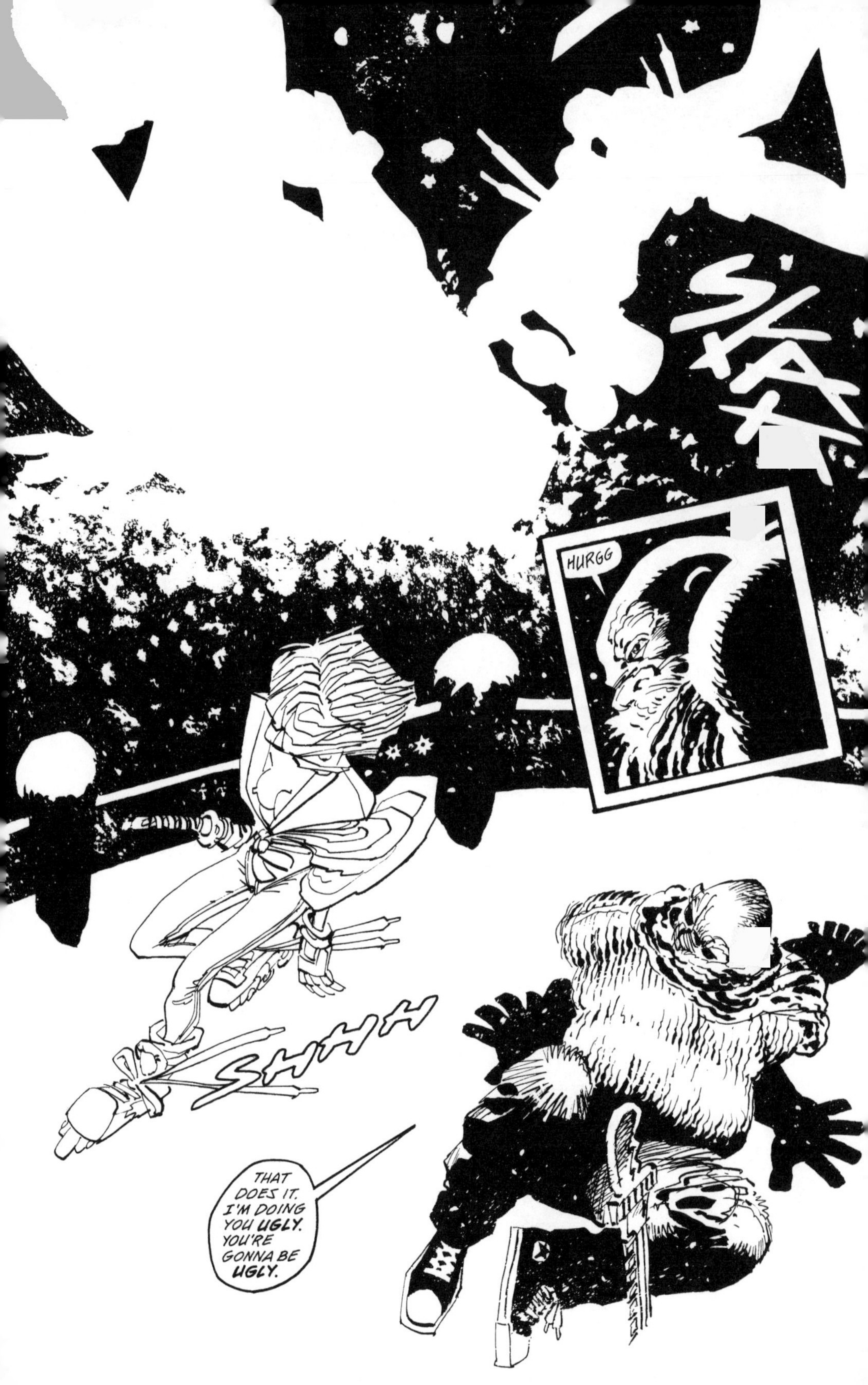
SHAK
HURGG
SHHHH
THAT DOES IT. I'M DOING YOU UGLY. YOU'RE GONNA BE UGLY.

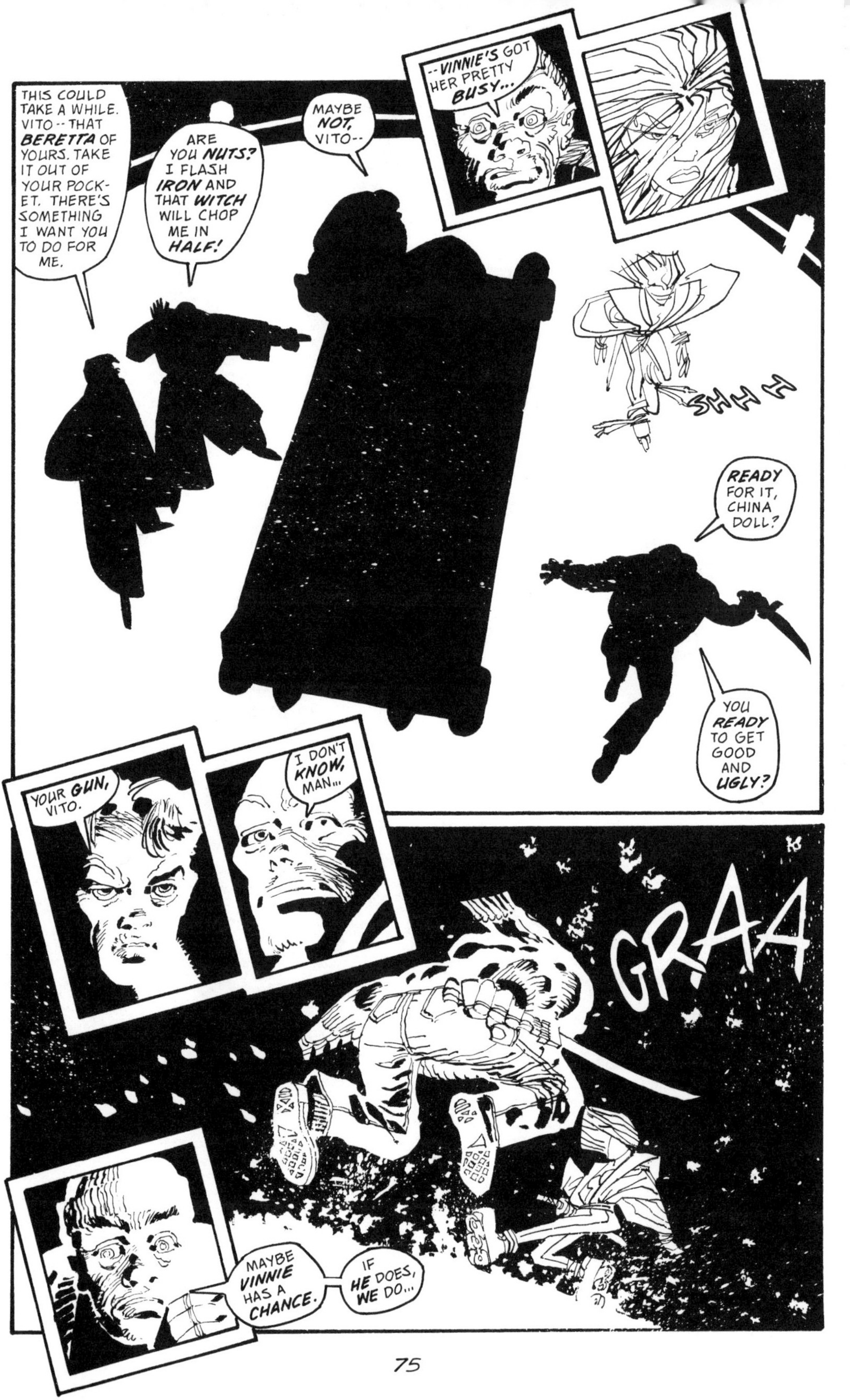

THIS COULD TAKE A WHILE. VITO -- THAT BERETTA OF YOURS. TAKE IT OUT OF YOUR POCKET. THERE'S SOMETHING I WANT YOU TO DO FOR ME.
ARE YOU NUTS? I FLASH IRON AND THAT WITCH WILL CHOP ME IN HALF!
MAYBE NOT, VITO--
--VINNIE'S GOT HER PRETTY BUSY...
SHHH
READY FOR IT, CHINA DOLL?
YOU READY TO GET GOOD AND UGLY?
YOUR GUN, VITO.
I DON'T KNOW, MAN...
GRAA
MAYBE VINNIE HAS A CHANCE.
IF HE DOES, WE DO...

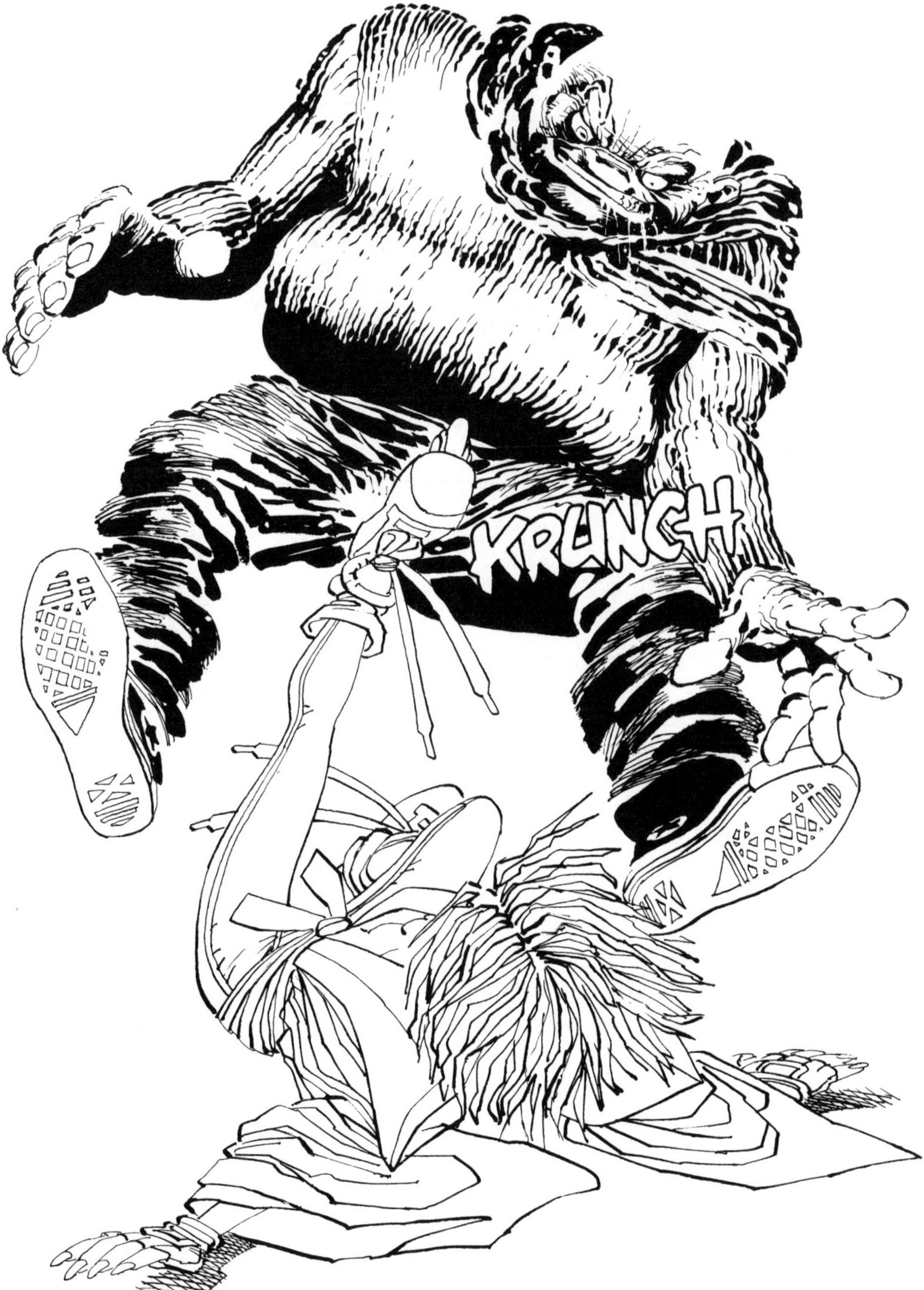
KRUNCH

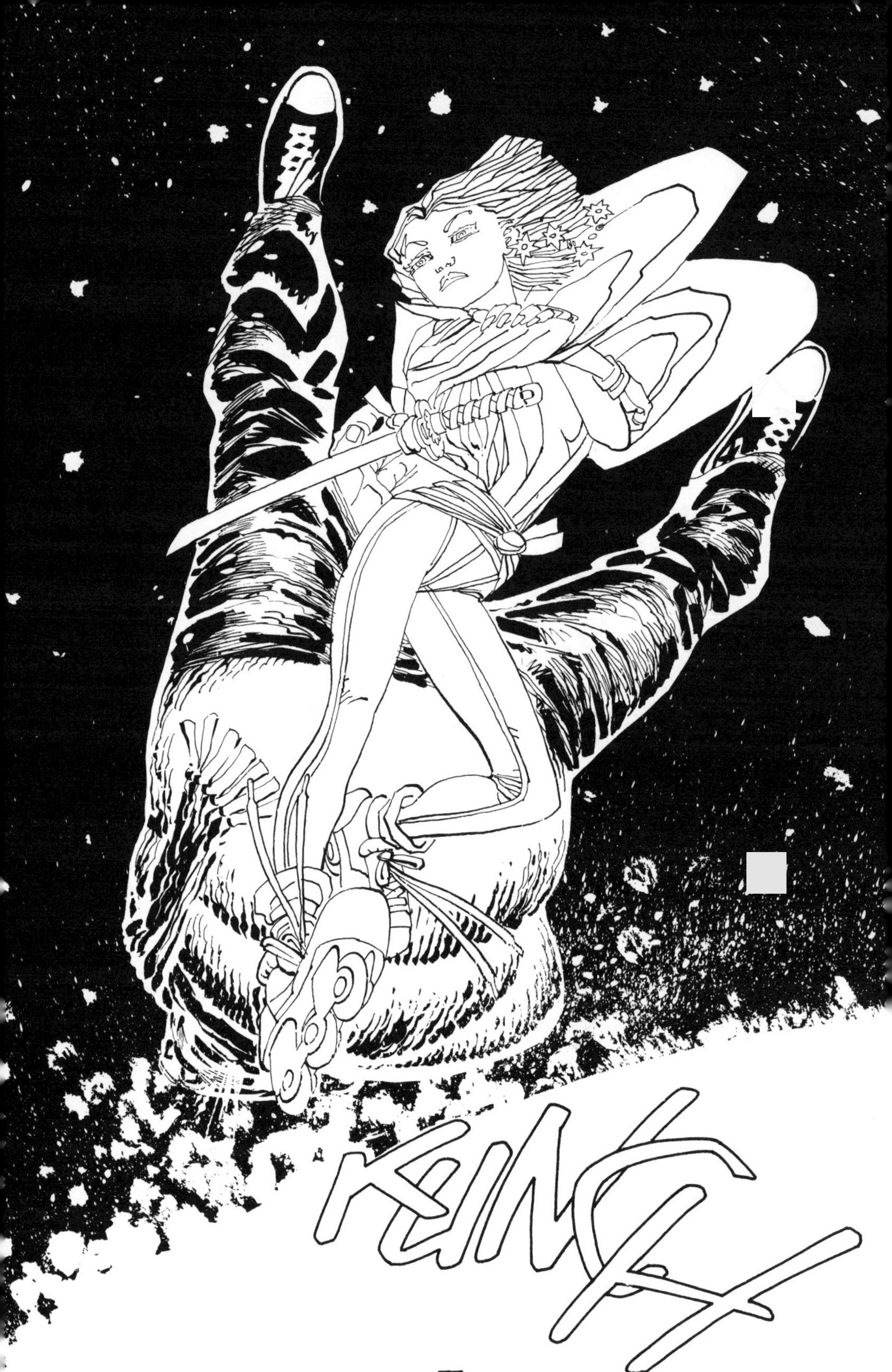
KLINCH

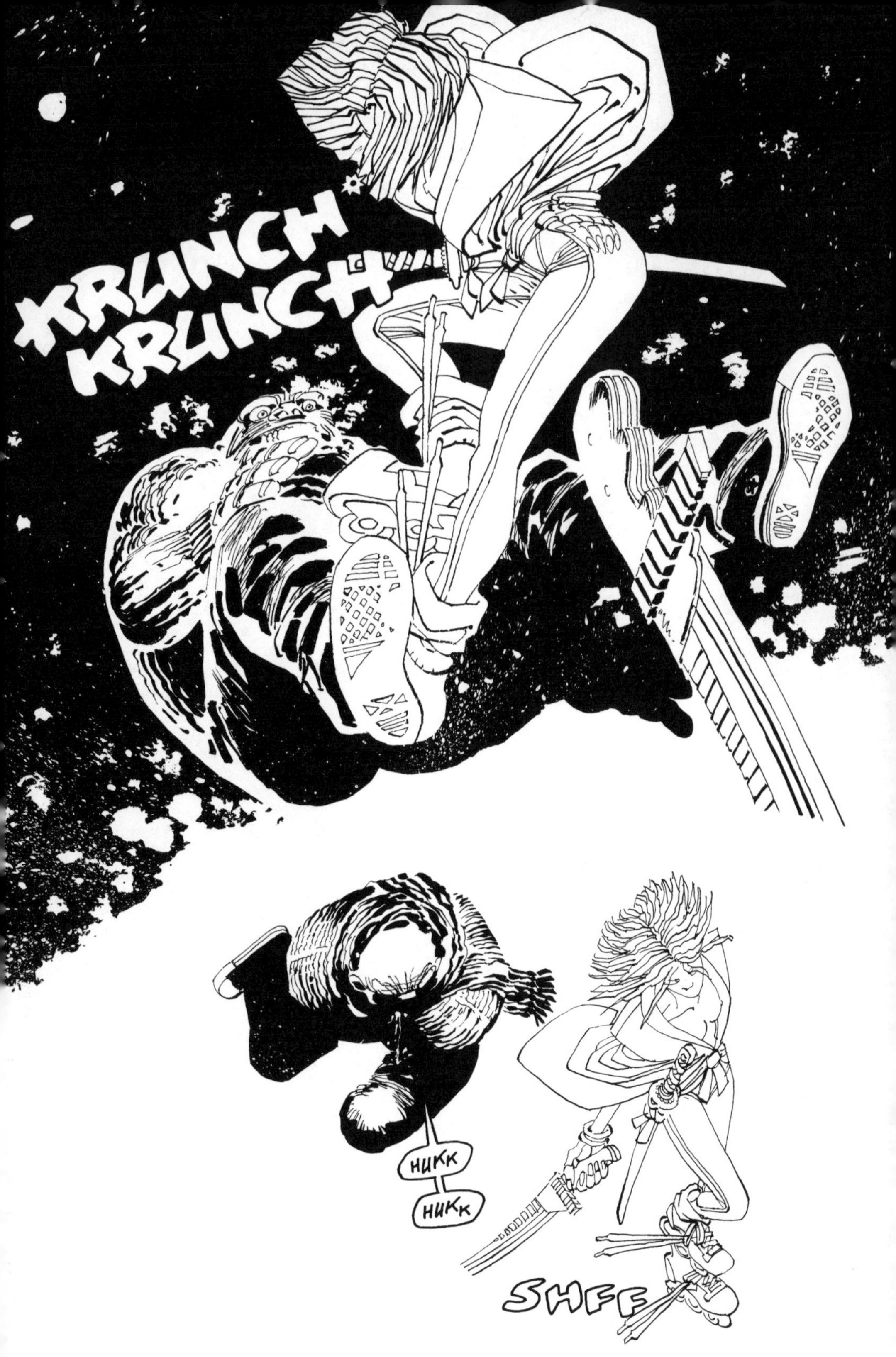
KRUNCH
KRUNCH
HUKK
HUKK
SHFF

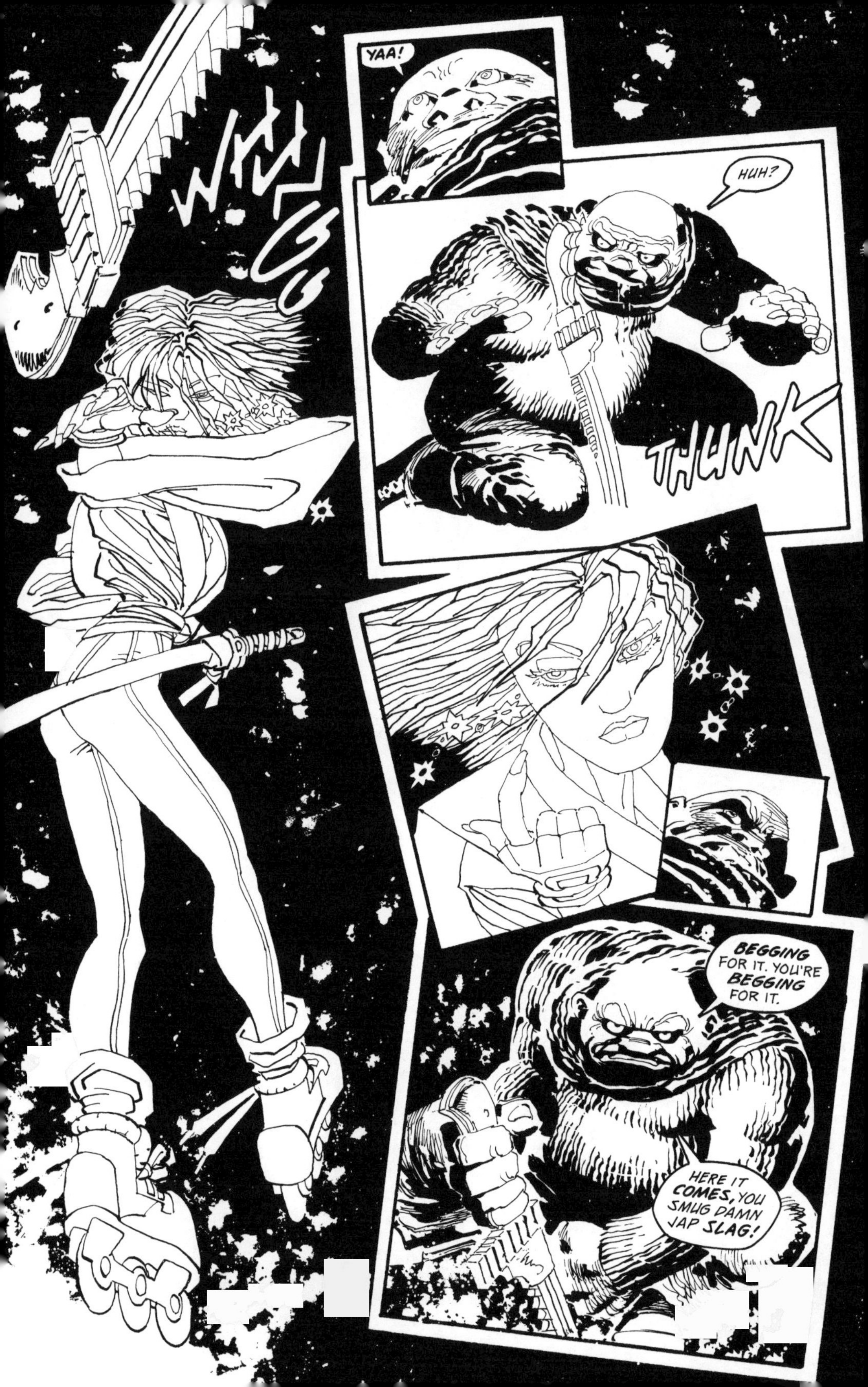
WHUG
YAA!
HUH?
THUNK
BEGGING FOR IT. YOU'RE BEGGING FOR IT.
HERE IT COMES, YOU SMUG DAMN JAP SLAG!

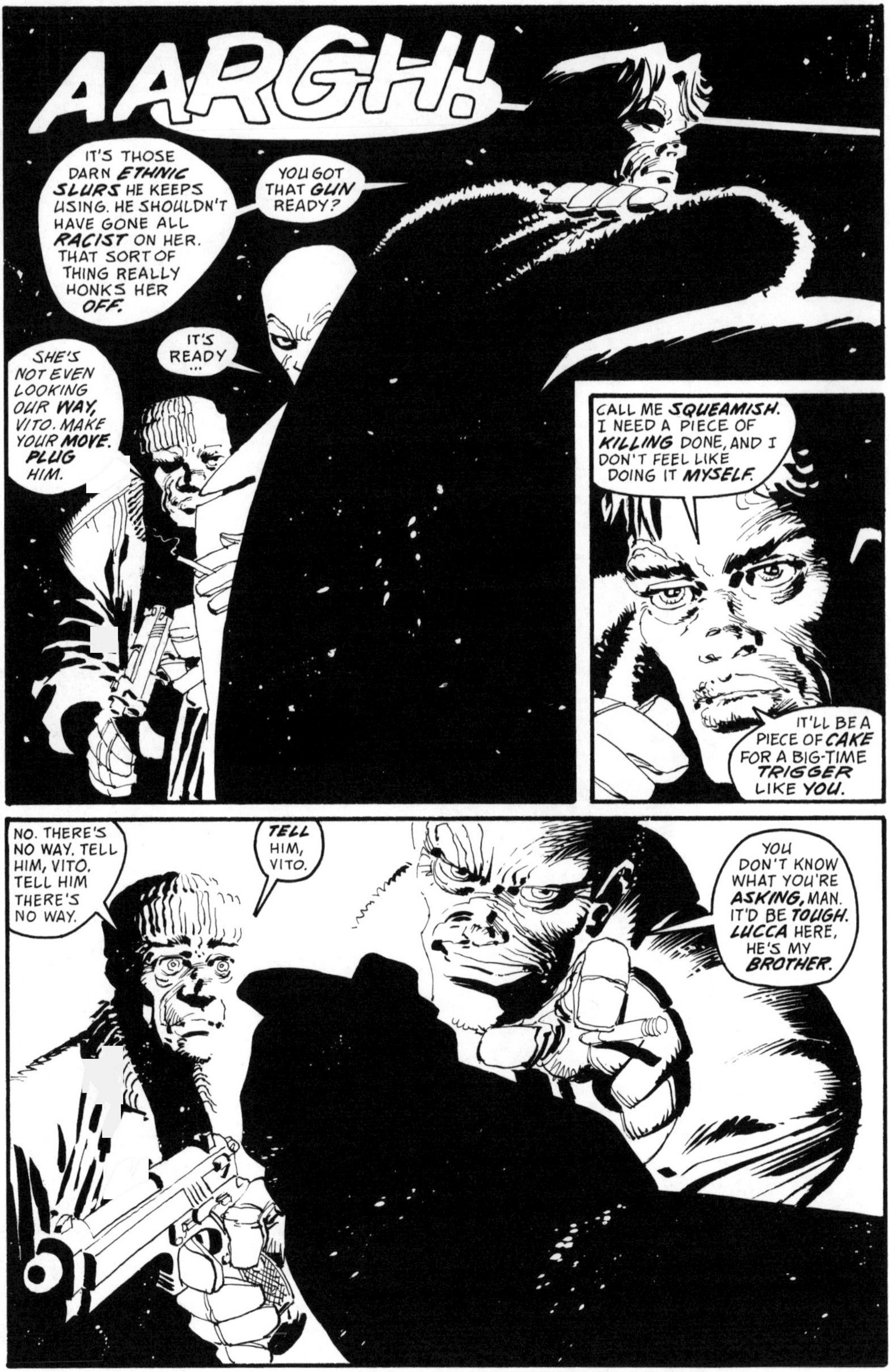
AARGH!
IT'S THOSE DARN ETHNIC SLURS HE KEEPS USING. HE SHOULDN'T HAVE GONE ALL RACIST ON HER. THAT SORT OF THING REALLY HONKS HER OFF.
YOU GOT THAT GUN READY?
SHE'S NOT EVEN LOOKING OUR WAY, VITO. MAKE YOUR MOVE. PLUG HIM.
IT'S READY ...
CALL ME SQUEAMISH. I NEED A PIECE OF KILLING DONE, AND I DON'T FEEL LIKE DOING IT MYSELF.
IT'LL BE A PIECE OF CAKE FOR A BIG-TIME TRIGGER LIKE YOU.
NO. THERE'S NO WAY. TELL HIM, VITO. TELL HIM THERE'S NO WAY.
TELL HIM, VITO.
YOU DON'T KNOW WHAT YOU'RE ASKING, MAN. IT'D BE TOUGH. LUCCA HERE, HE'S MY BROTHER.

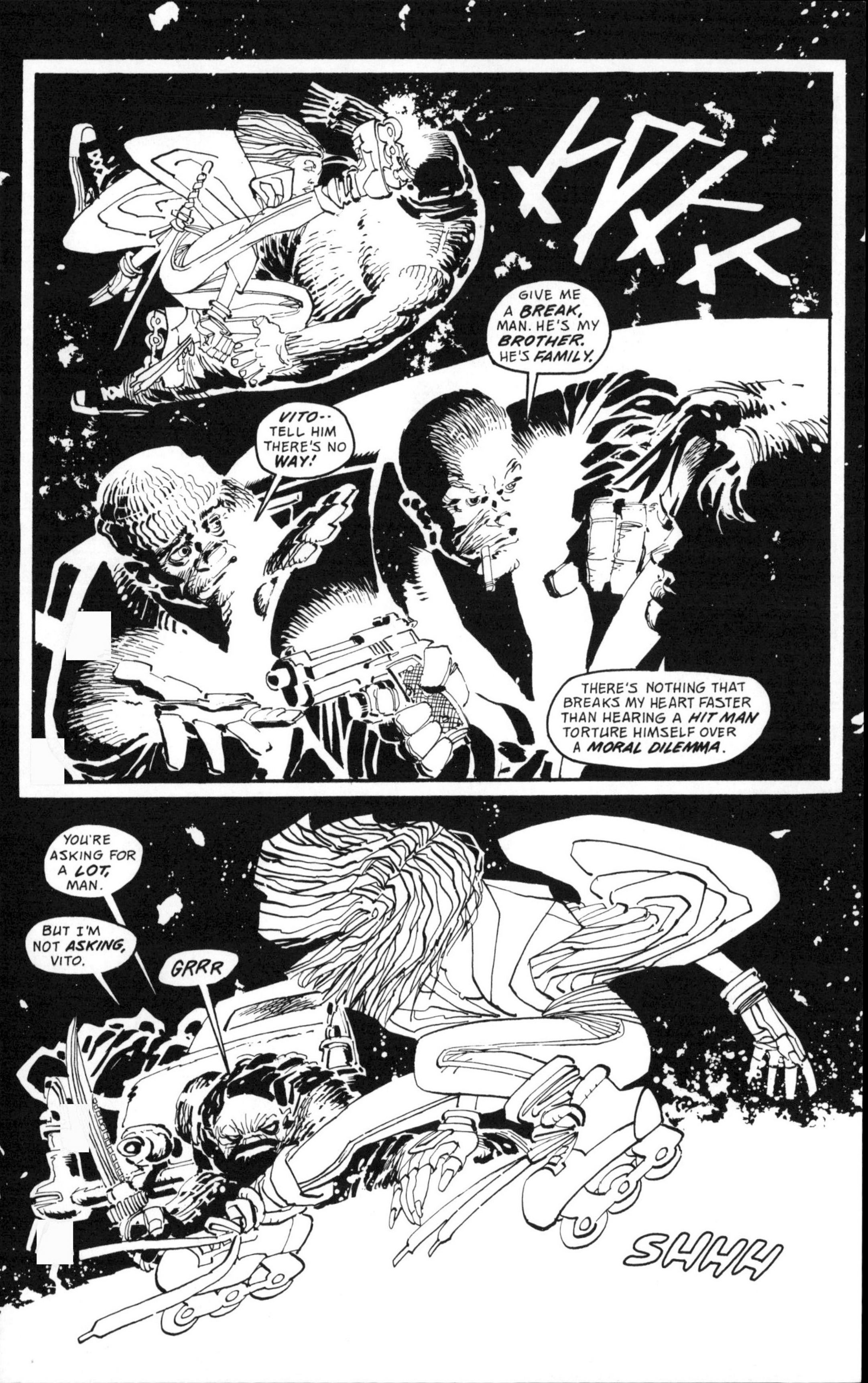
KKKK
GIVE ME A BREAK, MAN. HE'S MY BROTHER. HE'S FAMILY.
VITO-- TELL HIM THERE'S NO WAY!
THERE'S NOTHING THAT BREAKS MY HEART FASTER THAN HEARING A HIT MAN TORTURE HIMSELF OVER A MORAL DILEMMA.
YOU'RE ASKING FOR A LOT, MAN.
BUT I'M NOT ASKING, VITO.
GRRR
SHHH

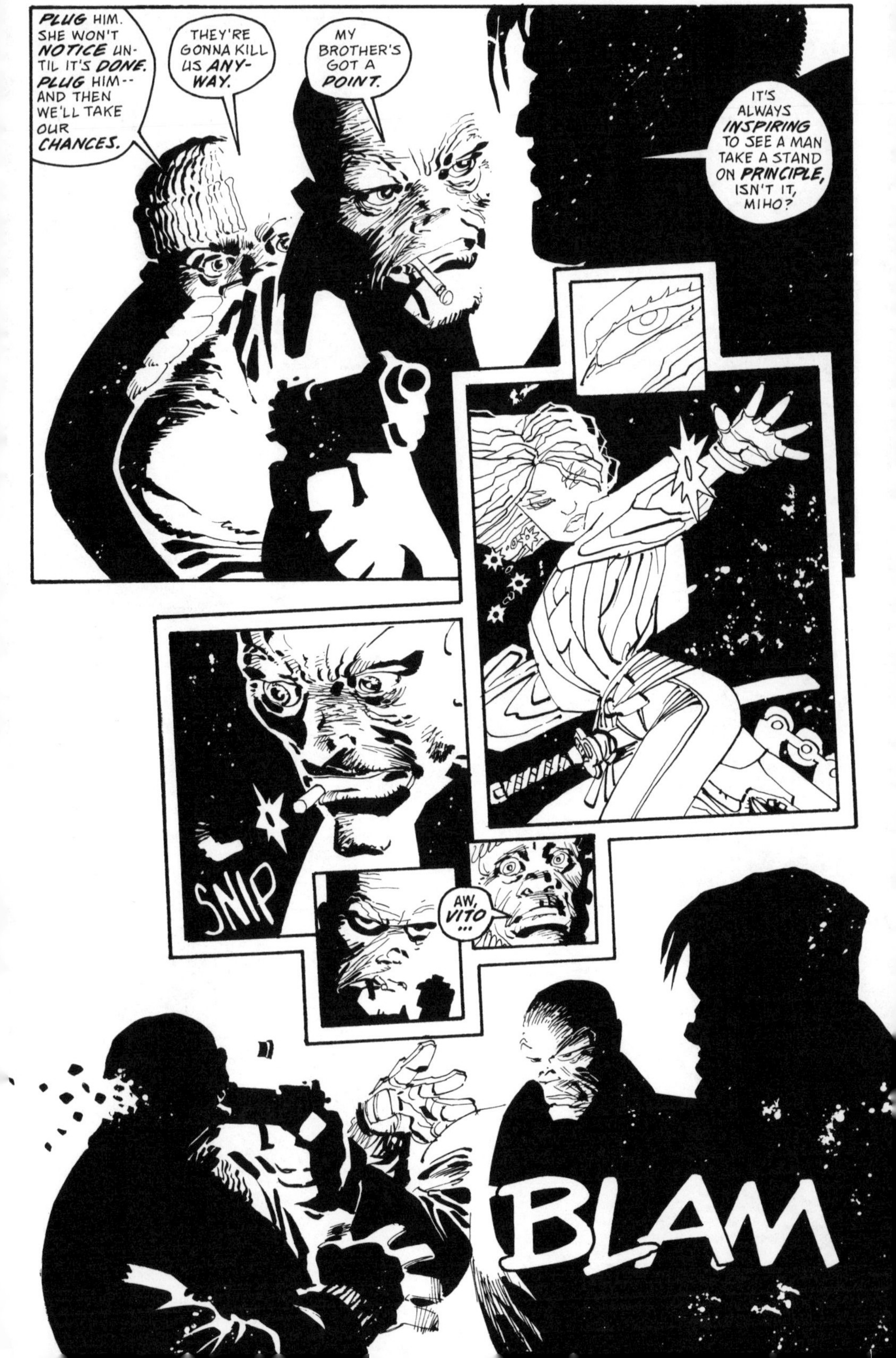
PLUG HIM. SHE WON'T NOTICE UNTIL IT'S DONE. PLUG HIM-- AND THEN WE'LL TAKE OUR CHANCES.
THEY'RE GONNA KILL US ANYWAY.
MY BROTHER'S GOT A POINT.
IT'S ALWAYS INSPIRING TO SEE A MAN TAKE A STAND ON PRINCIPLE, ISN'T IT, MIHO?
SNIP
AW, VITO ...
BLAM

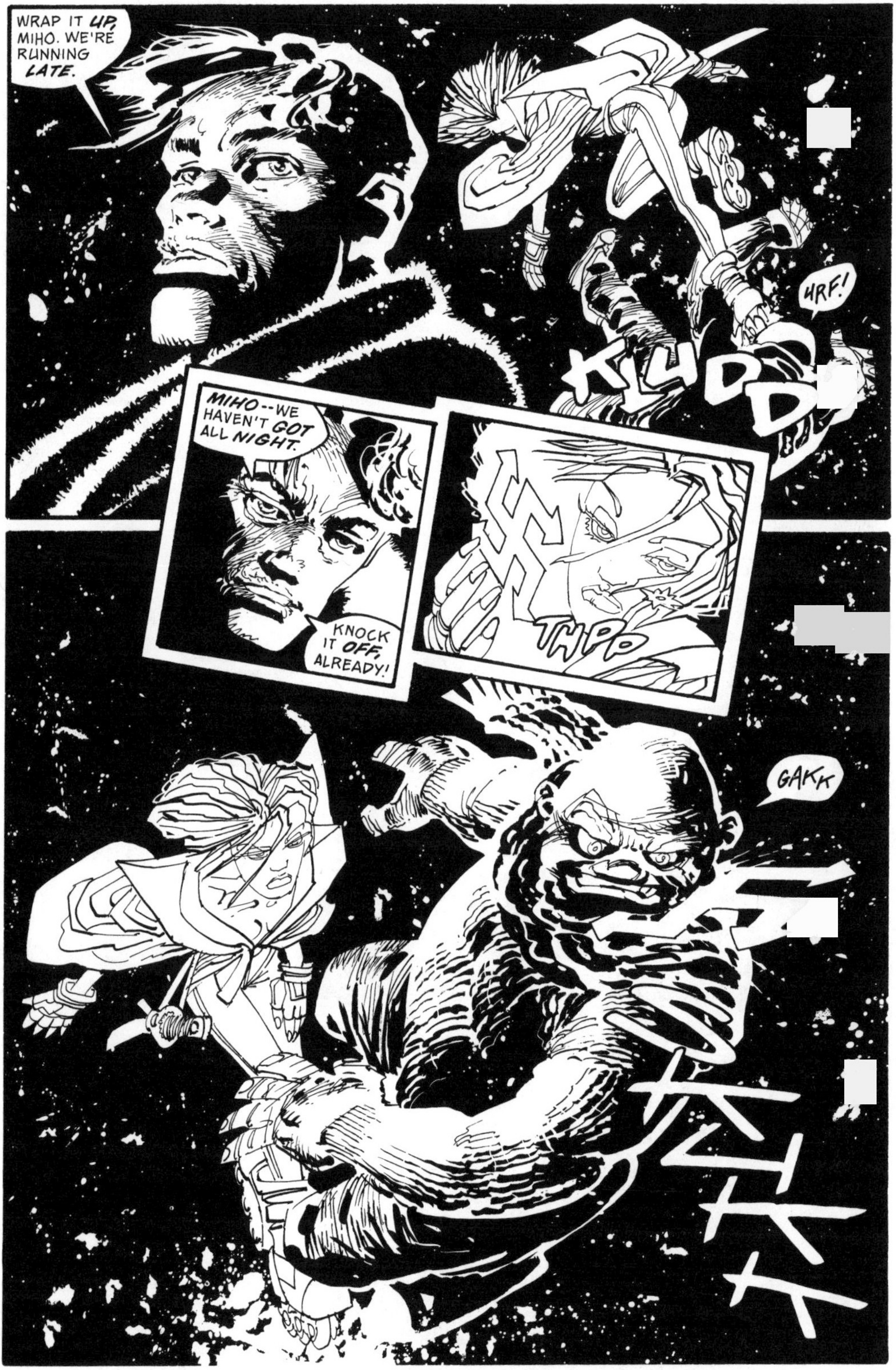
WRAP IT UP, MIHO. WE'RE RUNNING LATE.
URF!
KLUDD
MIHO--WE HAVEN'T GOT ALL NIGHT.
KNOCK IT OFF, ALREADY!
THPD
GAKK

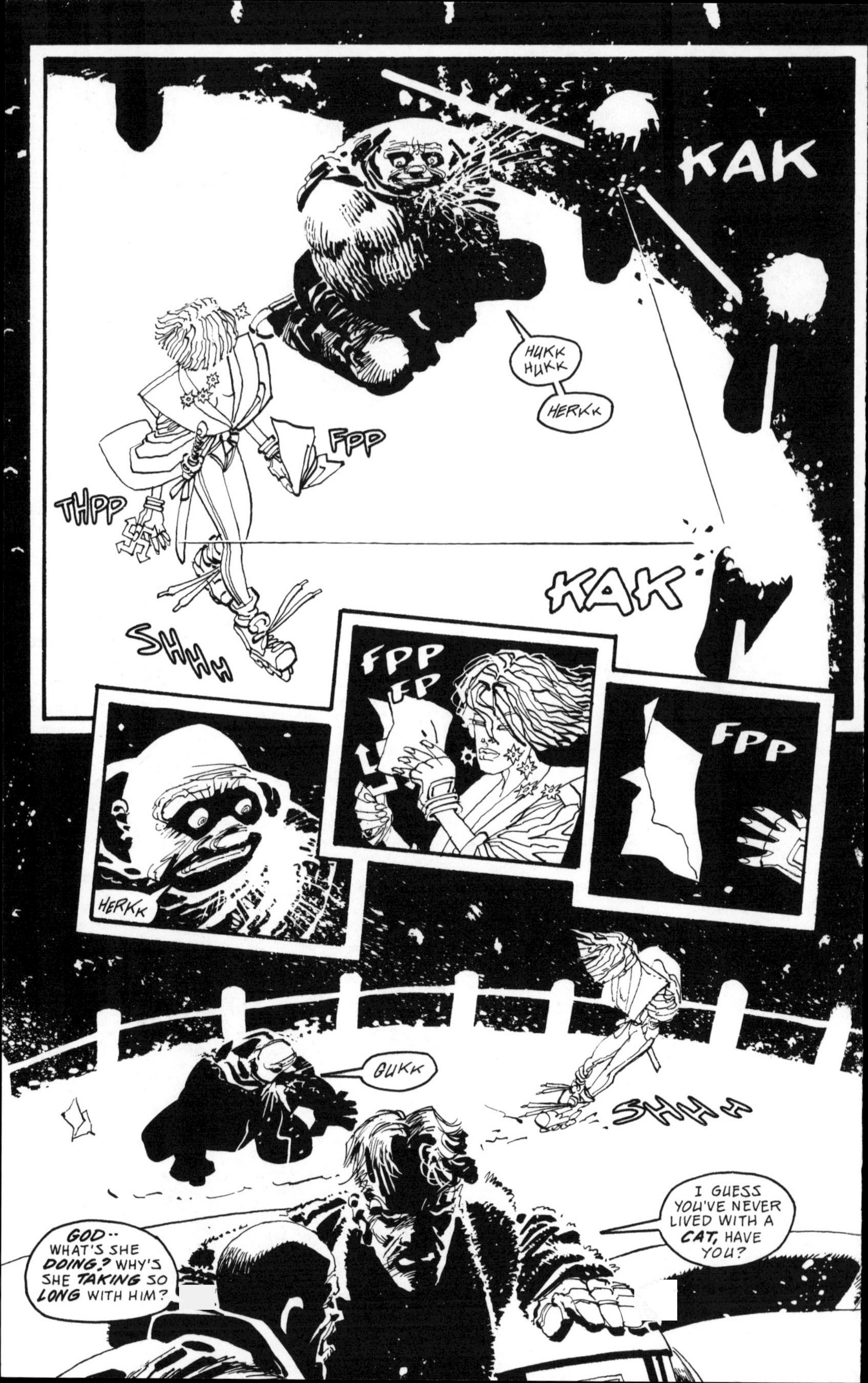
KAK
HUKK HUKK
HERKK
FPP
THPP
KAK
SHHHH
FPP FP
FPP
HERKK
GUKK
SHHHH
GOD.. WHAT'S SHE DOING? WHY'S SHE TAKING SO LONG WITH HIM?
I GUESS YOU'VE NEVER LIVED WITH A CAT, HAVE YOU?

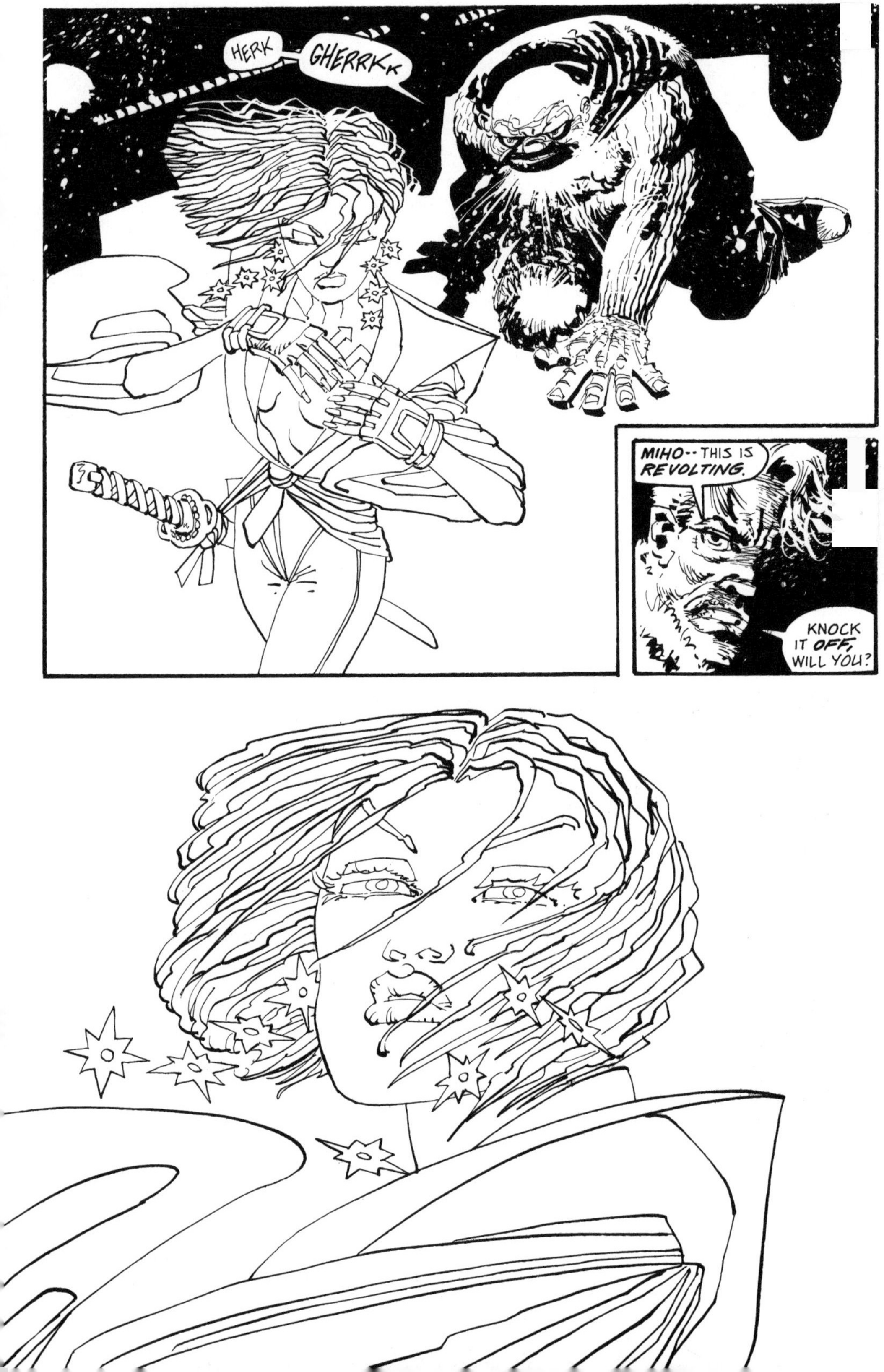
HERK
GHERRKK
MIHO-- THIS IS REVOLTING.
KNOCK IT OFF, WILL YOU?

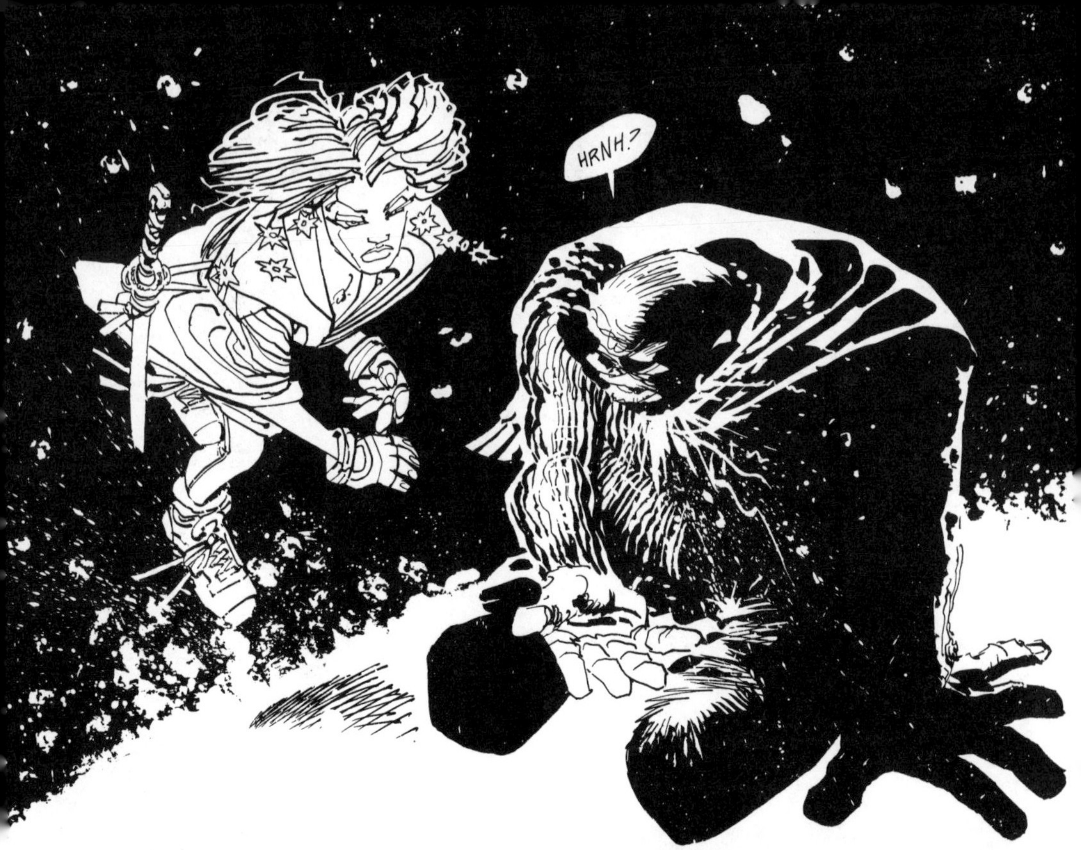
HRNH?

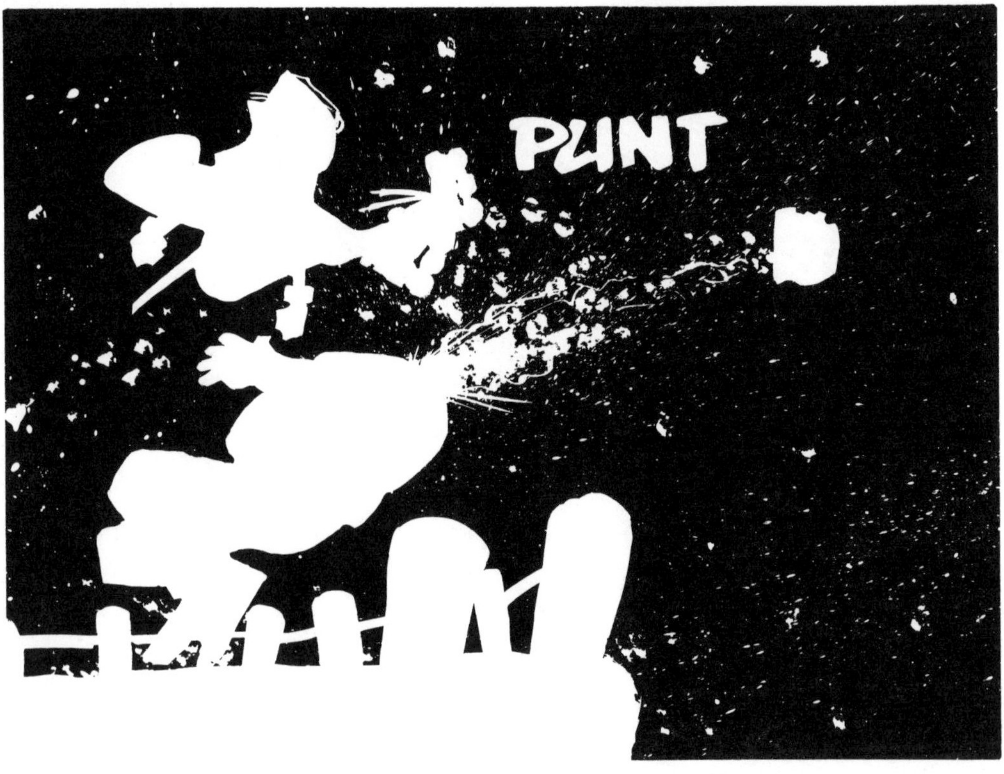
PLINT

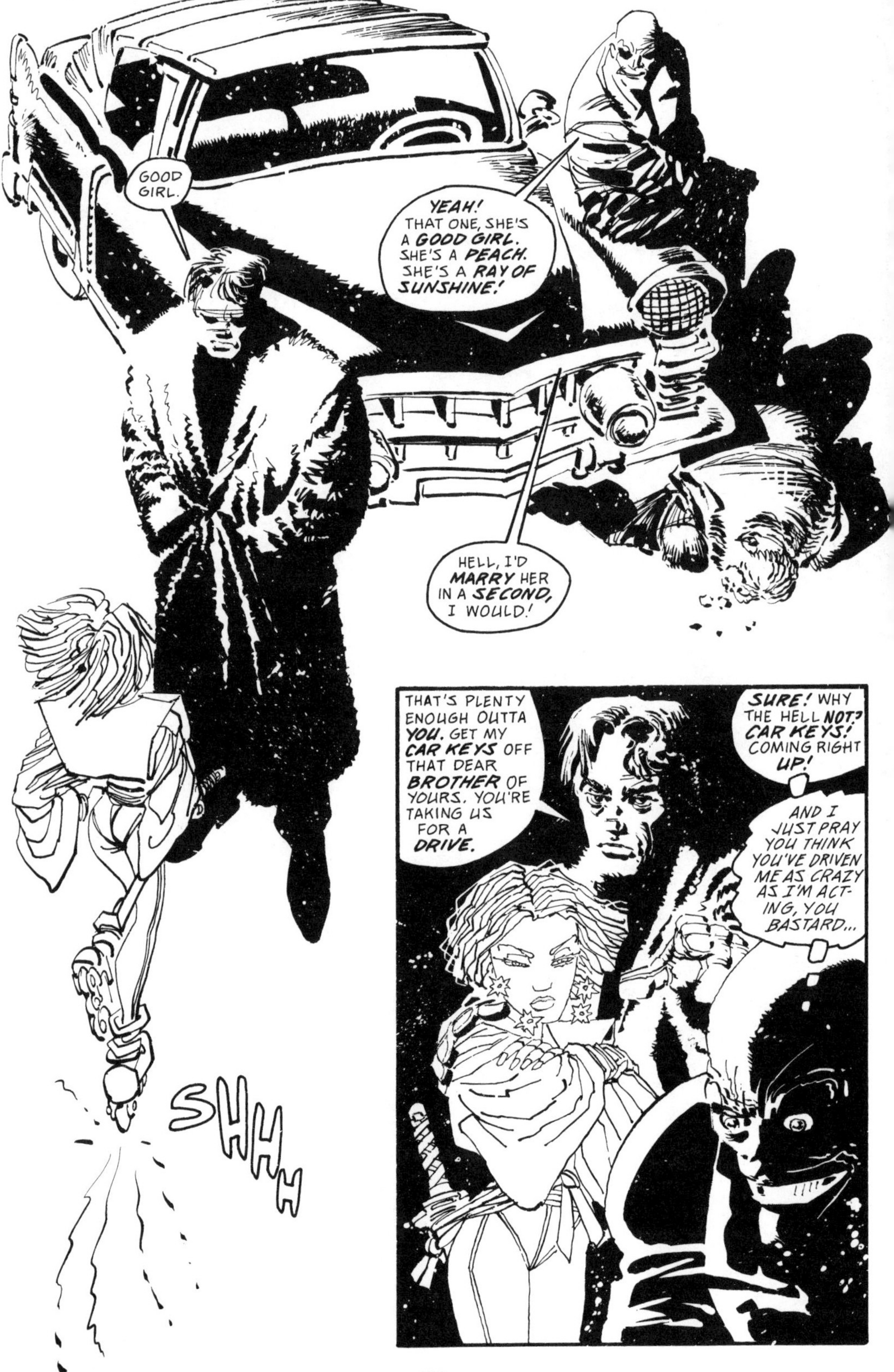
GOOD GIRL.
YEAH! THAT ONE, SHE'S A GOOD GIRL. SHE'S A PEACH. SHE'S A RAY OF SUNSHINE!
HELL, I'D MARRY HER IN A SECOND, I WOULD!
SHHHH
THAT'S PLENTY ENOUGH OUTTA YOU. GET MY CAR KEYS OFF THAT DEAR BROTHER OF YOURS. YOU'RE TAKING US FOR A DRIVE.
SURE! WHY THE HELL NOT? CAR KEYS! COMING RIGHT UP!
AND I JUST PRAY YOU THINK YOU'VE DRIVEN ME AS CRAZY AS I'M ACTING, YOU BASTARD...

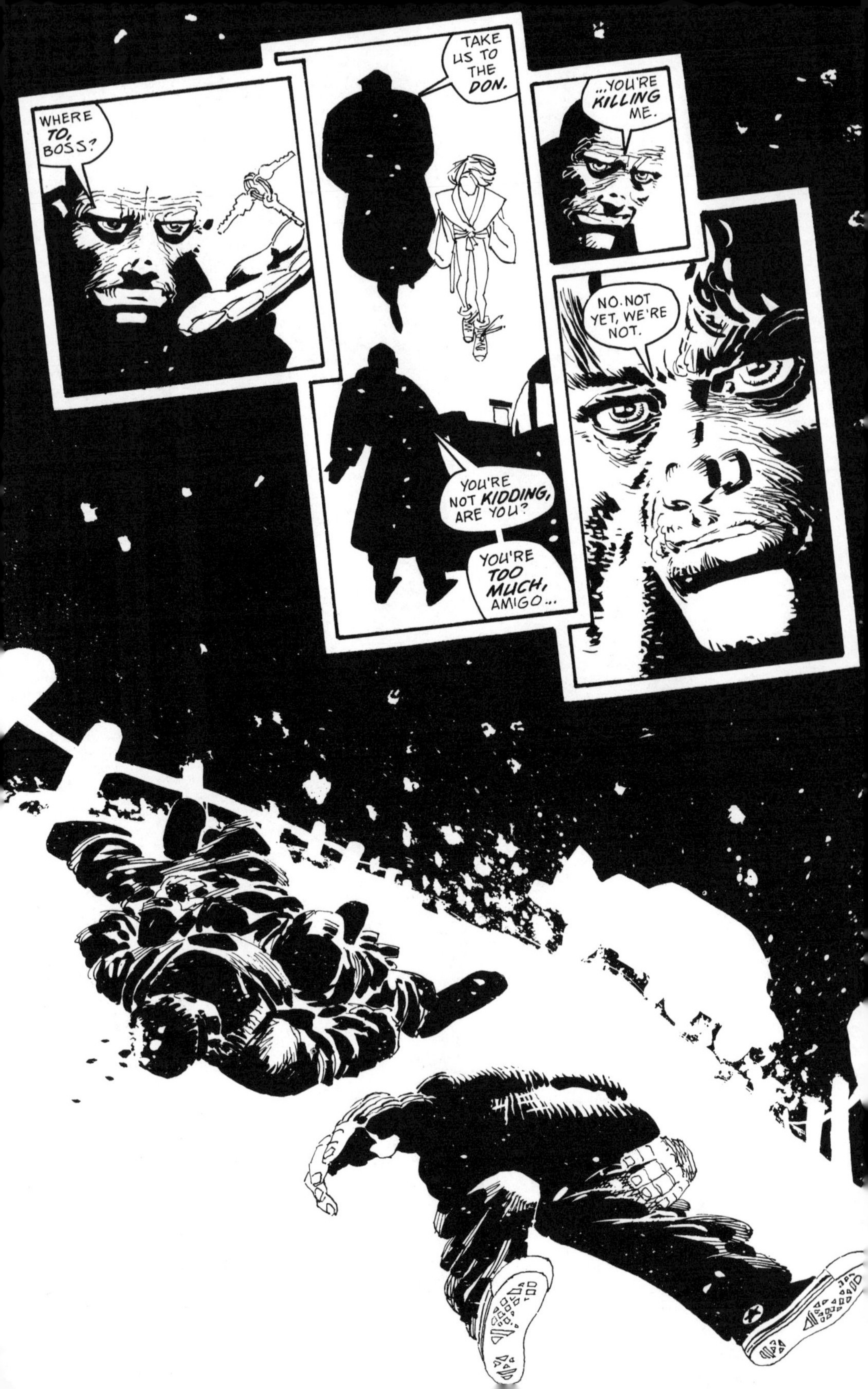
WHERE TO, BOSS?
TAKE US TO THE DON.
...YOU'RE KILLING ME.
NO. NOT YET, WE'RE NOT.
YOU'RE NOT KIDDING, ARE YOU?
YOU'RE TOO MUCH, AMIGO...

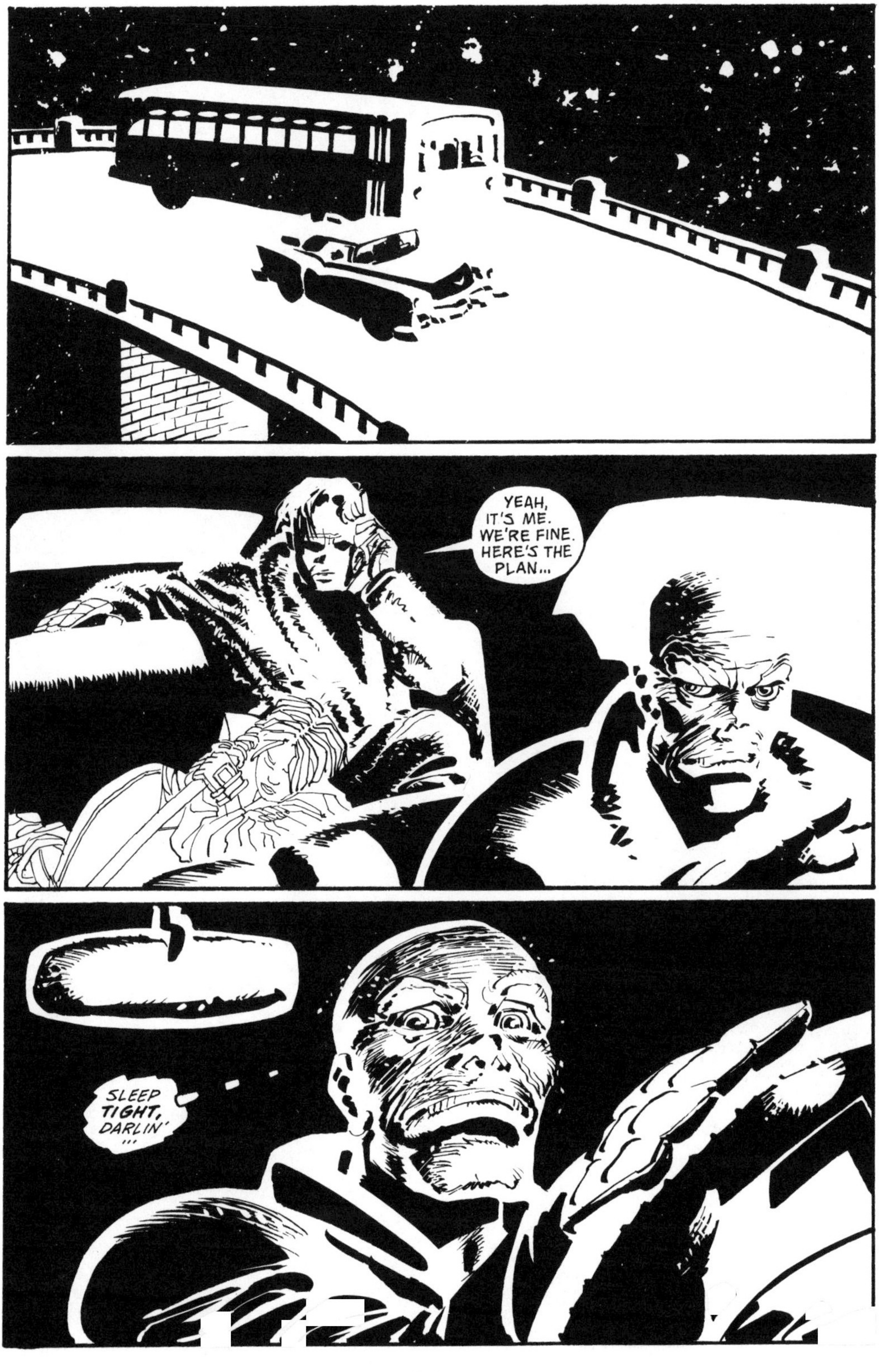
YEAH, IT'S ME. WE'RE FINE. HERE'S THE PLAN...
SLEEP TIGHT, DARLIN' ...

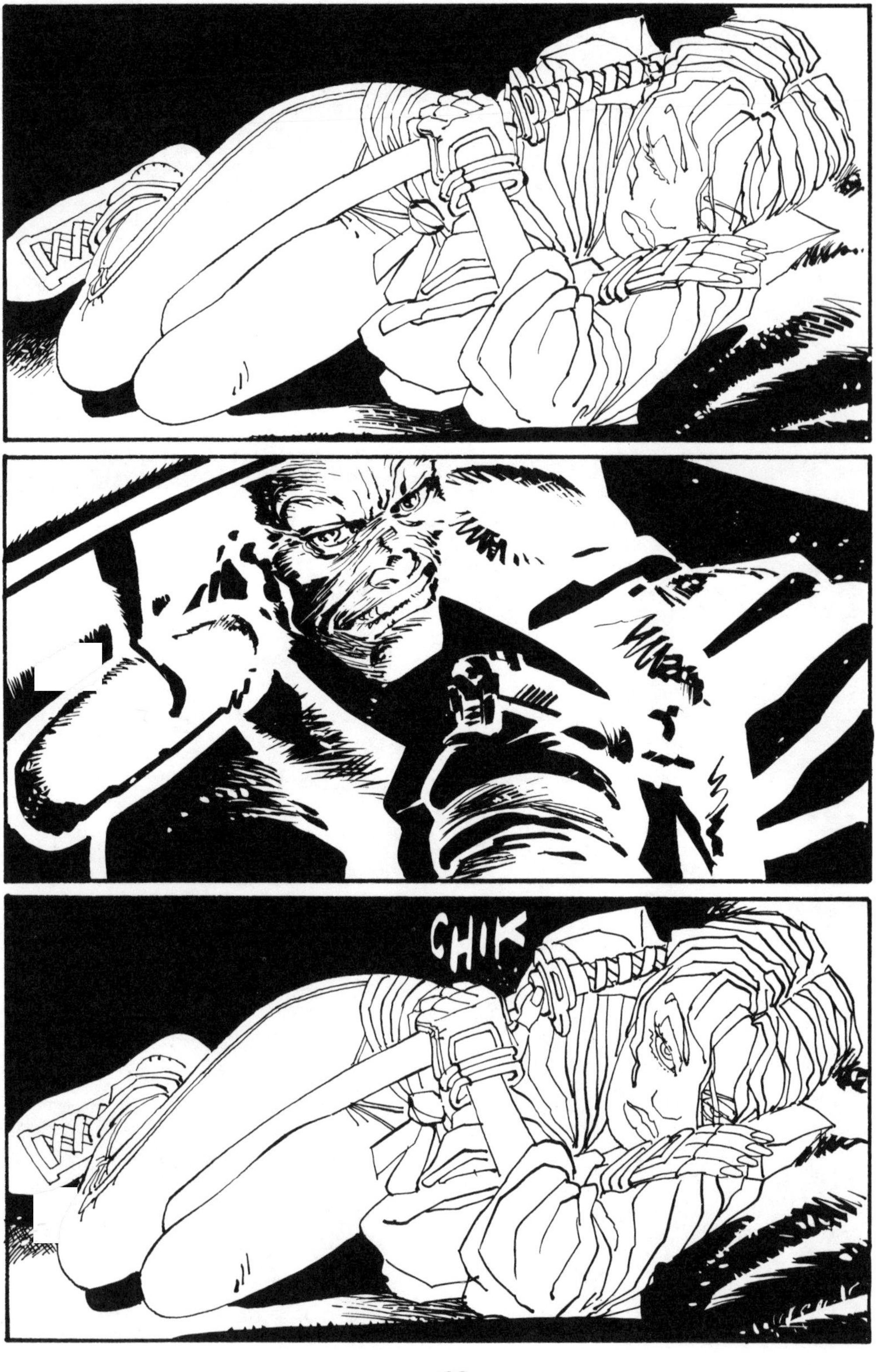
CHIK

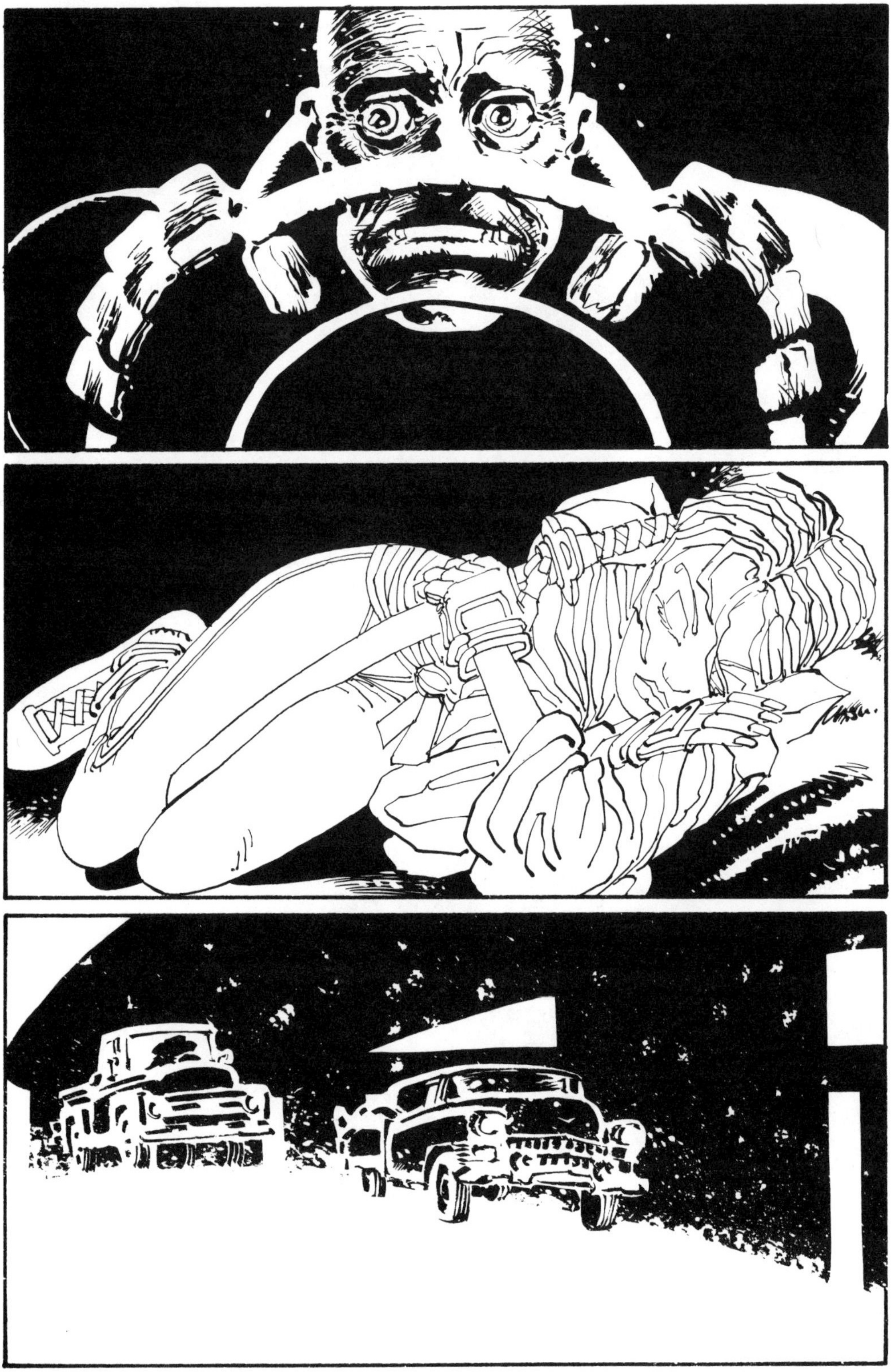

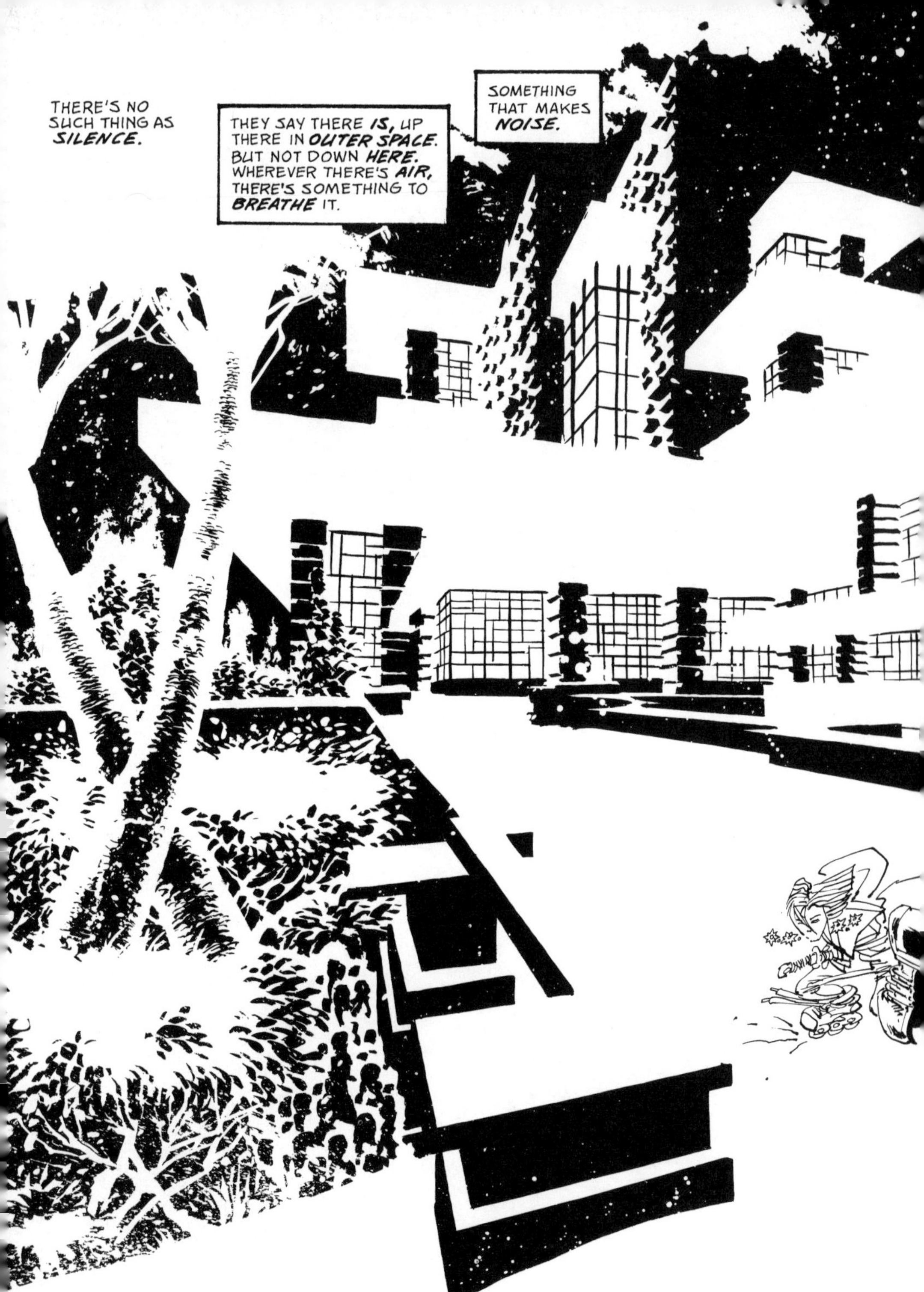
THERE'S NO SUCH THING AS *SILENCE.*
THEY SAY THERE *IS,* UP THERE IN *OUTER SPACE.* BUT NOT DOWN *HERE.* WHEREVER THERE'S *AIR,* THERE'S SOMETHING TO *BREATHE* IT.
SOMETHING THAT MAKES *NOISE.*

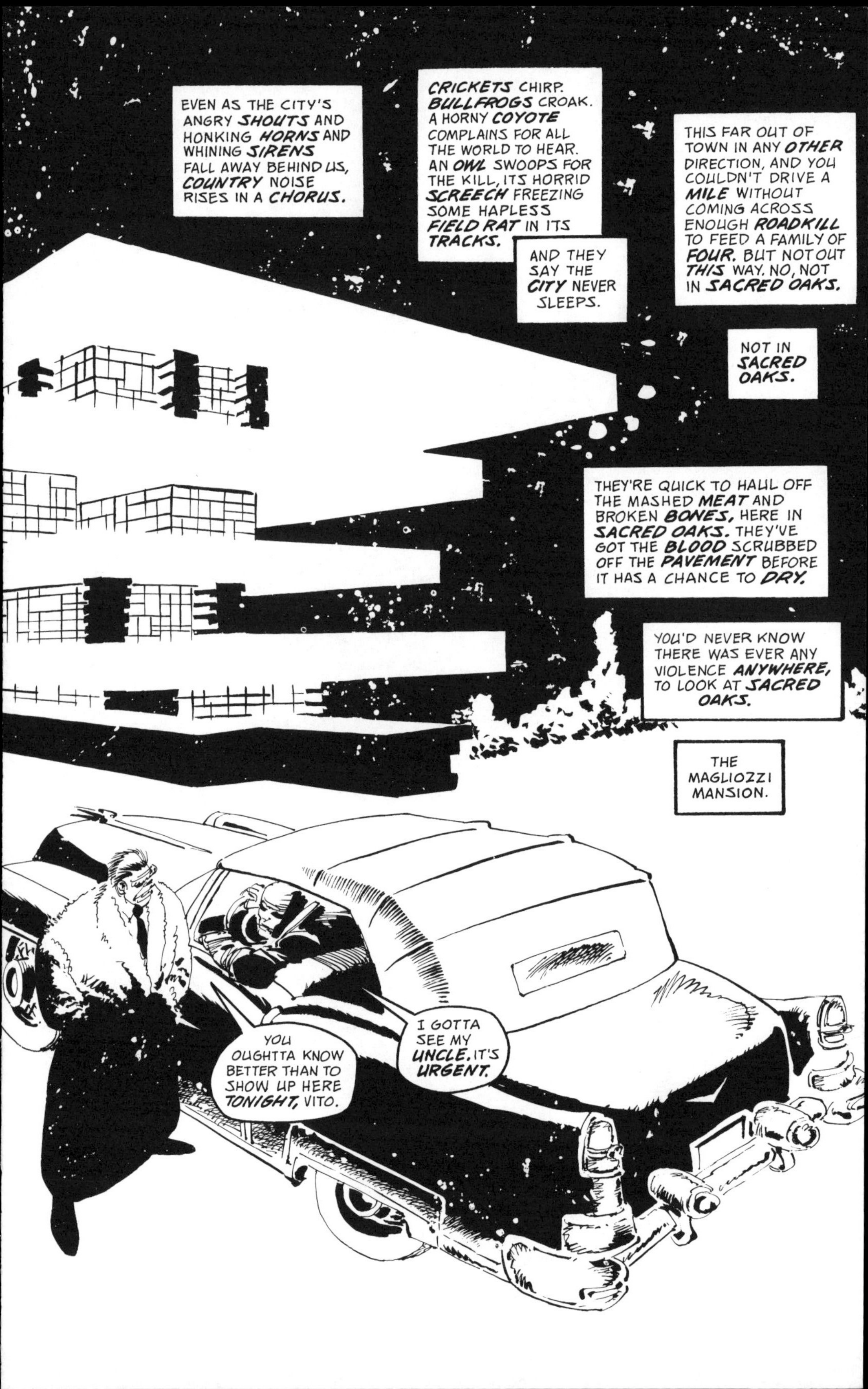
EVEN AS THE CITY'S ANGRY SHOUTS AND HONKING HORNS AND WHINING SIRENS FALL AWAY BEHIND US, COUNTRY NOISE RISES IN A CHORUS.
CRICKETS CHIRP. BULLFROGS CROAK. A HORNY COYOTE COMPLAINS FOR ALL THE WORLD TO HEAR. AN OWL SWOOPS FOR THE KILL, ITS HORRID SCREECH FREEZING SOME HAPLESS FIELD RAT IN ITS TRACKS.
AND THEY SAY THE CITY NEVER SLEEPS.
THIS FAR OUT OF TOWN IN ANY OTHER DIRECTION, AND YOU COULDN'T DRIVE A MILE WITHOUT COMING ACROSS ENOUGH ROADKILL TO FEED A FAMILY OF FOUR. BUT NOT OUT THIS WAY. NO, NOT IN SACRED OAKS.
NOT IN SACRED OAKS.
THEY'RE QUICK TO HAUL OFF THE MASHED MEAT AND BROKEN BONES, HERE IN SACRED OAKS. THEY'VE GOT THE BLOOD SCRUBBED OFF THE PAVEMENT BEFORE IT HAS A CHANCE TO DRY.
YOU'D NEVER KNOW THERE WAS EVER ANY VIOLENCE ANYWHERE, TO LOOK AT SACRED OAKS.
THE MAGLIOZZI MANSION.
YOU OUGHTTA KNOW BETTER THAN TO SHOW UP HERE TONIGHT, VITO.
I GOTTA SEE MY UNCLE. IT'S URGENT.

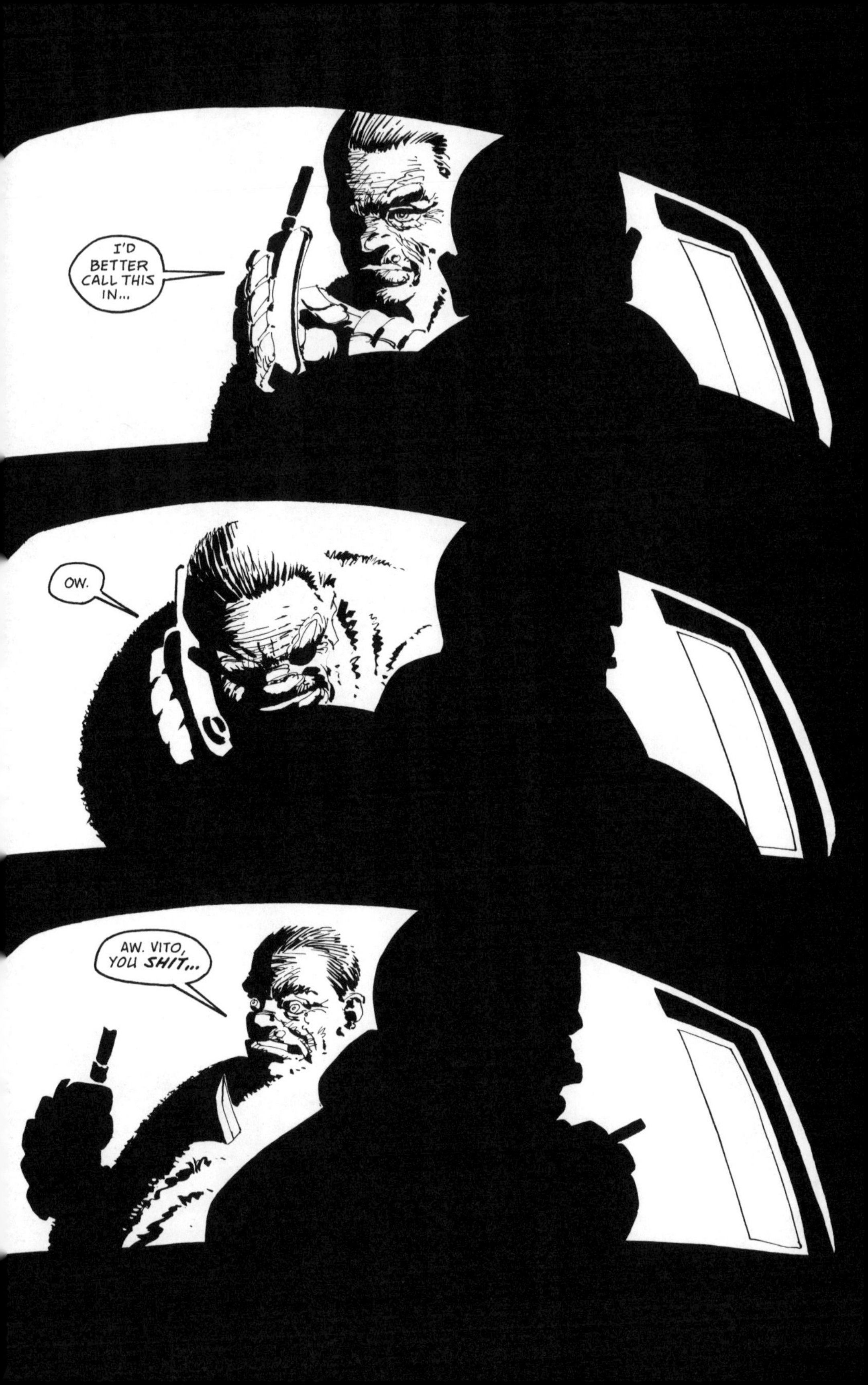
I'D BETTER CALL THIS IN...
OW.
AW. VITO, YOU SHIT...

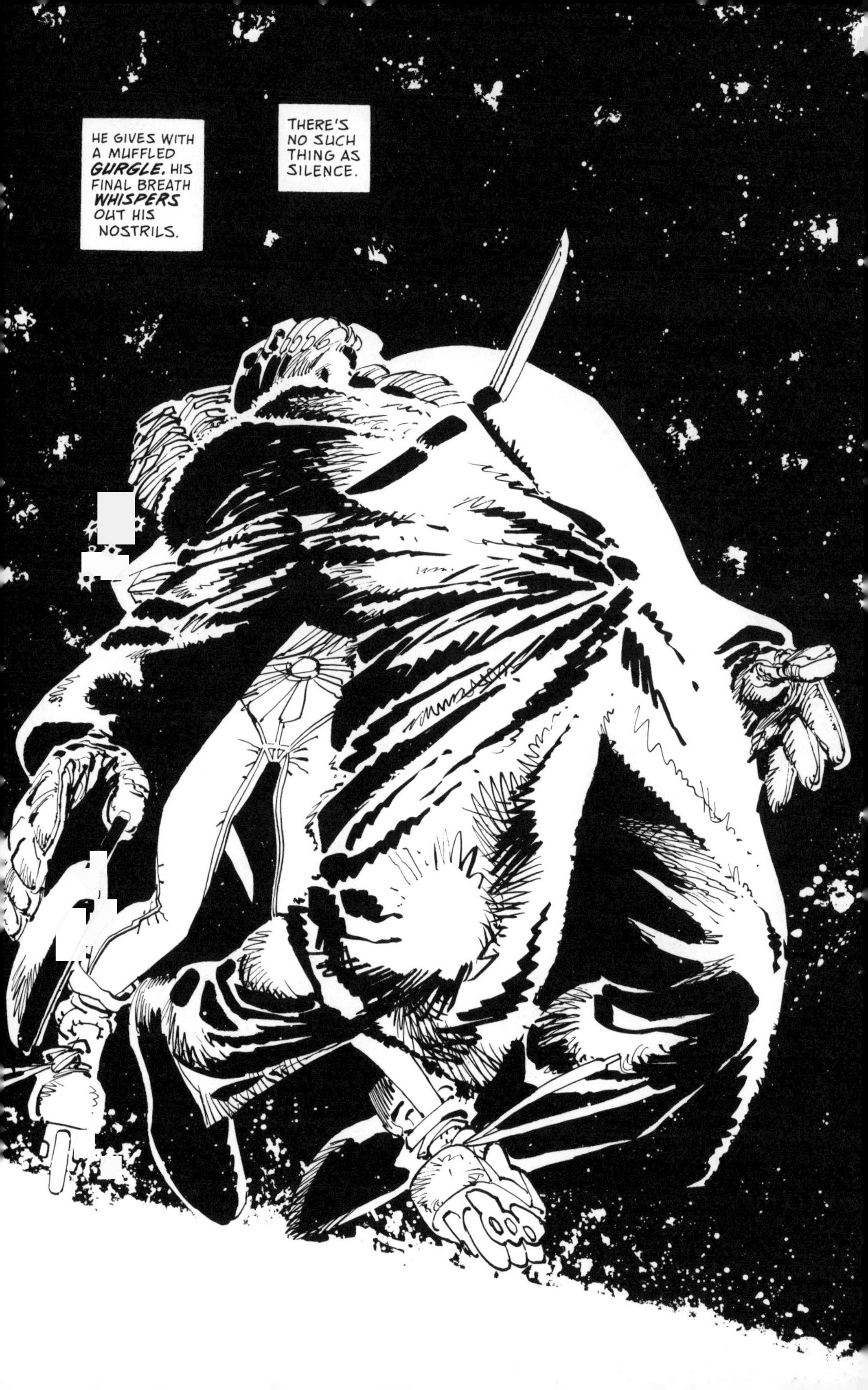
HE GIVES WITH A MUFFLED **GURGLE.** HIS FINAL BREATH **WHISPERS** OUT HIS NOSTRILS.
THERE'S NO SUCH THING AS SILENCE.

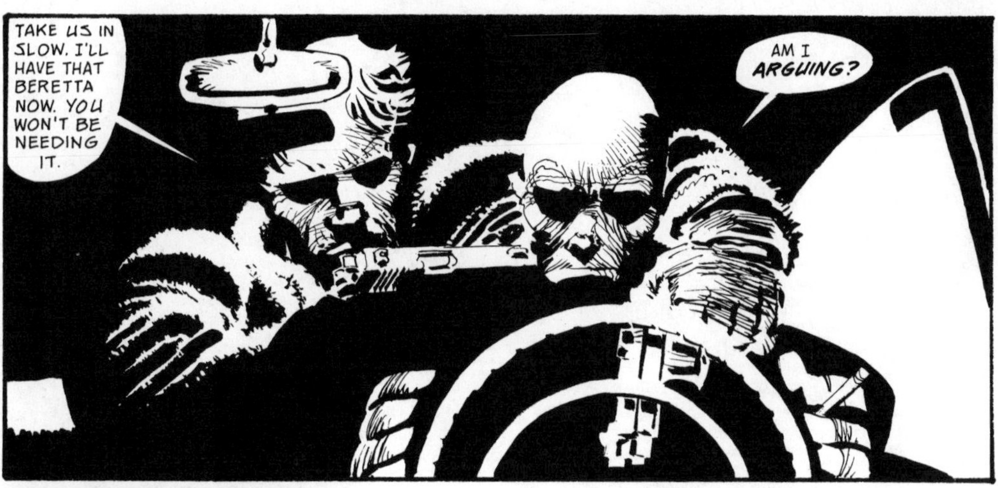
TAKE US IN SLOW. I'LL HAVE THAT BERETTA NOW. YOU WON'T BE NEEDING IT.
AM I ARGUING?

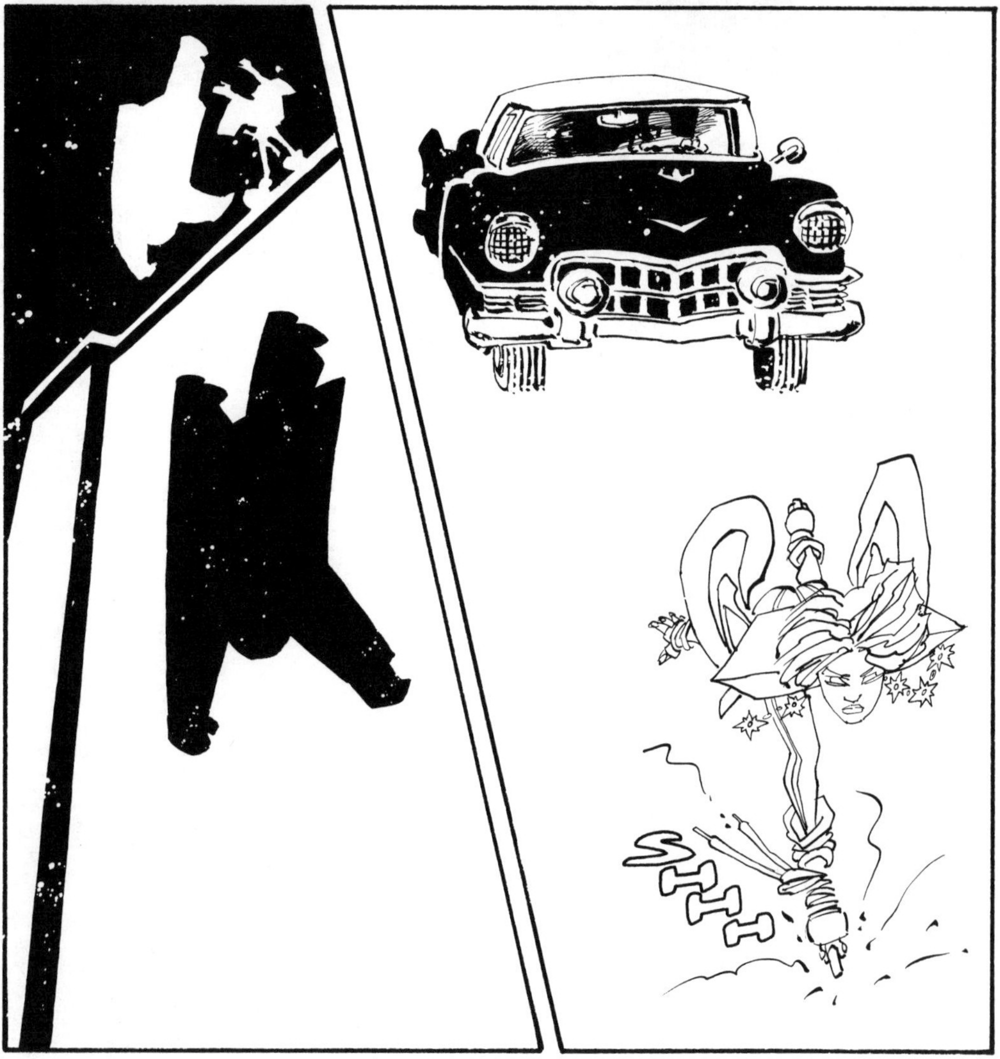

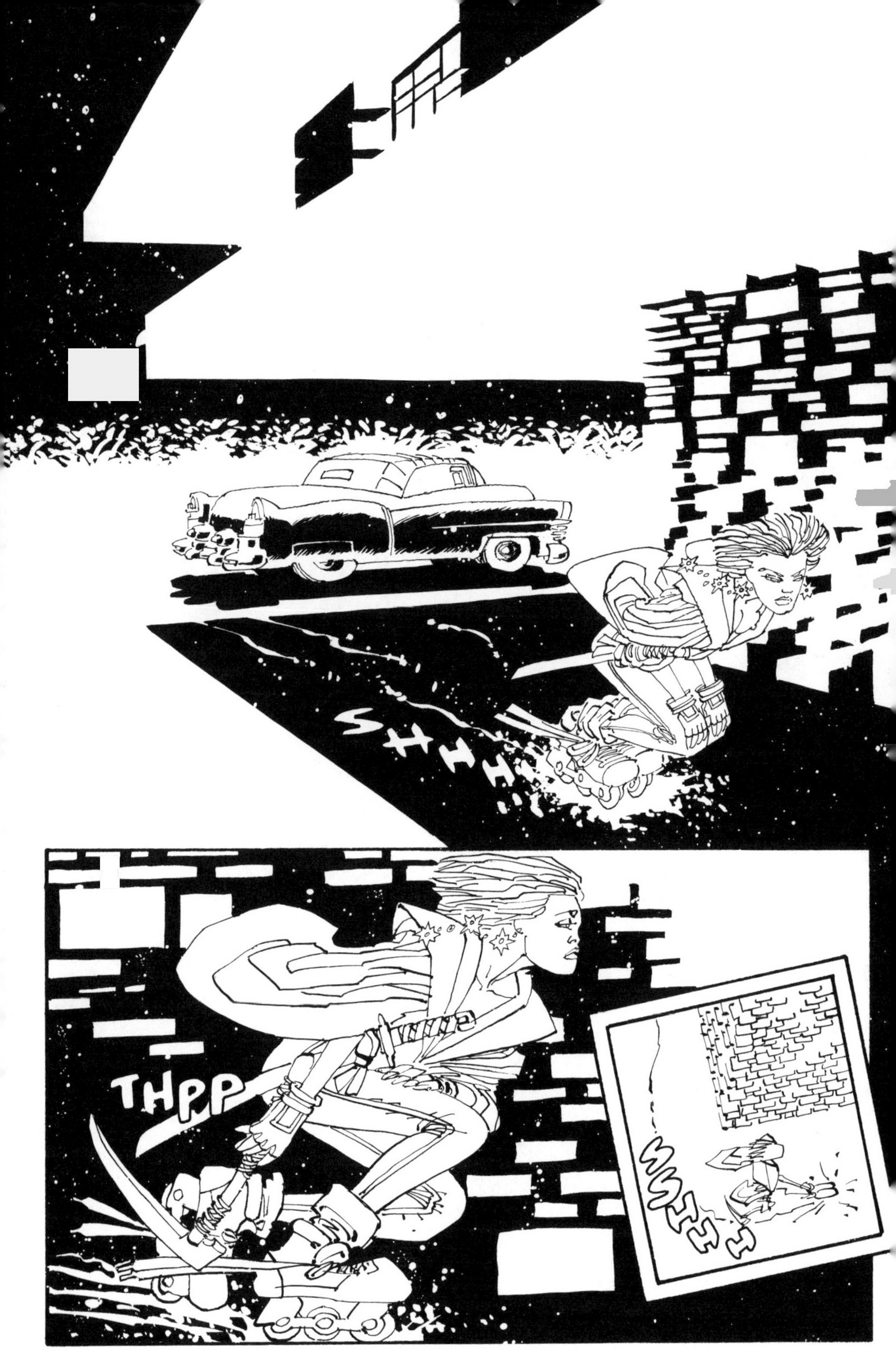
SHHH
THPP

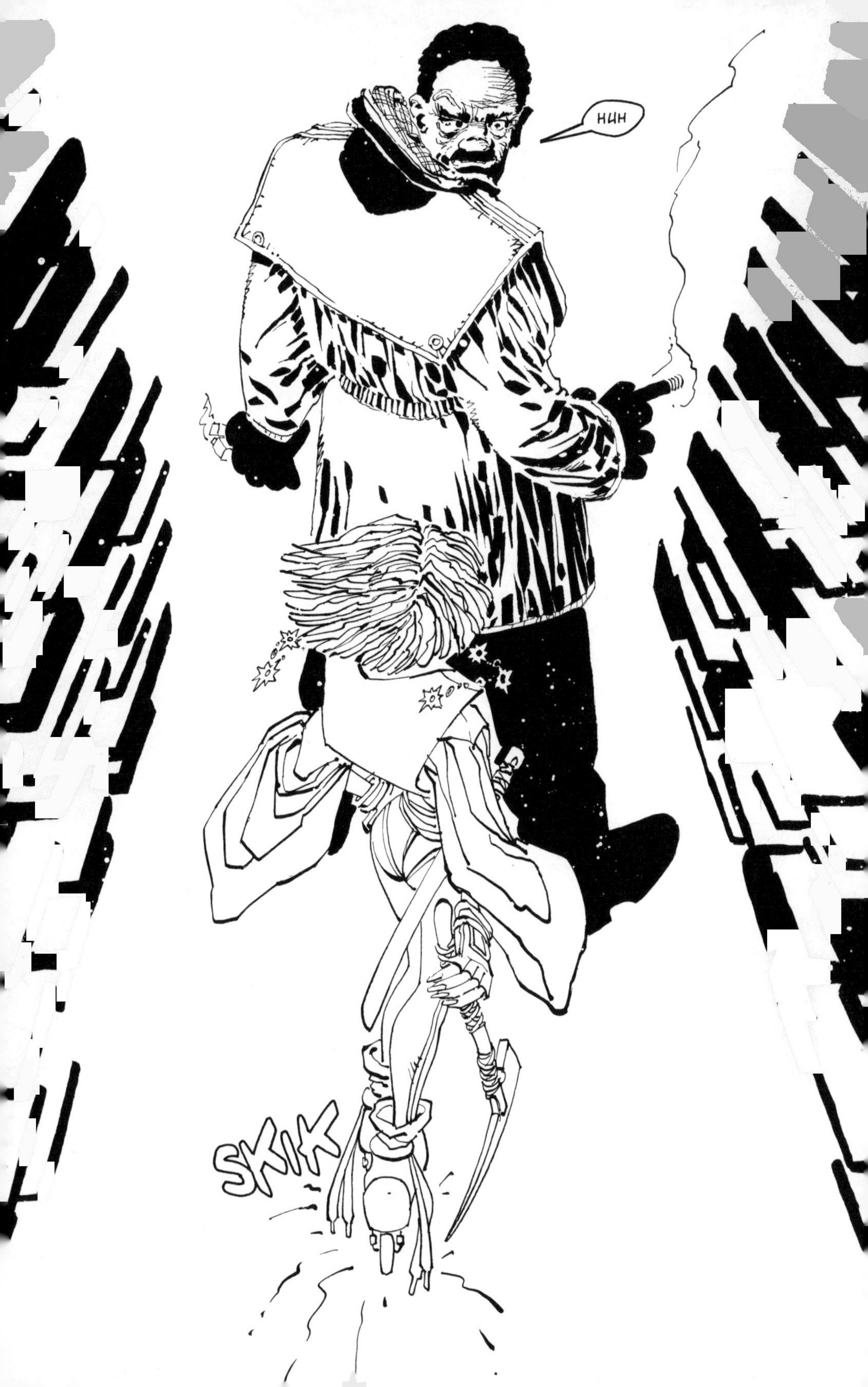
HUH
SKIK

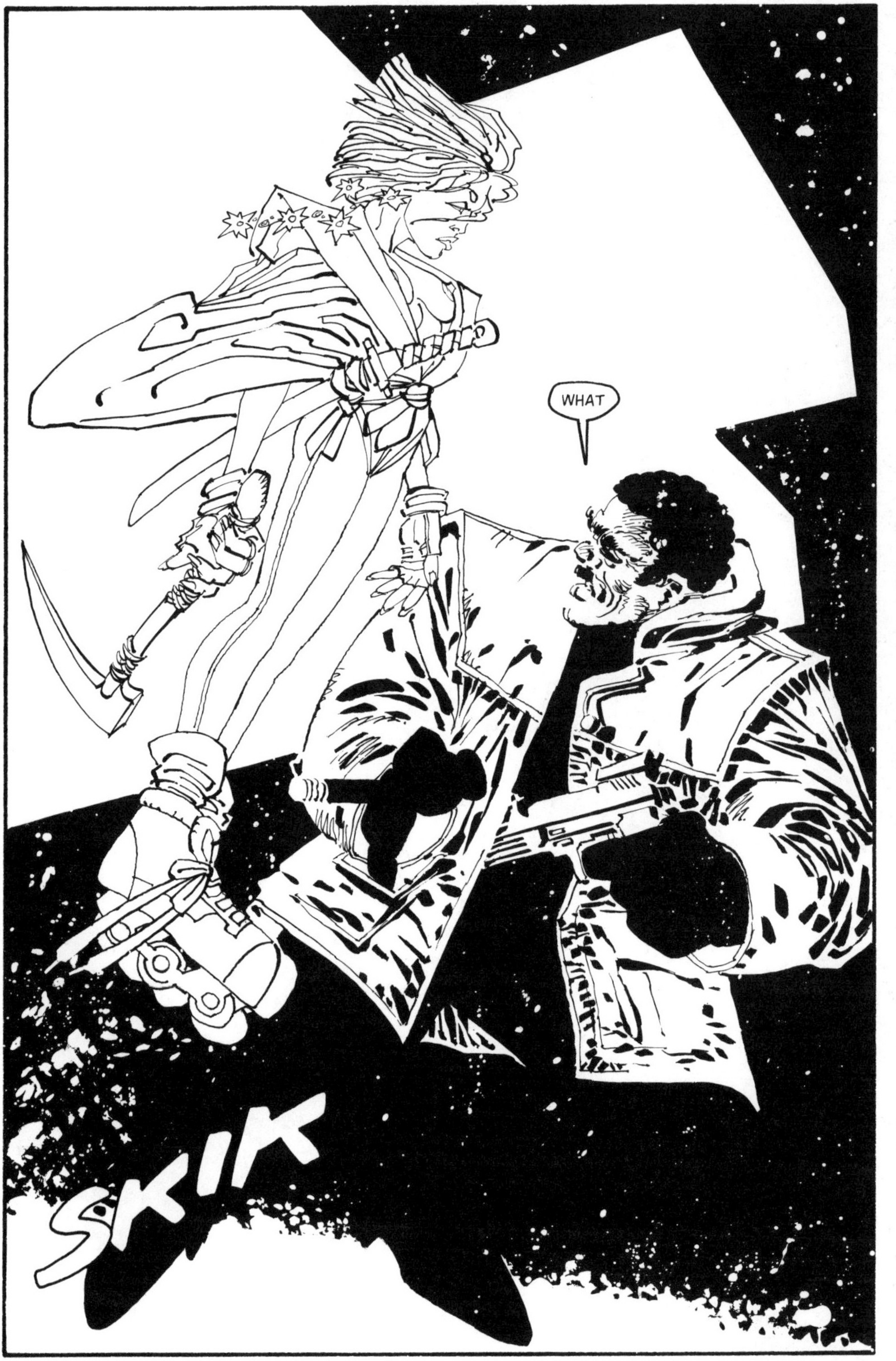
WHAT
SKIK

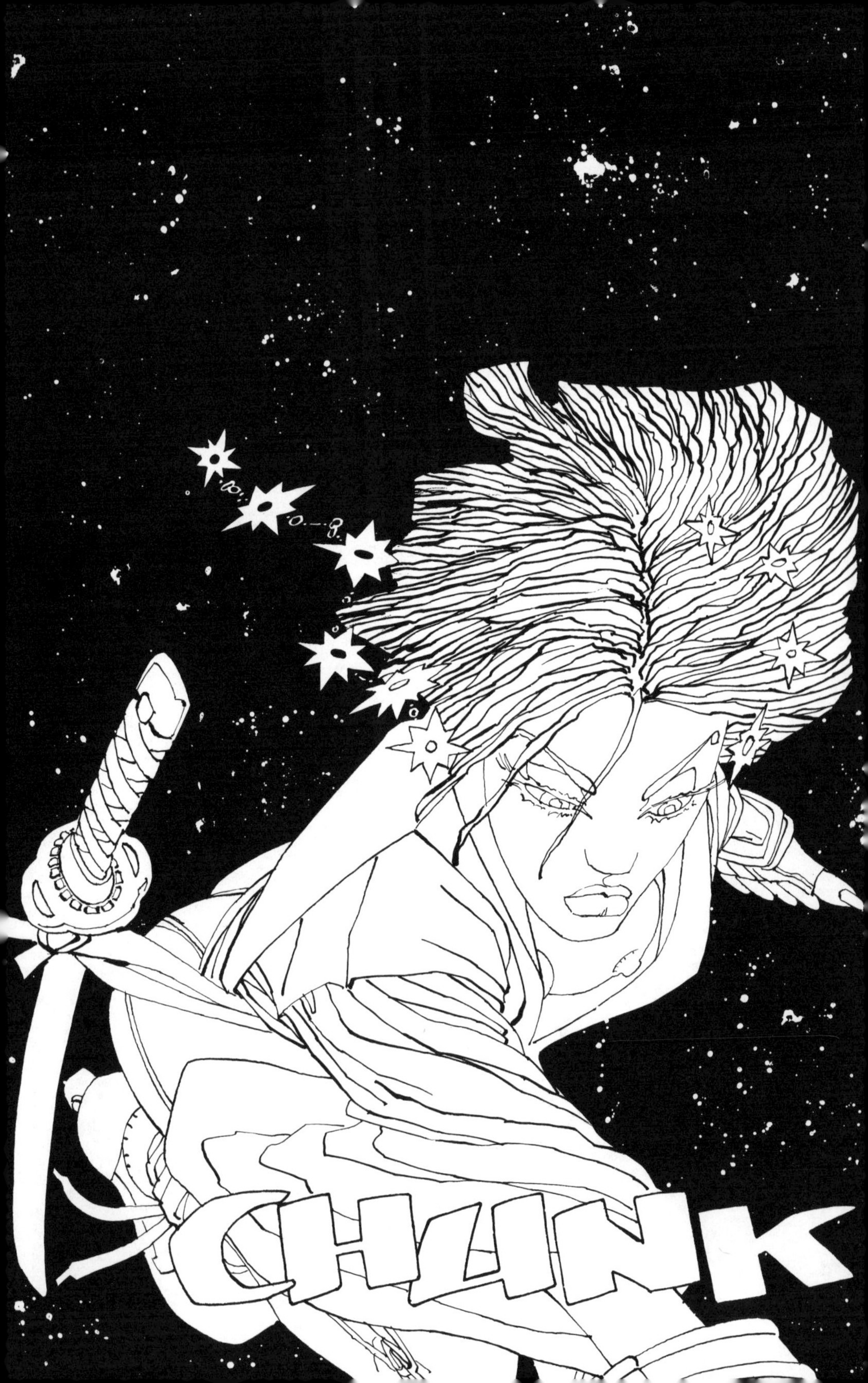
CHUNK

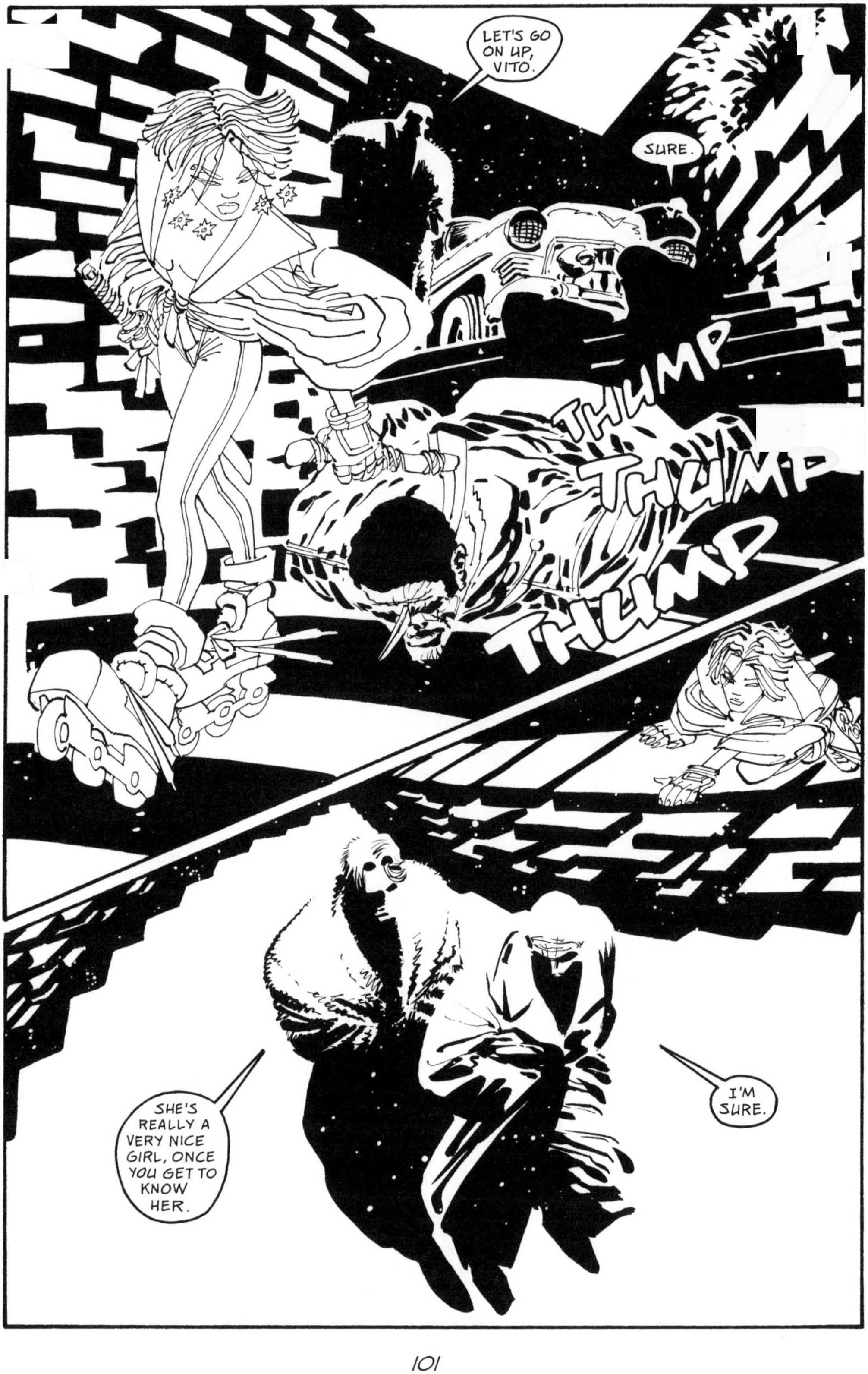
LET'S GO ON UP, VITO.
SURE.
THUMP
THUMP
THUMP
SHE'S REALLY A VERY NICE GIRL, ONCE YOU GET TO KNOW HER.
I'M SURE.

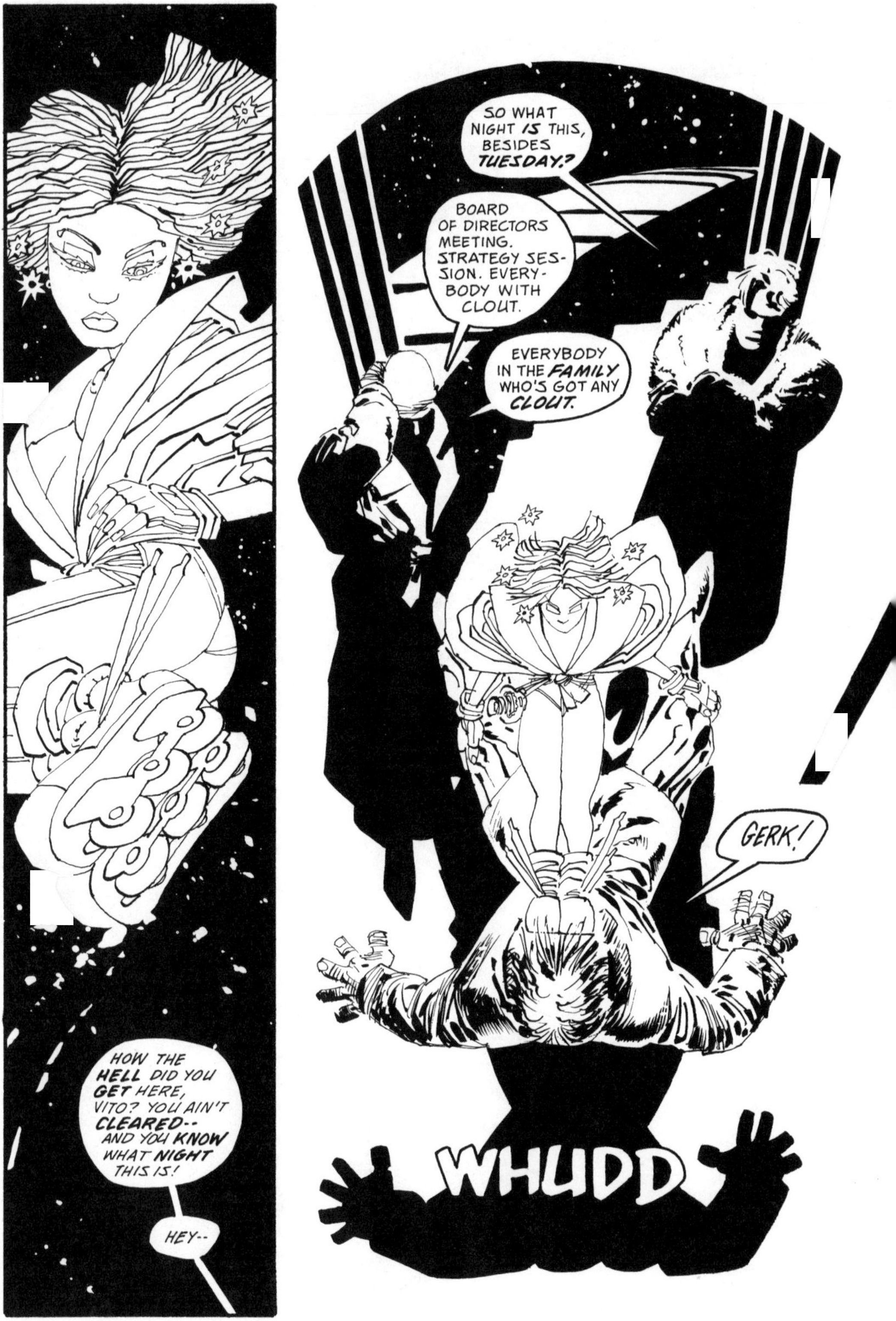
HOW THE HELL DID YOU GET HERE, VITO? YOU AIN'T CLEARED-- AND YOU KNOW WHAT NIGHT THIS IS!
HEY--
SO WHAT NIGHT IS THIS, BESIDES TUESDAY?
BOARD OF DIRECTORS MEETING. STRATEGY SESSION. EVERYBODY WITH CLOUT.
EVERYBODY IN THE FAMILY WHO'S GOT ANY CLOUT.
GERK!
WHUDD

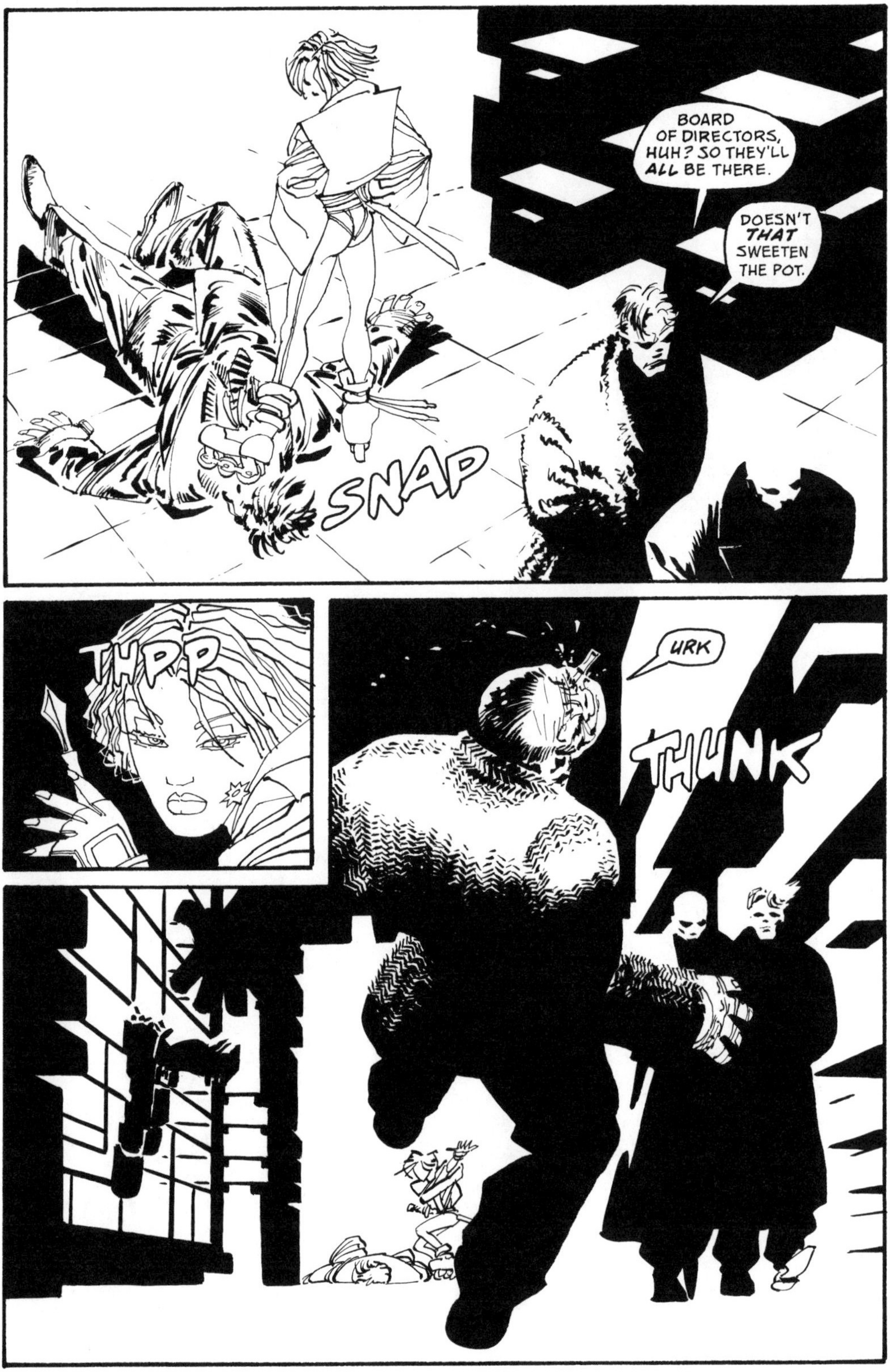
BOARD OF DIRECTORS, HUH? SO THEY'LL ALL BE THERE.
DOESN'T THAT SWEETEN THE POT.
SNAP
THPP
URK
THUNK

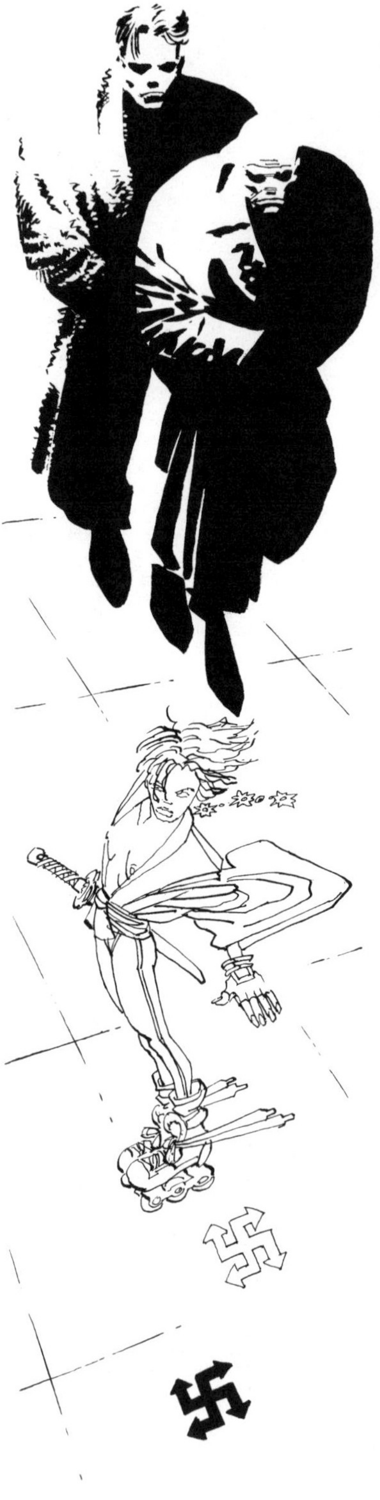

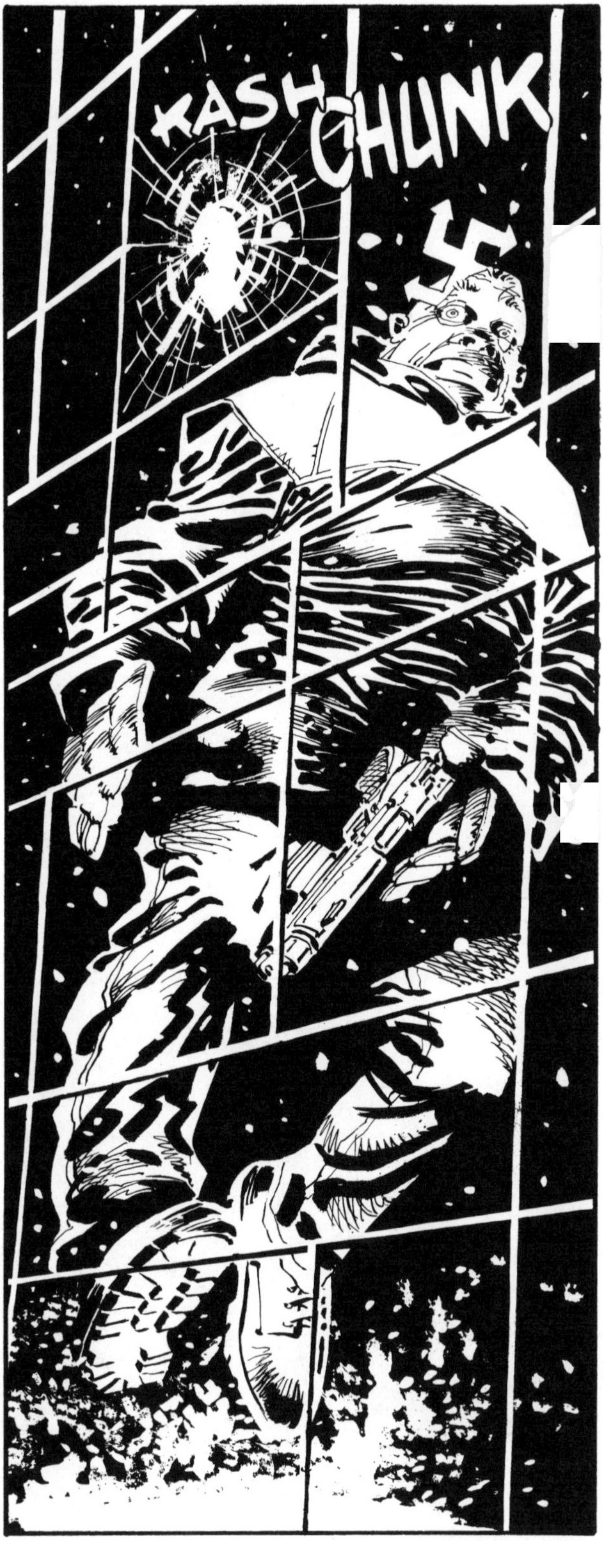
KASH
CHUNK

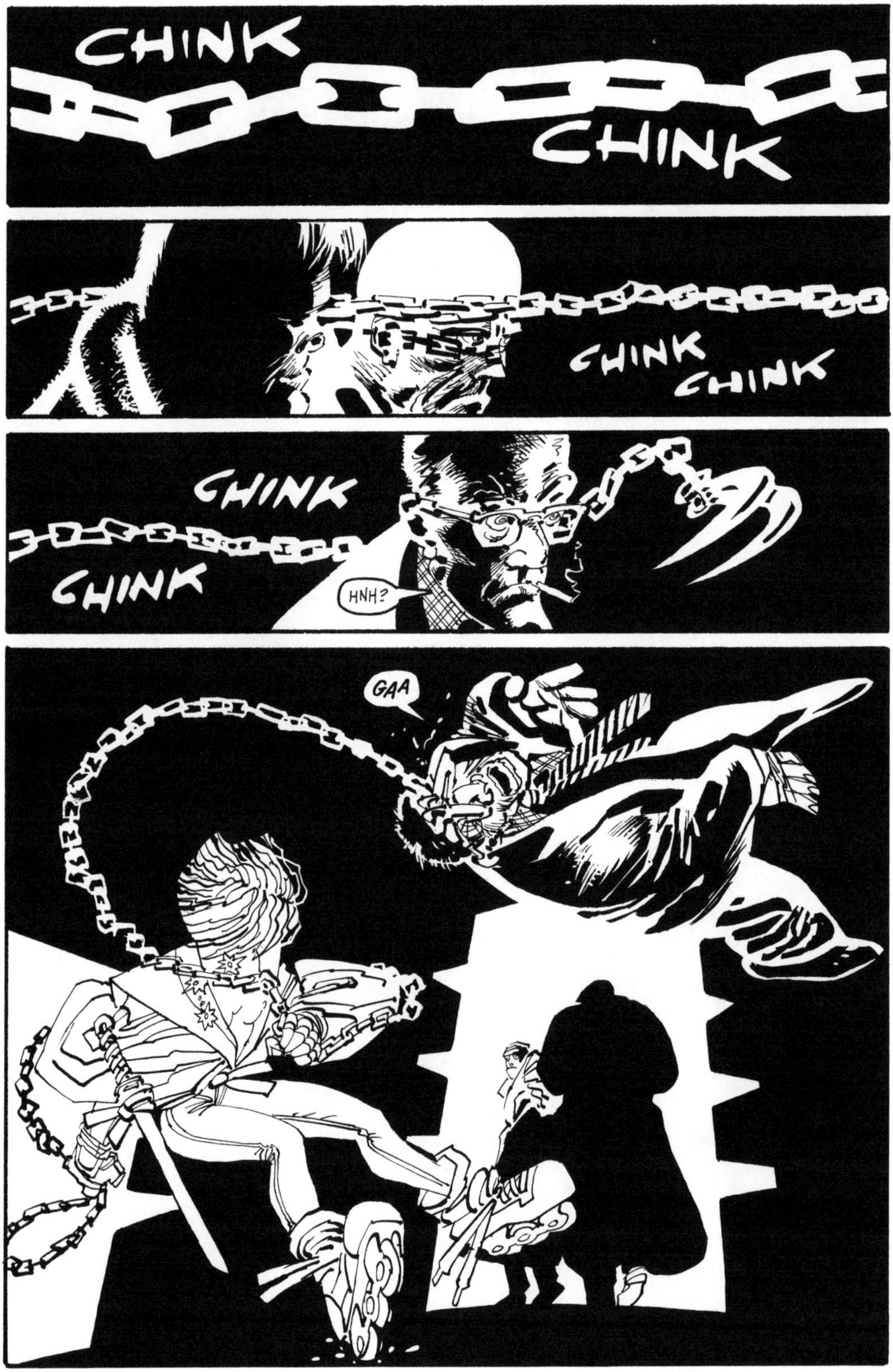
CHINK
CHINK
CHINK
CHINK
CHINK
CHINK
HNH?
GAA

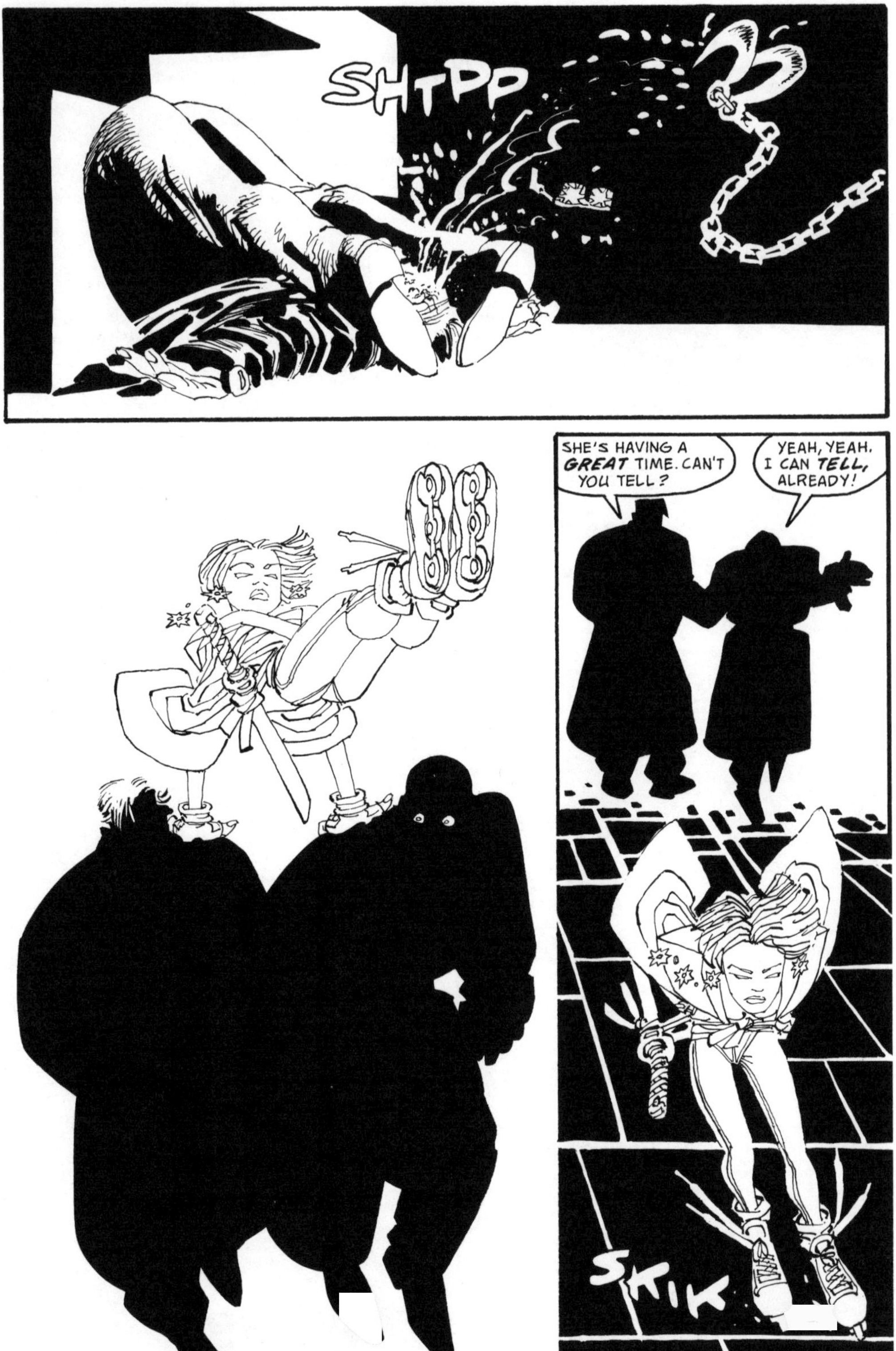
SHTPP
SHE'S HAVING A GREAT TIME. CAN'T YOU TELL?
YEAH, YEAH. I CAN TELL, ALREADY!
SKIK

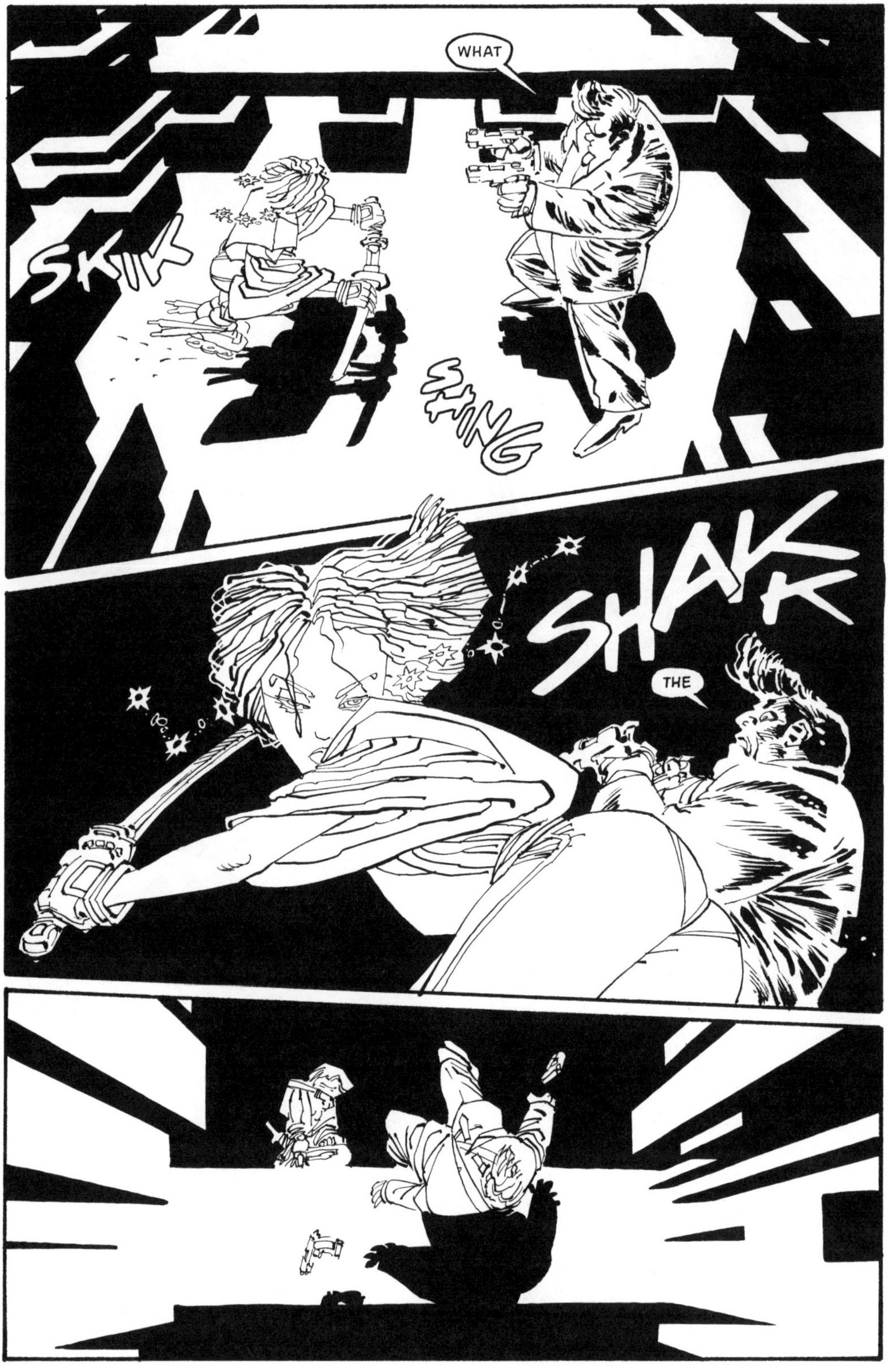
WHAT
SKIK
SHING
SHAK
THE

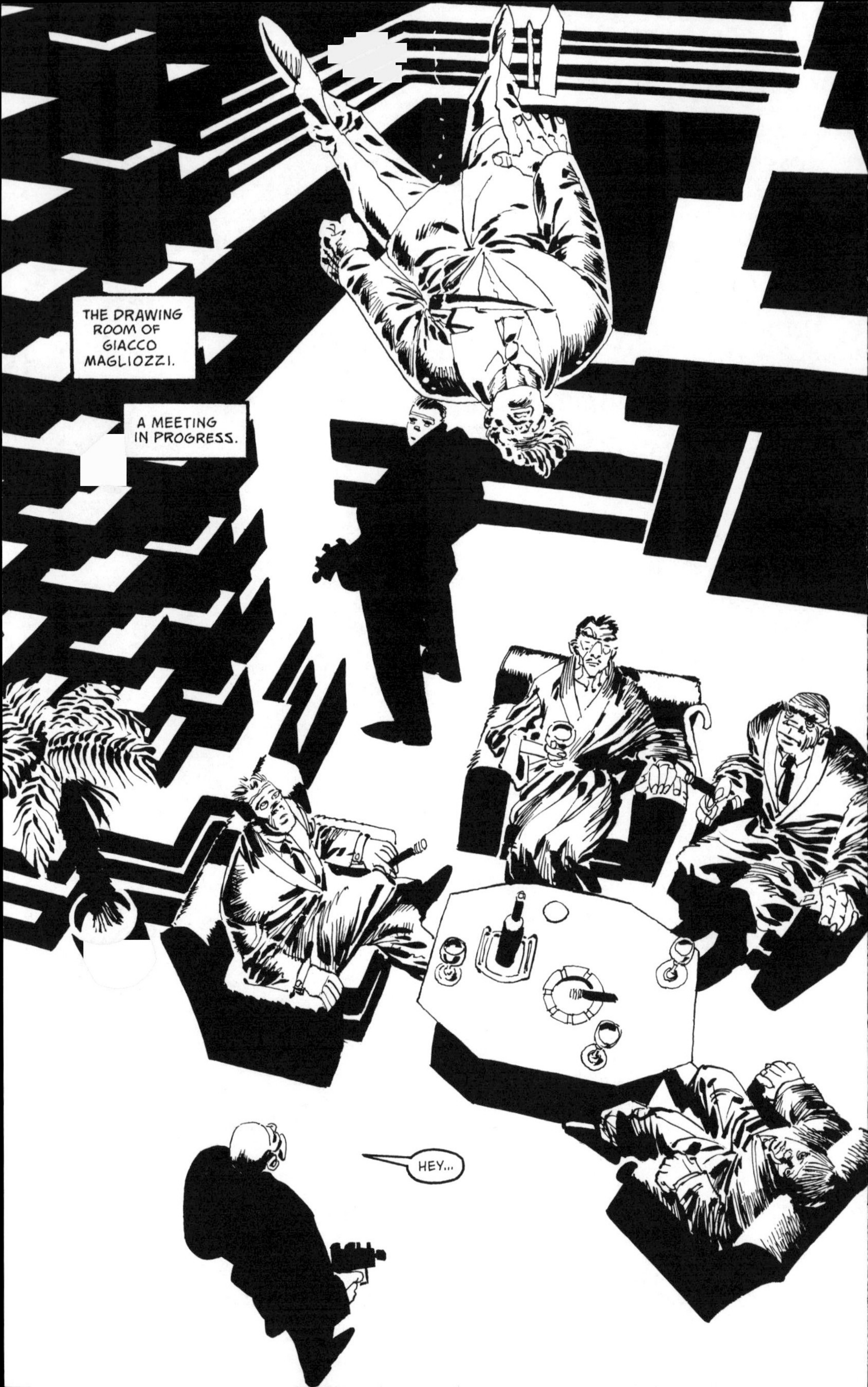
THE DRAWING ROOM OF GIACCO MAGLIOZZI.
A MEETING IN PROGRESS.
HEY...

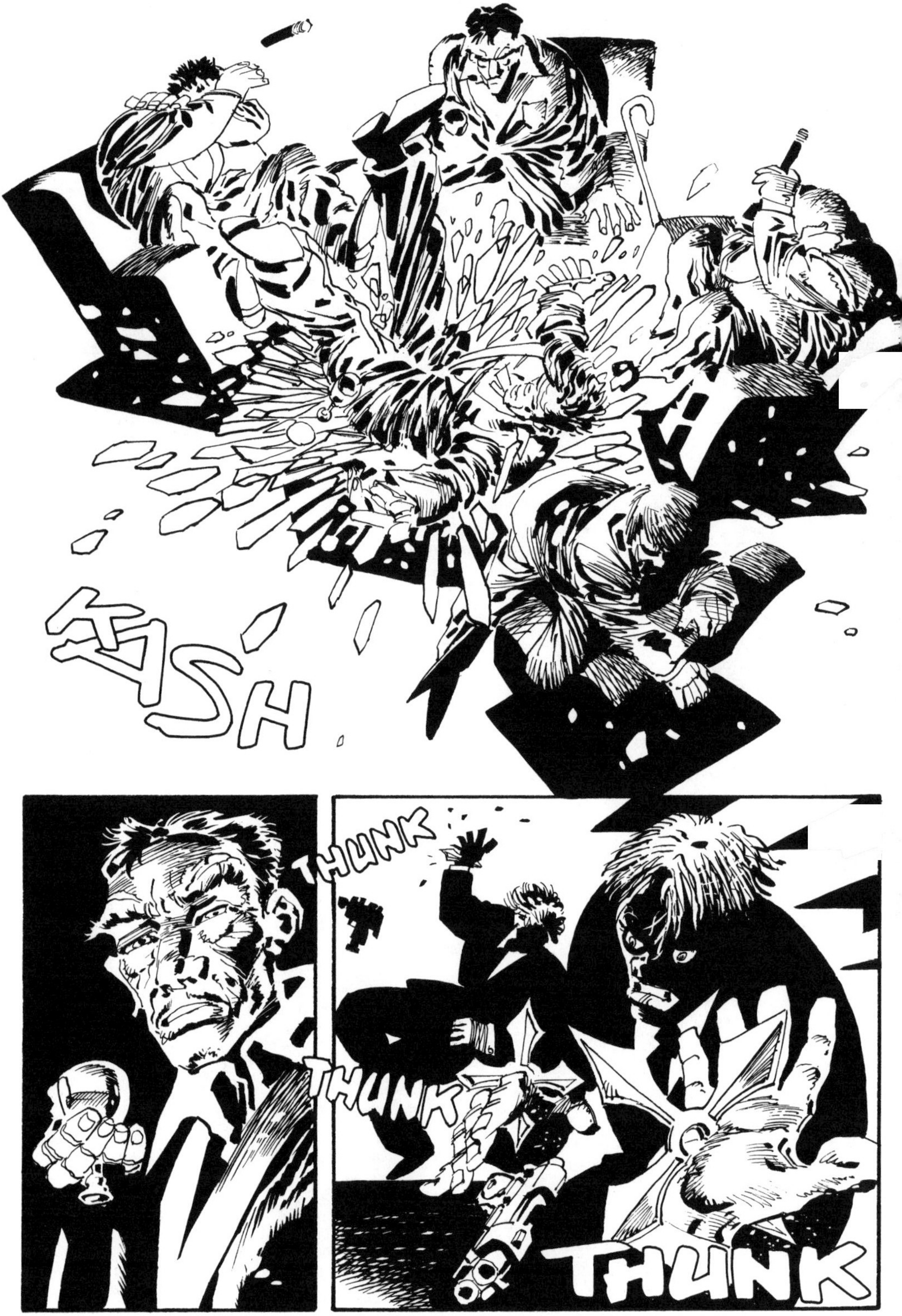
KASH
THUNK
THUNK
THUNK

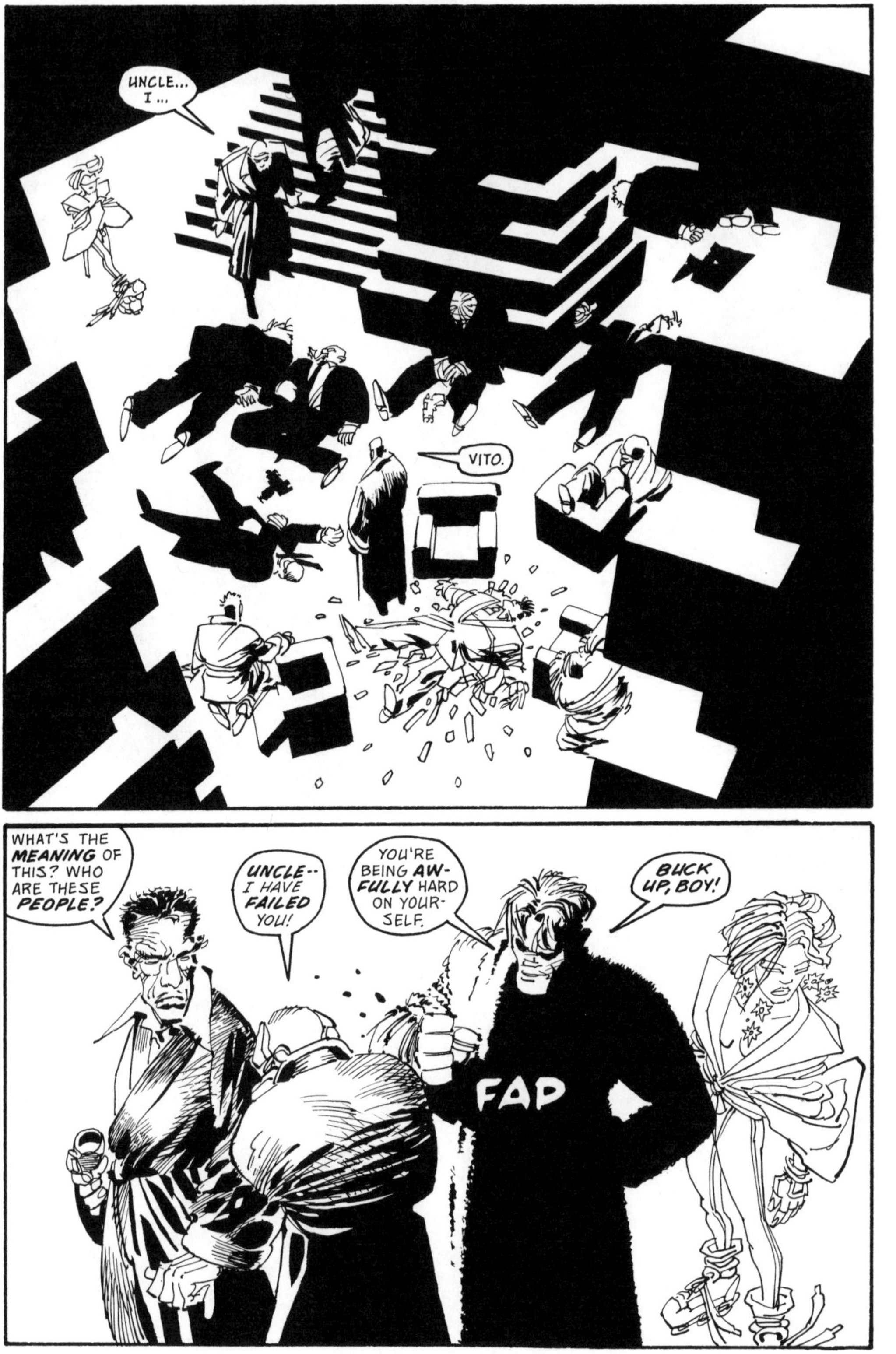
UNCLE... I...
VITO.
WHAT'S THE MEANING OF THIS? WHO ARE THESE PEOPLE?
UNCLE-- I HAVE FAILED YOU!
YOU'RE BEING AW-FULLY HARD ON YOUR-SELF.
BUCK UP, BOY!
FAP

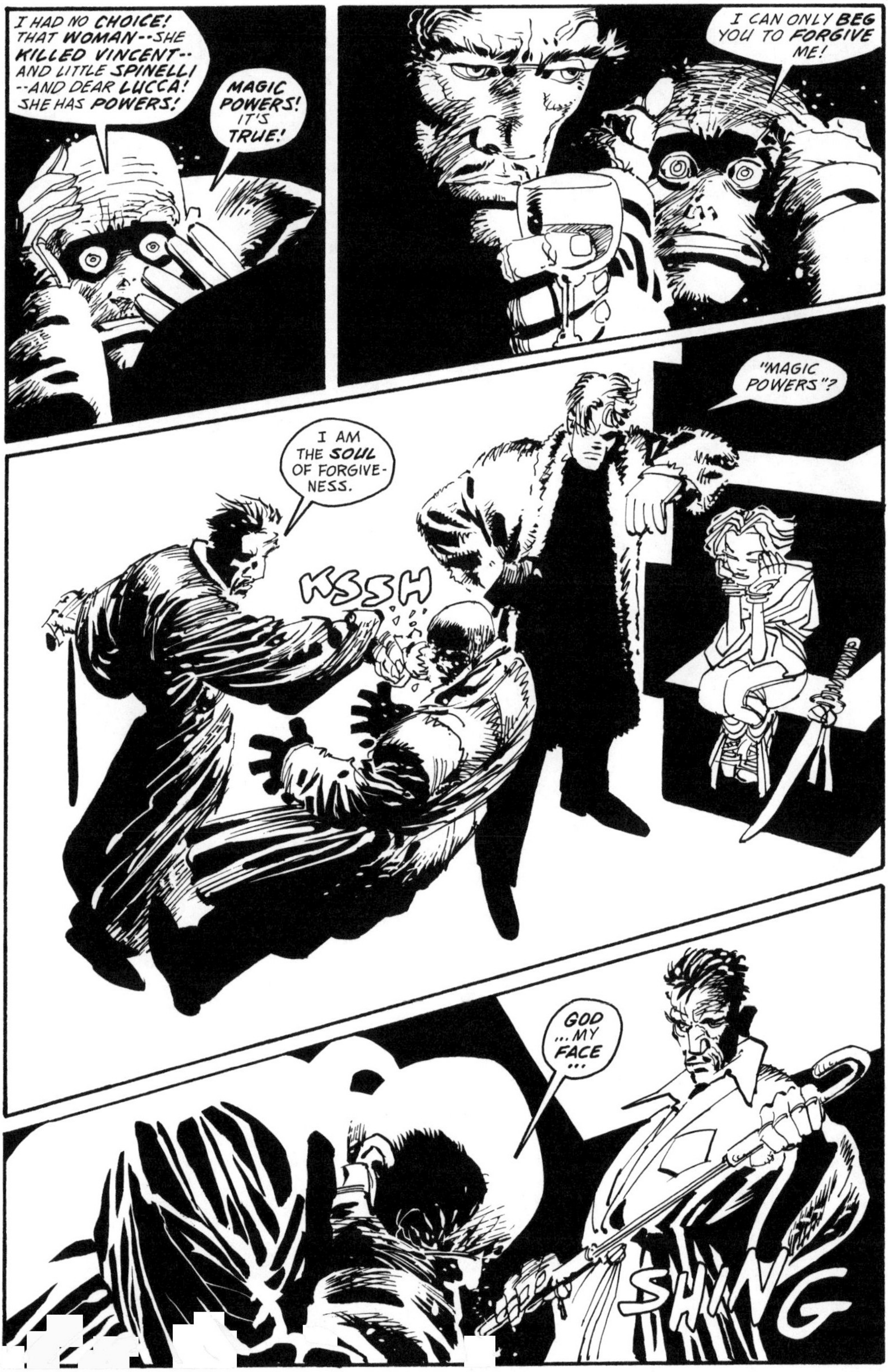
I HAD NO CHOICE! THAT WOMAN--SHE KILLED VINCENT-- AND LITTLE SPINELLI --AND DEAR LUCCA! SHE HAS POWERS!
MAGIC POWERS! IT'S TRUE!
I CAN ONLY BEG YOU TO FORGIVE ME!
"MAGIC POWERS"?
I AM THE SOUL OF FORGIVE-NESS.
KSSH
GOD ...MY FACE ...
SHING

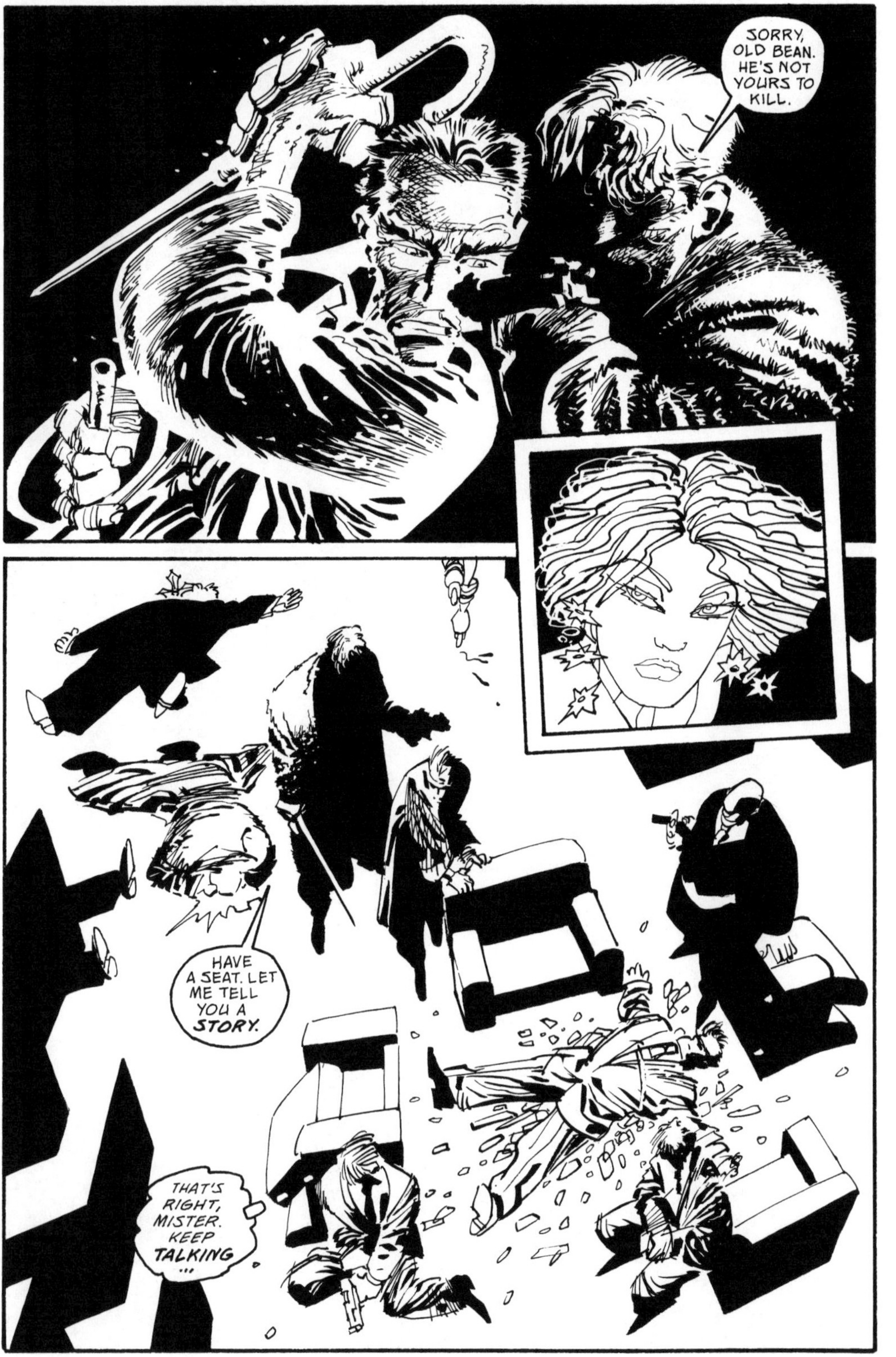
SORRY, OLD BEAN. HE'S NOT YOURS TO KILL.
HAVE A SEAT. LET ME TELL YOU A STORY.
THAT'S RIGHT, MISTER. KEEP TALKING ...

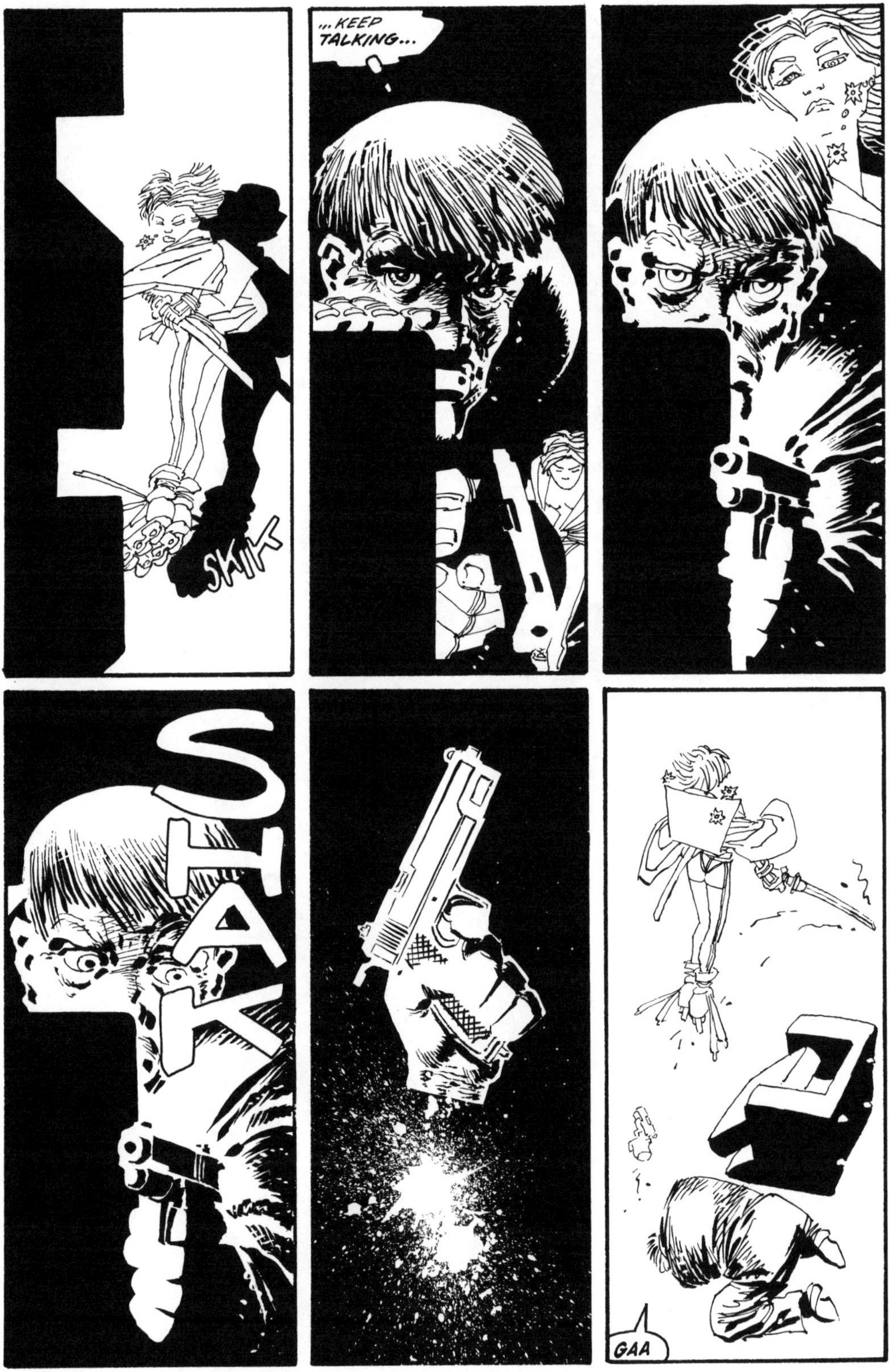
SKIK
...KEEP TALKING...
SHAK
GAA

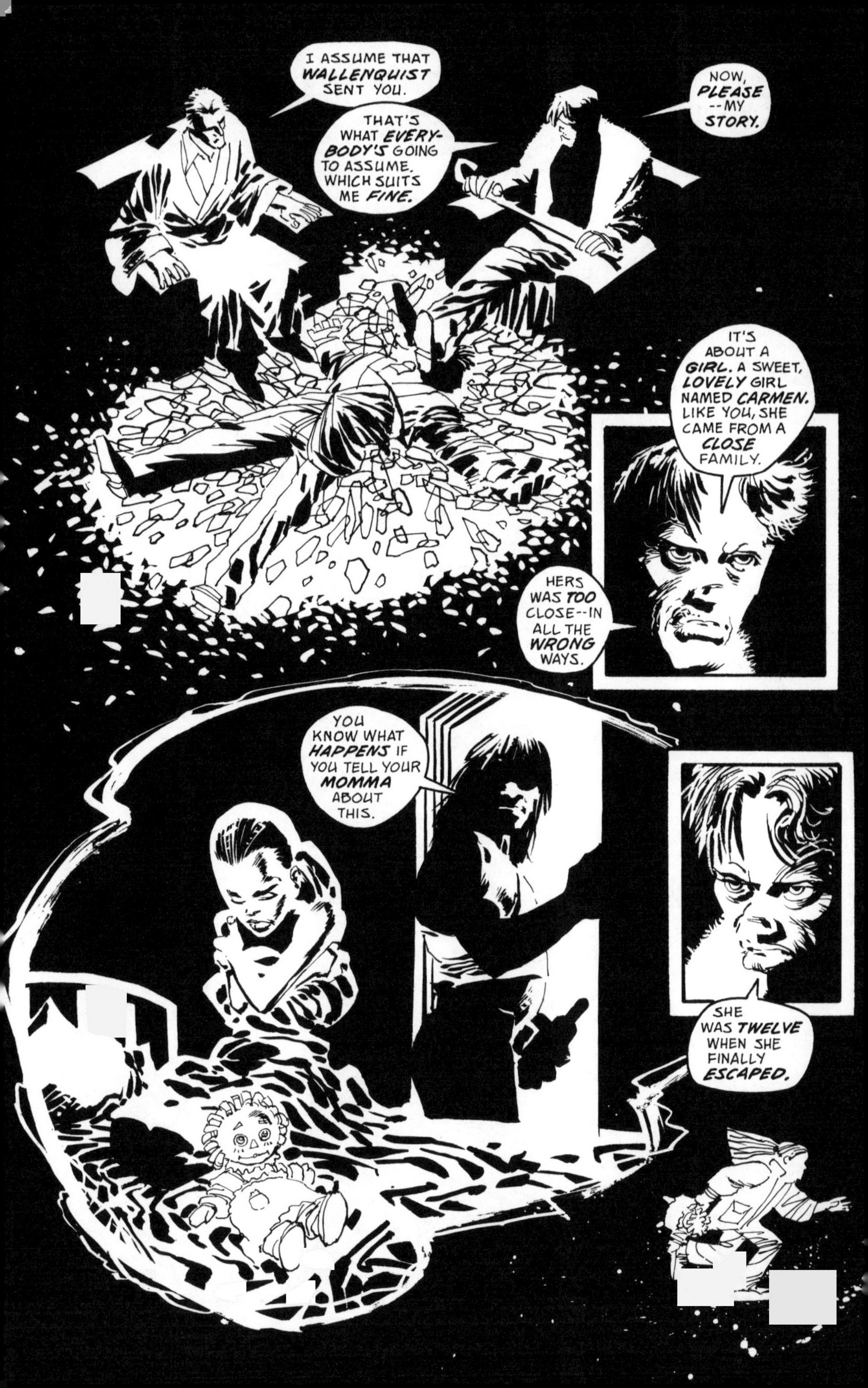
I ASSUME THAT WALLENQUIST SENT YOU.
THAT'S WHAT EVERY-BODY'S GOING TO ASSUME. WHICH SUITS ME FINE.
NOW, PLEASE --MY STORY.
IT'S ABOUT A GIRL. A SWEET, LOVELY GIRL NAMED CARMEN. LIKE YOU, SHE CAME FROM A CLOSE FAMILY.
HERS WAS TOO CLOSE--IN ALL THE WRONG WAYS.
YOU KNOW WHAT HAPPENS IF YOU TELL YOUR MOMMA ABOUT THIS.
SHE WAS TWELVE WHEN SHE FINALLY ESCAPED.

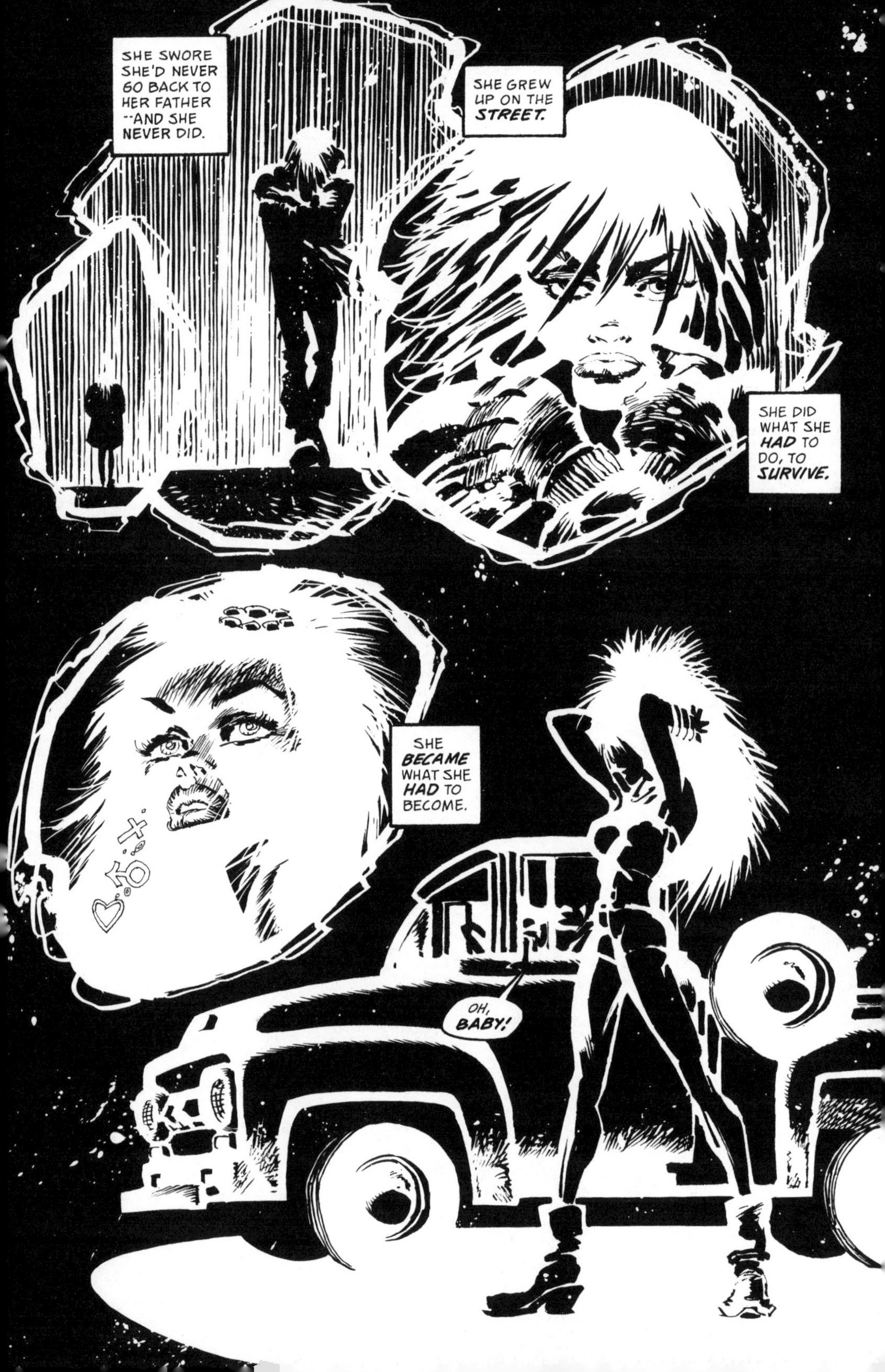
SHE SWORE SHE'D NEVER GO BACK TO HER FATHER --AND SHE NEVER DID.
SHE GREW UP ON THE ***STREET.***
SHE DID WHAT SHE ***HAD*** TO DO, TO ***SURVIVE.***
SHE ***BECAME*** WHAT SHE ***HAD*** TO BECOME.
OH, ***BABY!***

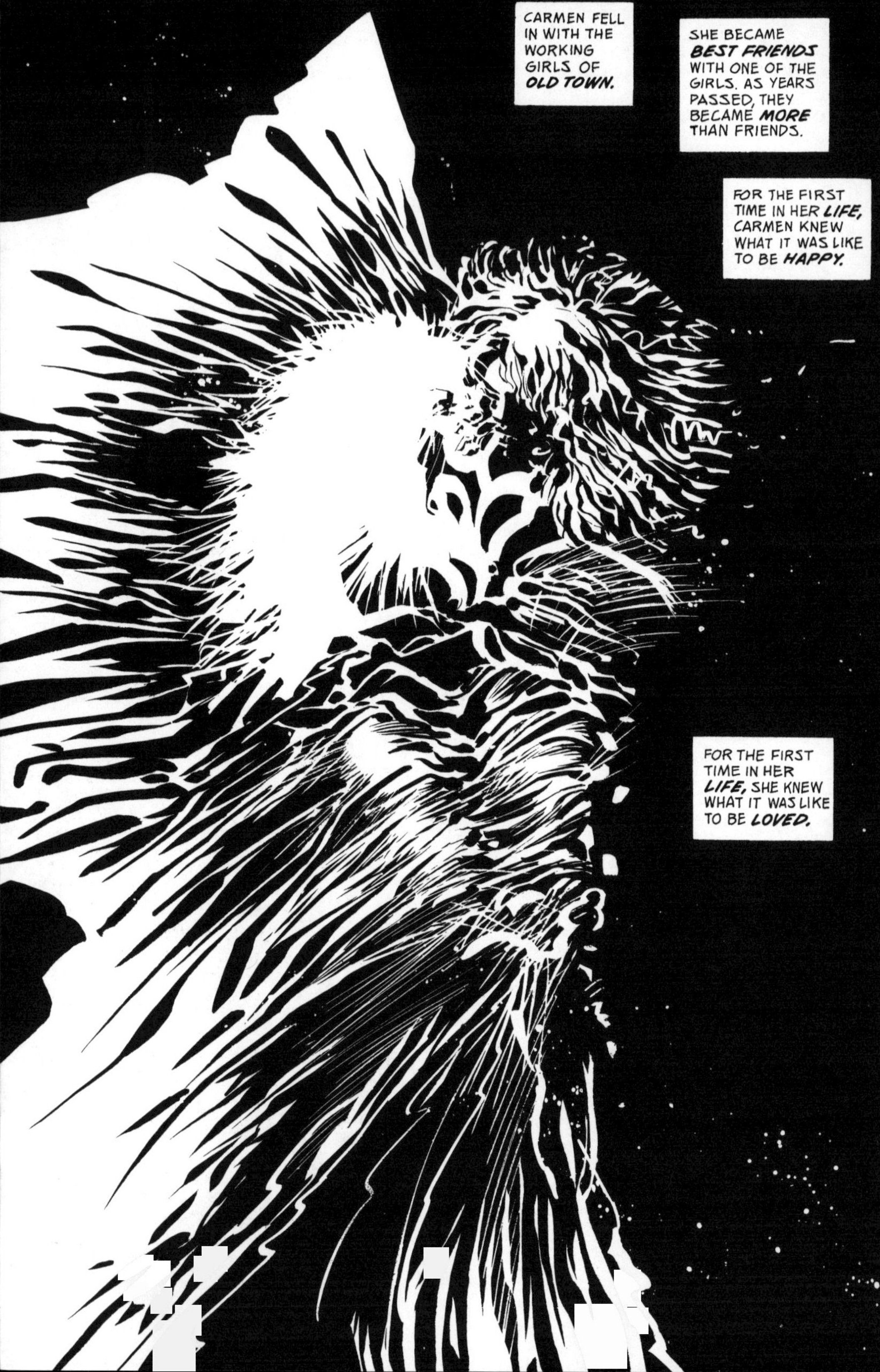

CARMEN FELL IN WITH THE WORKING GIRLS OF **OLD TOWN.**
SHE BECAME ***BEST FRIENDS*** WITH ONE OF THE GIRLS. AS YEARS PASSED, THEY BECAME ***MORE*** THAN FRIENDS.
FOR THE FIRST TIME IN HER ***LIFE,*** CARMEN KNEW WHAT IT WAS LIKE TO BE ***HAPPY.***
FOR THE FIRST TIME IN HER ***LIFE,*** SHE KNEW WHAT IT WAS LIKE TO BE ***LOVED.***

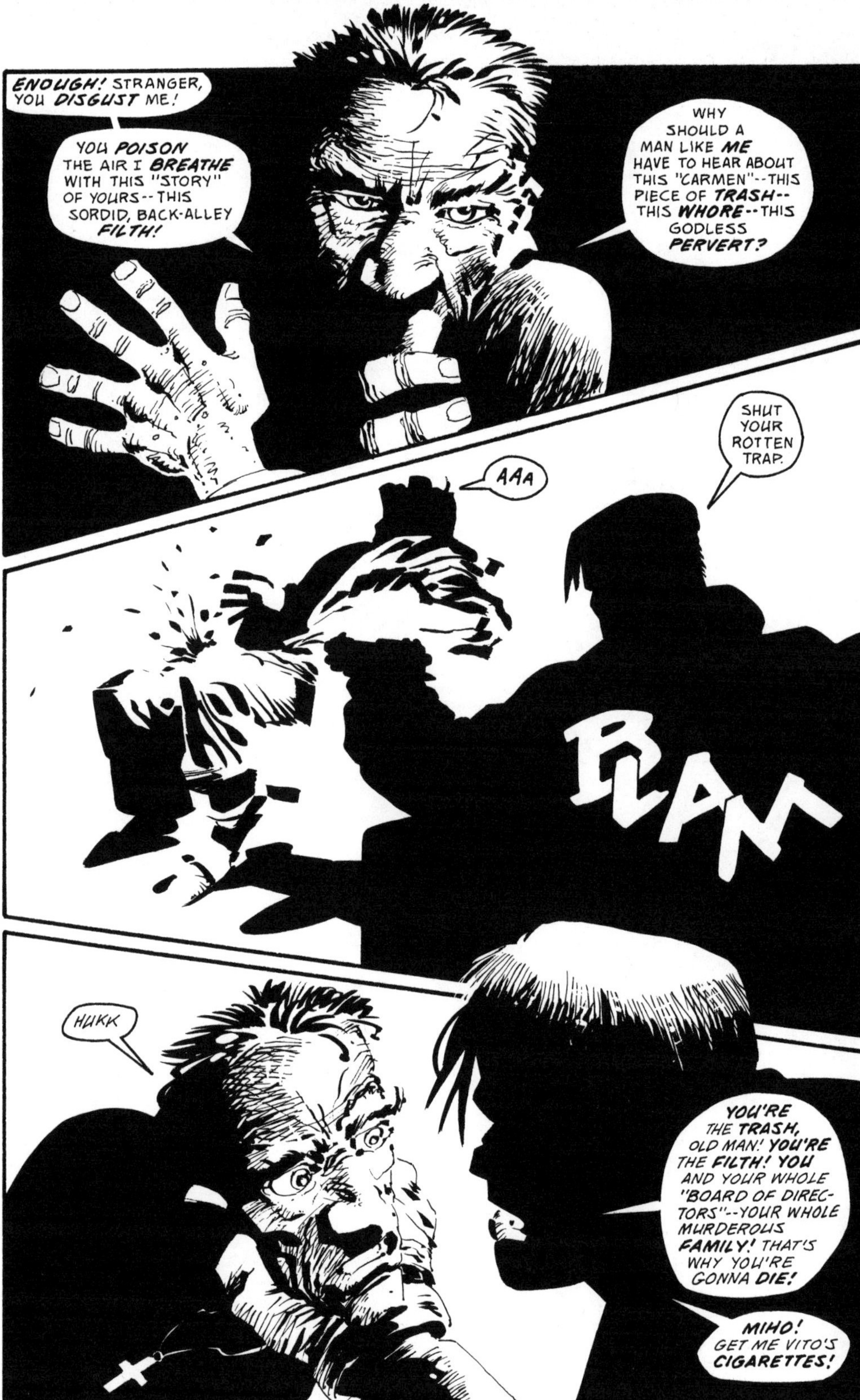
ENOUGH! STRANGER, YOU DISGUST ME!
YOU POISON THE AIR I BREATHE WITH THIS "STORY" OF YOURS--THIS SORDID, BACK-ALLEY FILTH!
WHY SHOULD A MAN LIKE ME HAVE TO HEAR ABOUT THIS "CARMEN"--THIS PIECE OF TRASH--THIS WHORE--THIS GODLESS PERVERT?
SHUT YOUR ROTTEN TRAP.
AAA
BLAM
HUKK
YOU'RE THE TRASH, OLD MAN! YOU'RE THE FILTH! YOU AND YOUR WHOLE "BOARD OF DIRECTORS"--YOUR WHOLE MURDEROUS FAMILY! THAT'S WHY YOU'RE GONNA DIE!
MIHO! GET ME VITO'S CIGARETTES!

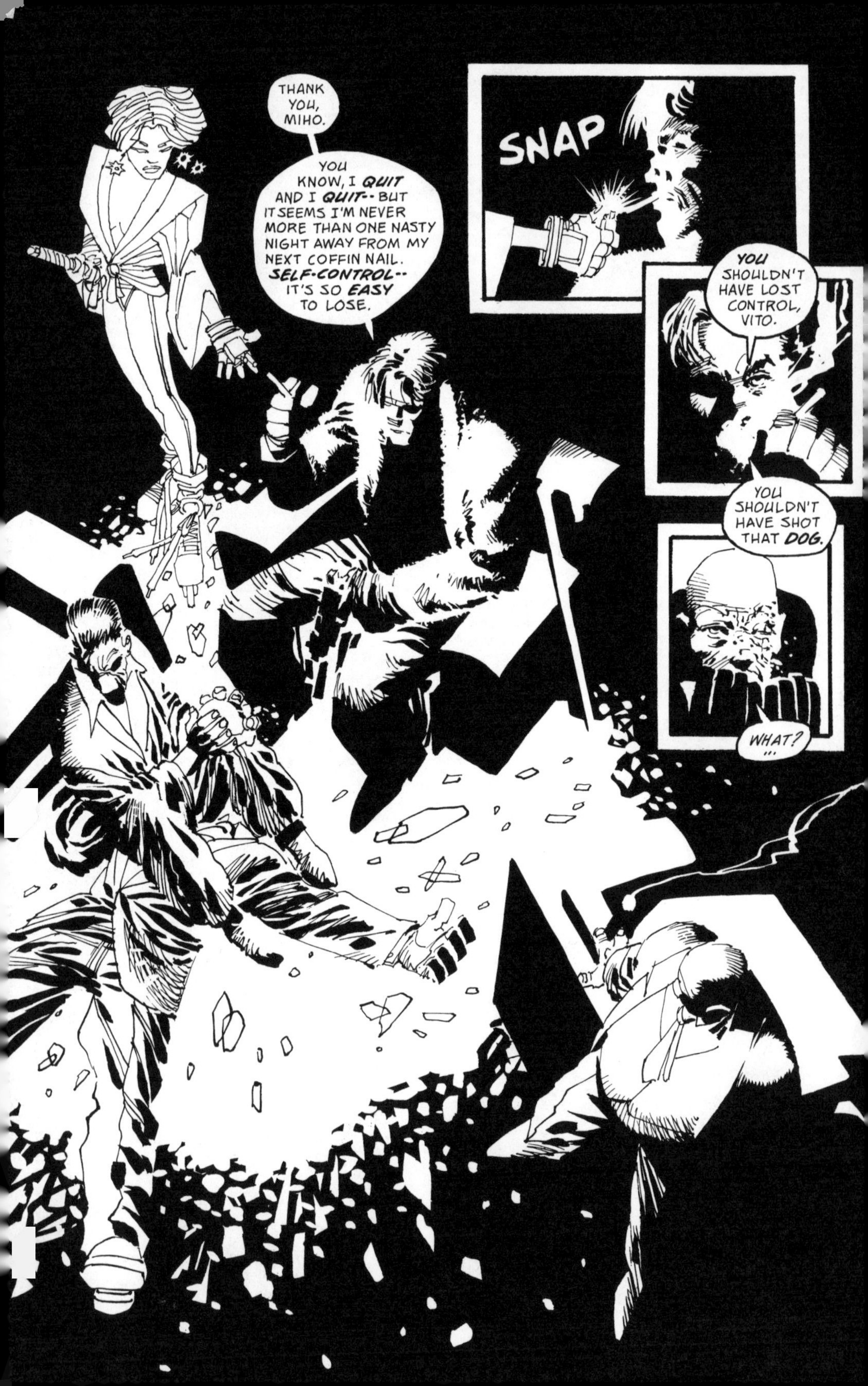
THANK YOU, MIHO.
YOU KNOW, I QUIT AND I QUIT-- BUT IT SEEMS I'M NEVER MORE THAN ONE NASTY NIGHT AWAY FROM MY NEXT COFFIN NAIL. SELF-CONTROL-- IT'S SO EASY TO LOSE.
SNAP
YOU SHOULDN'T HAVE LOST CONTROL, VITO.
YOU SHOULDN'T HAVE SHOT THAT DOG.
WHAT? ...

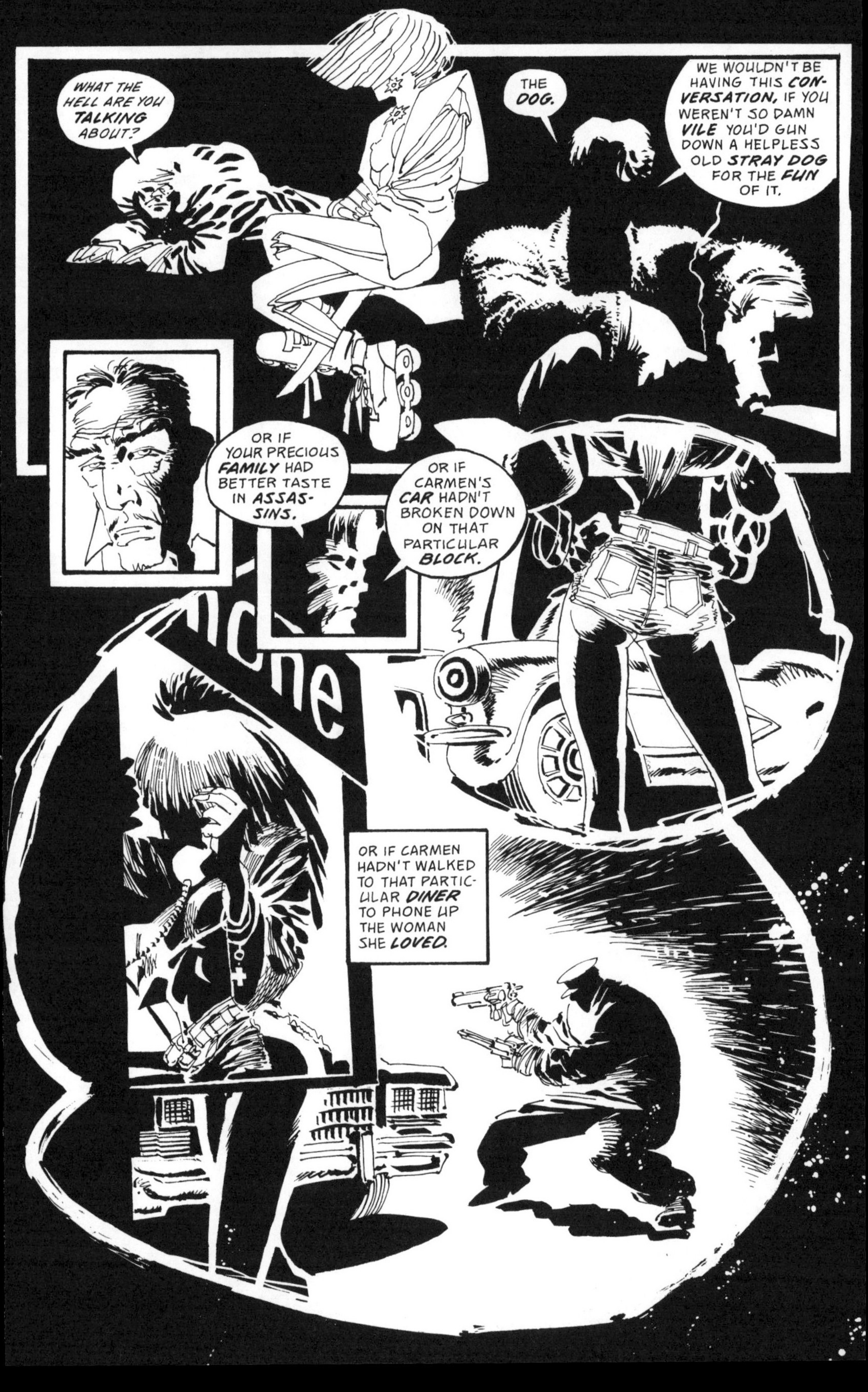
WHAT THE HELL ARE YOU TALKING ABOUT?
THE DOG.
WE WOULDN'T BE HAVING THIS CONVERSATION, IF YOU WEREN'T SO DAMN VILE YOU'D GUN DOWN A HELPLESS OLD STRAY DOG FOR THE FUN OF IT.
OR IF YOUR PRECIOUS FAMILY HAD BETTER TASTE IN ASSASSINS.
OR IF CARMEN'S CAR HADN'T BROKEN DOWN ON THAT PARTICULAR BLOCK.
OR IF CARMEN HADN'T WALKED TO THAT PARTICULAR DINER TO PHONE UP THE WOMAN SHE LOVED.

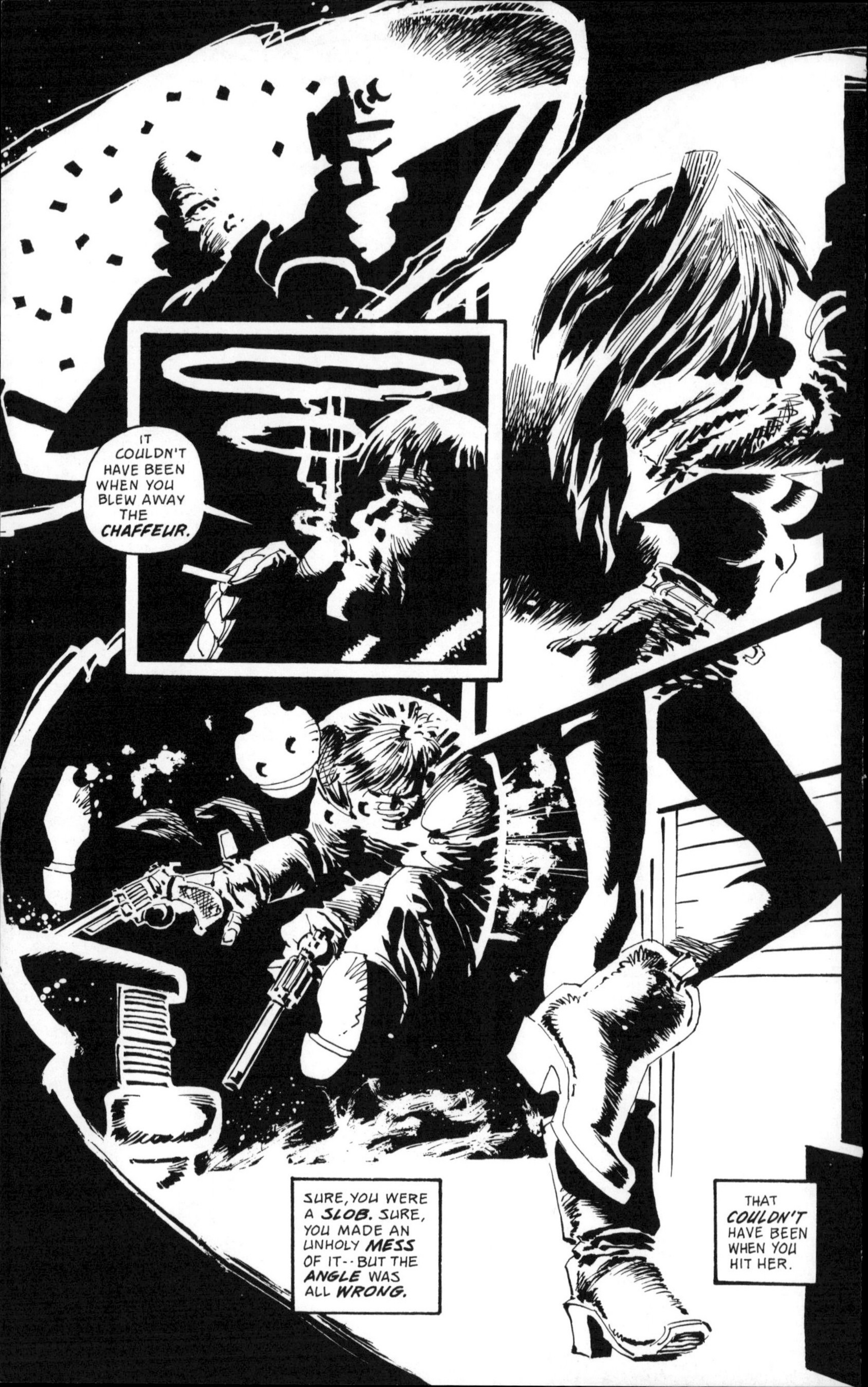
IT COULDN'T HAVE BEEN WHEN YOU BLEW AWAY THE CHAFFEUR.
SURE, YOU WERE A SLOB. SURE, YOU MADE AN UNHOLY MESS OF IT-- BUT THE ANGLE WAS ALL WRONG.
THAT COULDN'T HAVE BEEN WHEN YOU HIT HER.

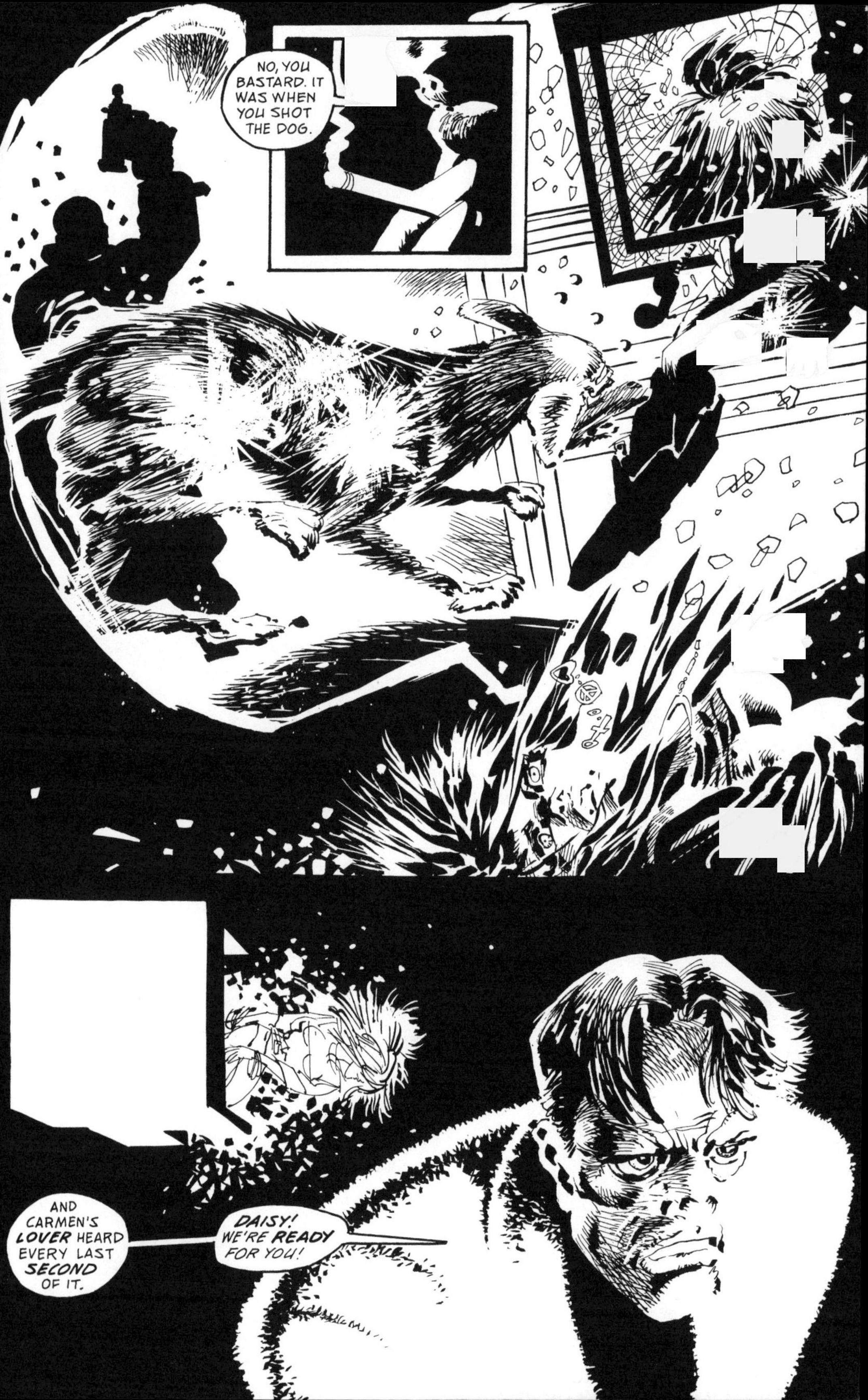
NO, YOU BASTARD. IT WAS WHEN YOU SHOT THE DOG.
AND CARMEN'S LOVER HEARD EVERY LAST SECOND OF IT.
DAISY! WE'RE READY FOR YOU!

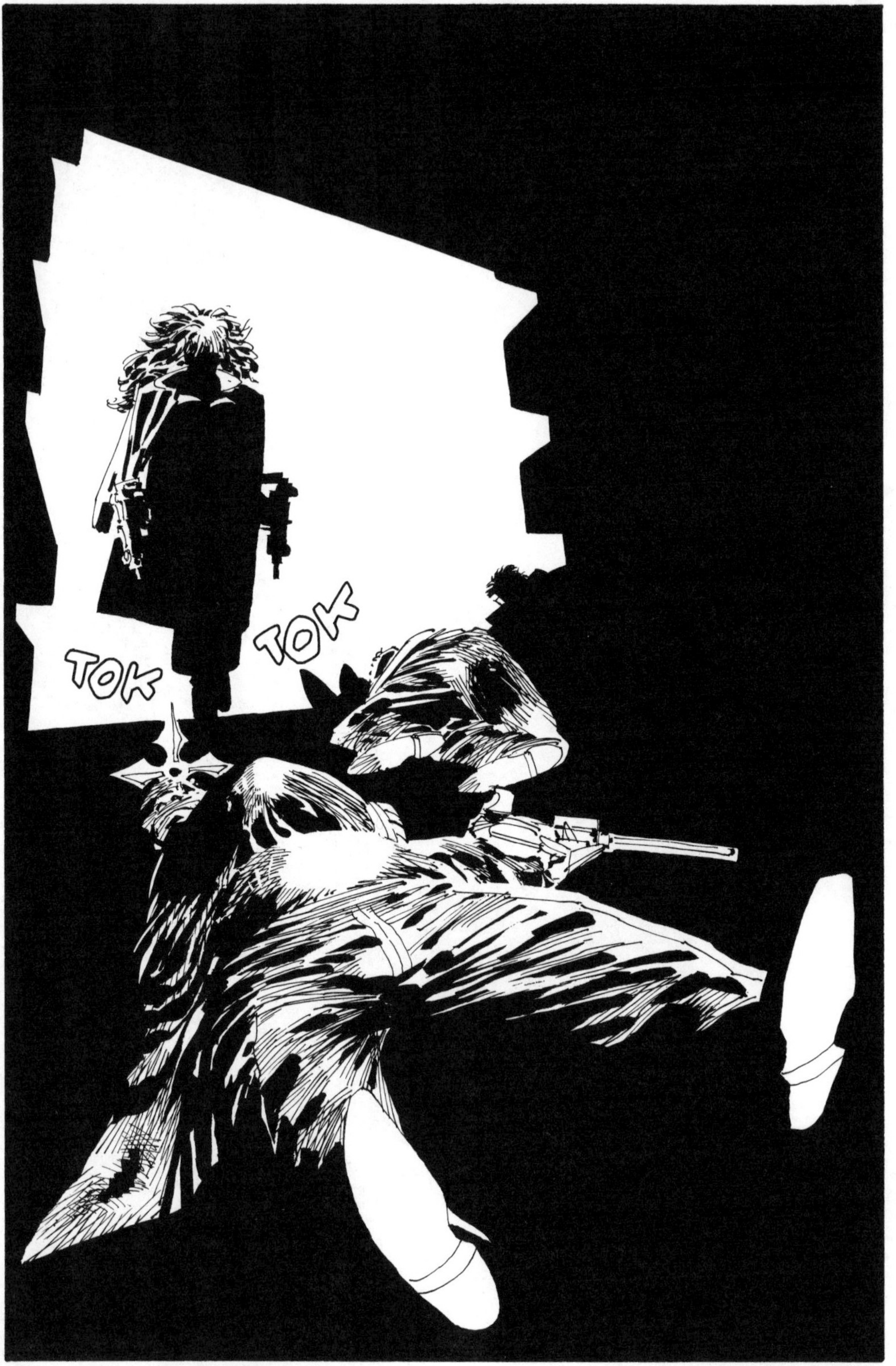
TOK
TOK

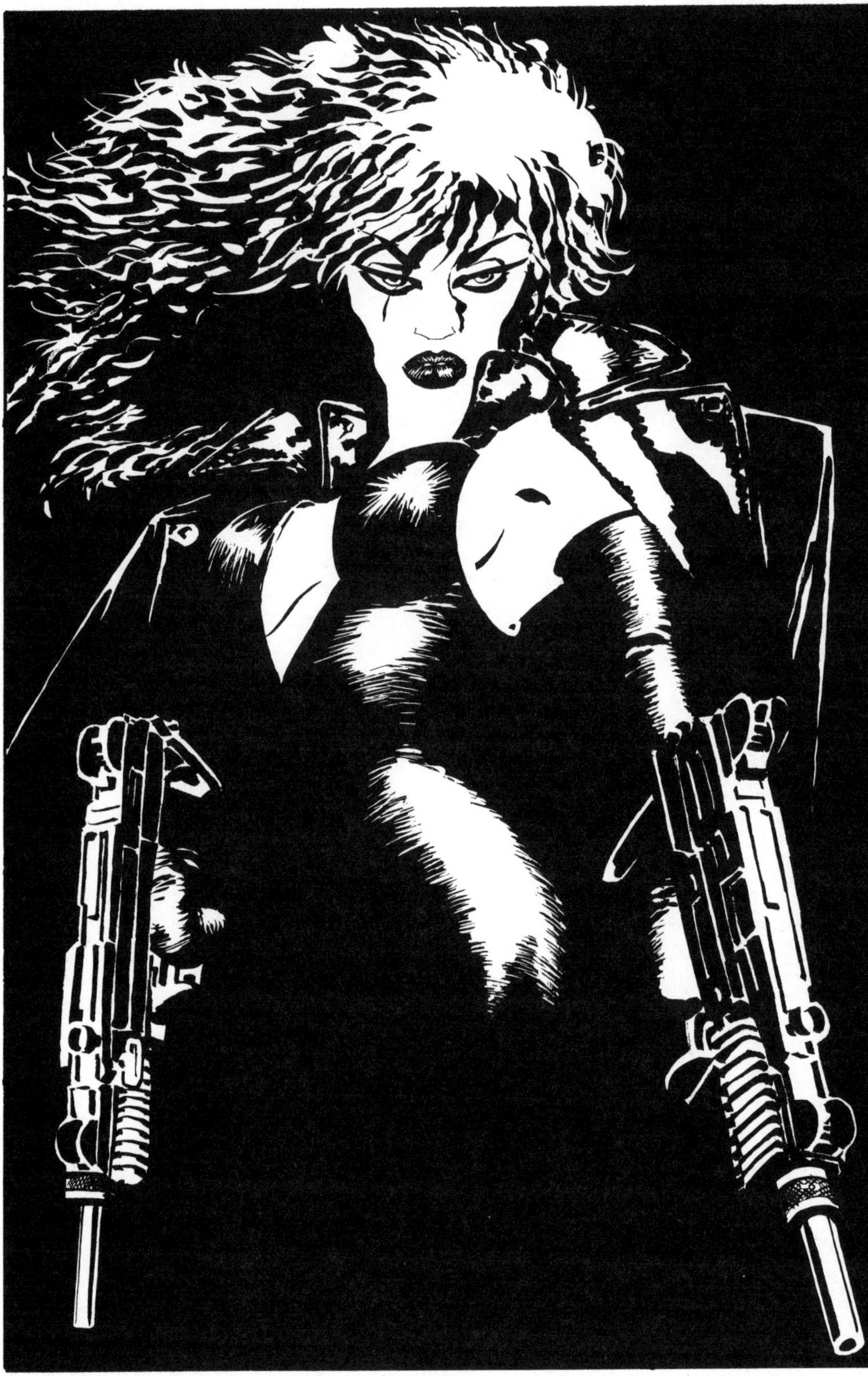

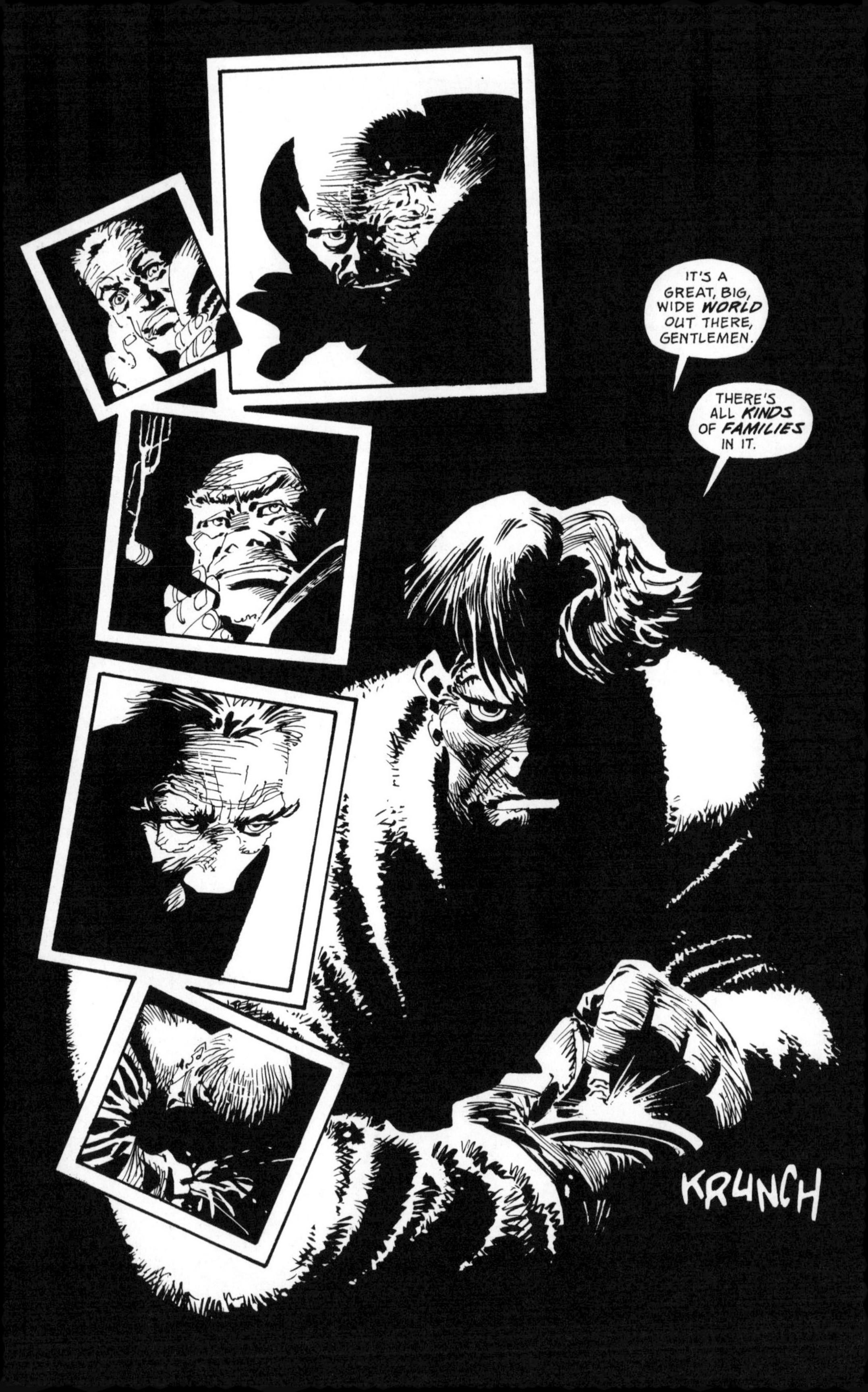
IT'S A GREAT, BIG, WIDE WORLD OUT THERE, GENTLEMEN.
THERE'S ALL KINDS OF FAMILIES IN IT.
KRUNCH

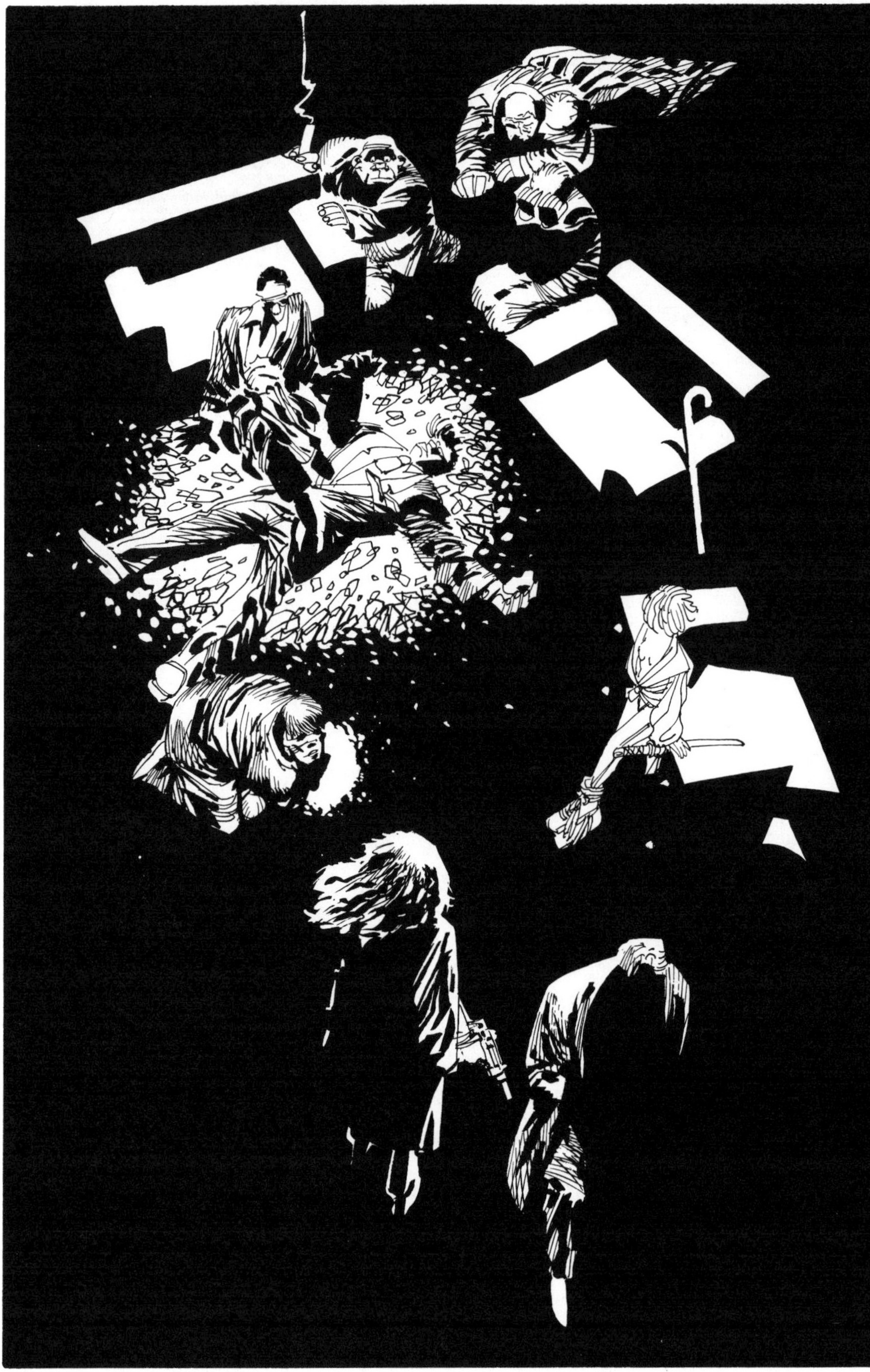

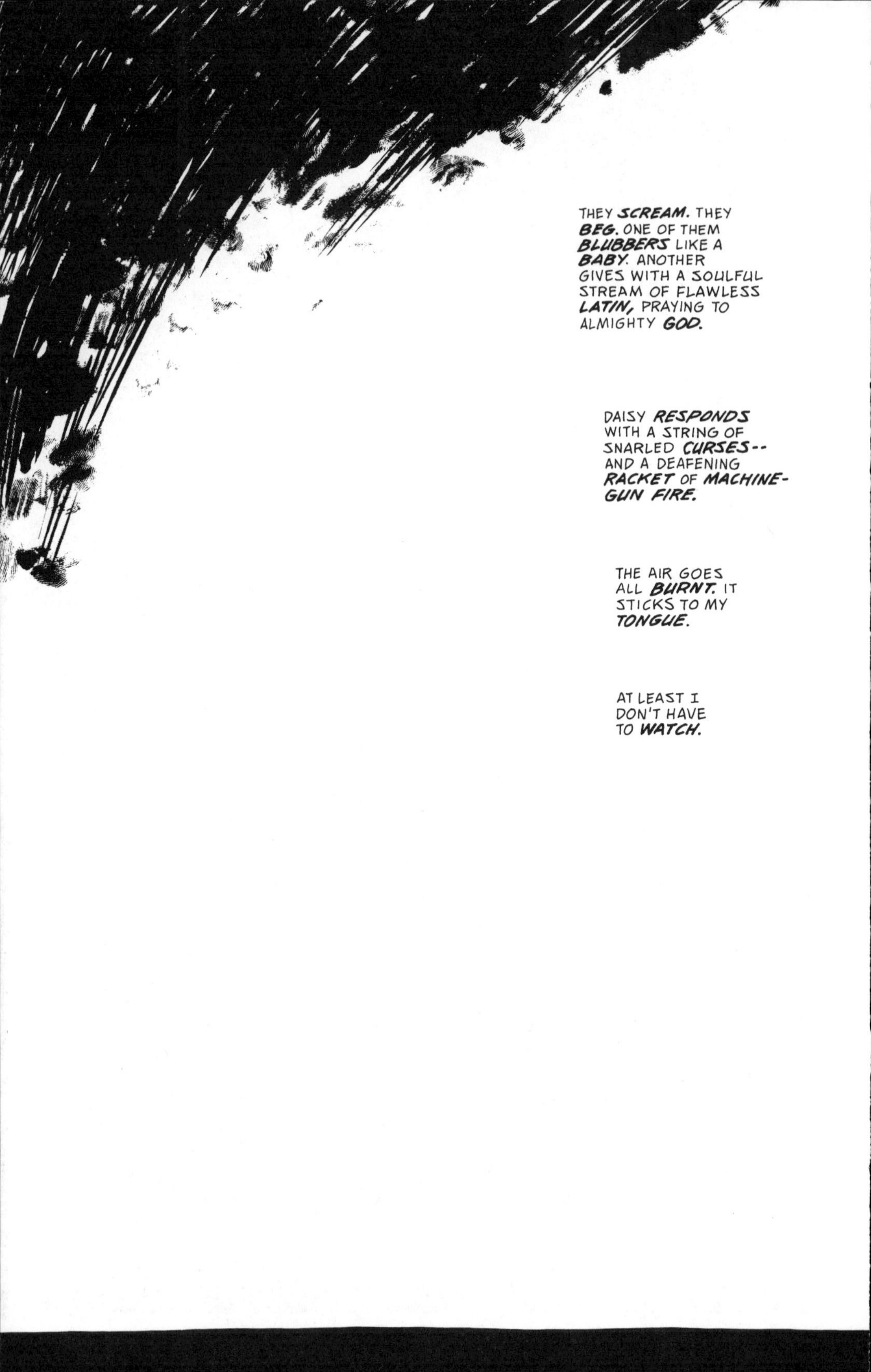
THEY **SCREAM.** THEY **BEG.** ONE OF THEM **BLUBBERS** LIKE A **BABY.** ANOTHER GIVES WITH A SOULFUL STREAM OF FLAWLESS **LATIN,** PRAYING TO ALMIGHTY **GOD.**
DAISY **RESPONDS** WITH A STRING OF SNARLED **CURSES**-- AND A DEAFENING **RACKET** OF **MACHINE-GUN FIRE.**
THE AIR GOES ALL **BURNT.** IT STICKS TO MY **TONGUE.**
AT LEAST I DON'T HAVE TO **WATCH.**